# Guide to Burma

# Guide to
# Burma

Nicholas Greenwood

*"For the temple-bells are callin', an' it's there that I would be
By the old Moulmein Pagoda, looking lazy at the sea."*

Kipling

BRADT PUBLICATIONS, UK
HUNTER PUBLISHING, USA

First published in 1993 by Bradt Publications, 41 Nortoft Rd, Chalfont St Peter, Bucks SL9 0LA, England. Distributed in the USA by Hunter Publishing Inc, 300 Raritan Center Parkway, CN94, Edison, NJ 08810.

**British Library Cataloguing in Publication data**

A catalogue record for this book is
available from the British Library

ISBN 0 946983 87 9

Illustrations by Rebecca Vanes
Cover photos: Front — 'Chinthe' standing guard at the foot of Mandalay Hill; back — Novice nun's initiation ('ear-piercing') ceremony, Eindawya Pagoda, Rangoon; Bespectacled Buddha image at the Shwemyethman Pagoda, Shwedaung.
Photographs by the author
Maps by Robert and Rhoda Burns
Typeset from the author's disc by Patti Taylor, London NW10 3BX
Printed by The Guernsey Press

This book is dedicated to the memory of my parents Walter and Agnes Greenwood and my grandmother Claire Herzbrun

'If there be any justification then for my books, it will perhaps be found in the purpose I have had at heart, of making the things I know about, however slightly, better understood of those with whom I share this marvellous heritage.'

V. C. Scott O'Connor, 1907.

## ABOUT THE AUTHOR

Former horse racing correspondent and broadcaster, Nicholas Greenwood has travelled extensively throughout Southeast Asia and numbers Burma, Laos, Cambodia and Vietnam amongst the countries he has visited. A specialist in Burmese affairs, he is a member of the *The Britain-Burma Society*, the *Liverpool Burma Support Group* and the *Burma Action Group UK*. He has contributed to three books on northern Thailand and in June 1992 his travelogue *Bound Tightly With Banana Leaves: A South East Asian Journal* was published by Right Now Books.

## ACKNOWLEDGEMENTS

I would like to thank all the Burmese people I met on my many travels who offered me invaluable advice and kindness; for example U Soe Myint from Bassein, whom I sat next to on one occasion for 14 hours on the Rangoon to Mandalay 'express'. A typically hospitable Burmese, his words of wisdom (and confectionery) helped pass the time.

Thanks also to my Burmese friends in the UK, including U Nyunt Aung, Aung Naing, Tun Tun, U Kyaw Zay-Ya and U Khin Maung Tun, to Thanomsil Khiansua, David Jefferis, Steve Kurdyak and Colleen Kirkham from Canada, Angela Parker and James Mort from Australia, Dr John Stewart of the British Airways Travel Clinic and Janine Boxall of Camrus Publishers Ltd.

# CONTENTS

# INTRODUCTION

'We're sailing to Burma ... yes the sea is blue, so blue — and everything's going as it should ...'

*Happy End*, Bertolt Brecht.

Burma (renamed Myanmar by the military junta) is an extraordinary country. The very moment you touch down at Rangoon's Mingaladon Airport on your flight from Bangkok, you set your watch back 30 minutes and your life back at least 30 years. For Burma is caught in a singular time-warp having been cut off from the outside world since Ne Win seized power in a *coup d'état* in 1962. Once the richest nation in Southeast Asia, Burma is now one of the poorest lands in the world. It lies practically untouched by modernisation, stifled by an inept government, yet is home to the kindest and friendliest people you could ever hope to meet. It is the land too of Pagan, the awe-inspiring amphitheatre of 5,000 temples, of Kipling's Mandalay and Moulmein, of the stunning Shwedagon Pagoda, the astonishing Golden Rock Pagoda and of "the sunshine an' the palm-trees an' the tinkly temple-bells." Burma is truly a unique and remarkable country.

Chapter One

# General Facts

## GEOGRAPHY, CLIMATE, TIME, DAYS AND DATES

'Burma is slightly bigger than the British Isles and much more elongated. It is shaped like a parrot facing west: Rangoon is where the parrot's claws would grip the perch, and Tenasserim is the long tail hanging down ...

Concerning the size of Burma there hangs a tale which is perhaps worth telling. Throughout Burmese history there has run a strong thread of self-confidence, intertwined with a mistrust of foreigners: traits of character which are still present to-day. During the Crimean War, King Mindon once asked to be shown Britain on a map of the world, and when he saw it commented: 'Yes, I always knew it was a very small country. Now show me Burma.' When he saw that it was much the same size, he flew into a rage, and was only pacified when his courtier, losing his nerve and fearful of losing his head, hastily added most of Asia to his sovereign's putative dominions.'

*Return to Burma*, Bernard Fergusson, 1962.

Burma, the second largest country in Southeast Asia, covers an area of 676,552km$^2$ or 262,000 square miles (roughly twice the size of Vietnam and approximately the size of France and Great Britain combined). It is bordered by India and Bangladesh in the northwest, China and Laos in the north and northeast and Thailand in the east and southeast. Burma's west coast is contiguous to both the Bay of

Bengal and the Andaman Sea and totals about 2,000 miles. The greatest length of the country from north to south is about 1,300 miles, and the greatest width from east to west is about 600 miles.

The country's major waterway is the Irrawaddy River which flows over 2,000km from the Kachin Hills in the north to its outflow into the Andaman Sea. Its biggest tributary is the Chindwin which runs from the northwest to join the Irrawaddy in central Burma. The country's other significant river, the Salween, has its course across the Shan Plateau and its mouth at Martaban. The Mekhong River forms the border between Burma and Laos.

Burma has a tropical climate with three general seasons. The rainy season during the southwest monsoons from mid-May to mid-October, the dry cool season from mid-October to mid-February and the hot season from mid-February until the onset of the rains in May. It can be exceptionally cold in the north where there are snow-capped mountains (Burma's highest peak, and the highest in Southeast Asia, Mount Hkakabo, known as Hkakabo Razi, reaches 5,887m or 19,314 feet) and quite cool in Shan State. In the rainy season about 200 inches of rain fall on the coastlands, about 100 inches in the Irrawaddy Delta and about 80 in the hills, but in the dry central zone only about 25 to 45 inches. Immediately before the rains begin the temperature reaches 100° or more in the Delta and the dry zone. The coolest months are December and January, when in southern Burma the maximum is not less than 60°.

Burma is 6½ hours ahead of GMT (as opposed to BST which, according to the locals, stands sardonically for 'Burmese Standard Time'), and thus half an hour behind Thailand, the country from which the majority of tourists arrive. A number of travellers are now coming from Singapore which is 1½ hours ahead of Burma in time, but probably 100 years ahead in terms of development!

The Burmese date is 638 years after the Christian era. Therefore, in order to obtain the Burmese year, you have to subtract that number from the Christian one. In practice, both eras are used: to distinguish one from the other the word *Thekkah-yit* is placed before the Burmese date. Both Burmese and English months are used; often the two together, in documents.

The month is divided into two parts *lah-zahn* (the waxing) and *lah-byee-jaw* or *lah-zohk* (the waning). The full moon (*lah-byee*) falls on the 15th of the waxing, the *lah-gweh* (hidden moon) on the 14th or 15th of the wane. The days of worship are the full moon, eighth of the wane, the hidden moon and the eighth waxing. Otherwise, the days of the week are noted but generally not observed, except by foreigners.

# HISTORY AND POLITICS

'IT is not too much to say that Burma contains more of interest than any
equal section of the Indian Empire. Many people think of Burma as a part
of India, and the Burmese as Indians, but they are no more Indians than
the Chinese are Americans. To be sure, Burma is a province of the Indian
Empire, though it ought to be as much a separate dominion as Australia
or Canada.

It is a three day's journey on a fast steamer from Calcutta to Rangoon;
and when one reaches the latter city he finds people of a totally different
race, different language, different customs, different complexion, different
costumes and different religion.'

Dr. Francis E. Clark, 1910.

Owing to the lack of reliable records, very little is known about
Burma's early history. Legends relate that a king of the Mons, a
people who had apparently migrated into Lower Burma from the
southeast, built the Shwedagon Pagoda on the site of modern
Rangoon during the lifetime of the Buddha (ca. 6th Century BC).
Another legend, that the 3rd Century BC Indian Emperor Ashoka (or
Asoka), a devout Buddhist, sent monks to Thaton, a Mon settlement
in Lower Burma on the Gulf of Martaban, suggests that they had
early contacts with the Indian subcontinent by sea. Indian ships
docked at Thaton, Pegu and other Lower Burma ports, and the
region became an outpost of Indian civilisation. India's chief
contribution to Burmese culture was Buddhism, and over the
centuries it was the axis around which Burmese life and national
identity evolved.

Chinese records from the 3rd Century AD mention a people known
as the Pyu who lived in the central Irrawaddy River area of Upper
Burma, having apparently migrated into the region from the Tibetan
Plateau. Chinese Buddhist pilgrims of the 7th Century AD describe
a Pyu city-state, known as Sri Ksetra (the 'Pleasant' or 'Fortunate
Field'), near the modern town of Prome on the banks of the
Irrawaddy. Sri Ksetra consisted of over 100 monasteries and its
finest monument still in existence today is the 200 feet high
Bawbawgyi Pagoda, constructed of brick in Indian style. According
to Burmese chronicles, the Pyu gained supremacy over the Mons,
sent ships to India, Ceylon (Sri Lanka), the Malay Peninsula and
Indonesia and claimed tributaries as far afield as Sumatra and Java.
According to records, the Pyu Kingdom came to an end in 832 AD.

Another group of states was established as early as the 4th Century AD in what is now Arakan State, on the Bay of Bengal. The Arakanese were related to the Burmans of Upper Burma and, because of their location on the coast, had close sea links with India.

The Burmans, a people akin to the Pyu, founded settlements at Pagan on the banks of the Irrawaddy River in Upper Burma as early as the 2nd Century AD (the first known date for the establishment of Pagan is 849 AD). Strategically located on the north-south and east-west trade routes and close to the irrigated plain of Kyaukse, which produced an abundance of rice, Pagan provided an economic base upon which a mighty kingdom was to evolve.

The founder of the Pagan Dynasty was King Anawrahta (1044-77) and he was the first to bring Lower and Upper Burma under unified rule. Starting from Pagan, at that time merely a cluster of small villages, he conquered the neighbouring principalities of the central Irrawaddy valley. In 1057 he captured Thaton, gaining control over Lower Burma and bringing back to his capital the Theravada scriptures in Pali, a large number of Buddhist monks and artists and craftsmen of every description. From the Mon monks the Burmese received their alphabet and religion. Thus it was from this momentous date that there began the extraordinary architectural and artistic activity which, in a little more than two centuries, covered the city and its surrounding areas with thousands of magnificent monuments of every shape and size imaginable.

Kyansittha (1084-1113), the second great king of Pagan, continued the work of Anawrahta, reunifying the Kingdom after a series of uprisings, fending off foreign invaders and maintaining diplomatic and ecclesiastical ties with Ceylon. Though influenced to a certain extent by Hinduism, Kyansittha considered himself primarily a Buddhist king and indeed was responsible for the construction of the Ananda Temple, deemed the finest example of Burmese religious architecture.

Pagan flourished for more than two and a half centuries (during which time as many as 13,000 pagodas, temples and monasteries were built) before being destroyed by the Mongol armies of Kublai Khan, who invaded Upper Burma from China in 1287. From the 14th to the mid-16th Centuries, Upper Burma came under the control of Shan princes in what was a period of disunity and foreign domination. Burman kings, however, ruled at Ava (near Mandalay) as Shan tributaries. In Lower Burma, a Shan named Wareru (1287-96) established a Kingdom at Martaban in 1281, subsequently gaining control of much of the Lower Burma region. There followed a golden age of Lower Burma culture. Binnya U (1353-85) set up a new capital at Pegu. Dhammazedi (1472-92), a former Buddhist monk, was a model Buddhist king who promoted the reform of the *sangha* (monkhood) through the introduction of orthodox ordination rites from Ceylon.

In the 16th Century, a resurgence of Burman power took place at Toungoo on the Sittang River. In 1280 a fortified town had been established there which subsequently became a political centre of some significance. After the capture of Ava by a Shan prince in 1527, many Burmans sought refuge in Toungoo. Tabinshwehti (1531-50) founded the second unified Burmese Kingdom known as the Toungoo Dynasty. Tabinshwehti conquered Pegu in 1539, extending his control to Martaban and the coastal area as far south as Tavoy. He seized Prome from the Shan forces and in 1546 had himself consecrated king of Burma with Pegu as his capital.

In 1548, however, he overstepped himself by attempting to invade Siam (now central Thailand) and he was assassinated two years later. Following a subsequent revolt in central Burma, his brother King Bayinnaung (1551-81) captured Ava in 1555, thus uniting Upper and Lower Burma. He then marched against the Shan principalities in eastern Burma and parts of what today are Thailand and Laos, and in 1569 captured the Siamese capital of Ayutthaya. However, during the reign of Bayinnaung's son Nanda Bayin (1581-99) the Toungoo Dynasty began to wane: Siam reasserted its independence and an Arakanese fleet laid siege to Pegu, capturing it in 1599. Later King Thalun (1629-48) moved the capital from Pegu to Ava, thus withdrawing effective Burman power from Lower Burma. Eventually in 1752 a Shan named Binnya Dala deposed the final Toungoo monarch, who was brought back (along with as many as 30,000 prisoners) to Pegu.

However a new leader, Maung Aung Zeya, appeared in Upper Burma and within eight years unified Upper and Lower Burma. He defeated Binnya Dala's troops and proclaimed himself king of Burma, assuming the title *Alaungpaya*, 'the embryo Buddha'. Alaungpaya founded the Konbaung Dynasty which ruled the country until the late 19th Century. He captured Ava in 1753 and two years later brought his forces down the Irrawaddy River in a large flotilla and occupied Dagon, the site of the greatly revered Shwedagon Pagoda. There he established a new town called *Yangon*, meaning the 'End of Strife', or Rangoon, the future capital of colonial and independent Burma. In 1756 Alaungpaya captured Syriam, Lower Burma's main trading port, and the following year took Binnya Dala's royal capital Pegu. Even the then Shan Kingdom of Chiang Mai was brought under his control.

Alaungpaya demanded that the king of Siam recognise his status as an 'embryo Buddha'. When the monarch refused, he laid siege to Ayutthaya, the Siamese capital, but the siege was cut short when Alaungpaya was struck down with fever. As a consequence his troops made an orderly retreat back to Burmese territory, but the king died in May 1760.

Ayutthaya, alas, was not safe from eager Burmese hands, for in April 1767 Hsinbyushin (1763-76), the Konbaung Dynasty's second great king, completely destroyed this once great city, killing the king of Siam in the process. Having re-established Ava as his royal capital, Hsinbyushin proceeded to become embroiled in numerous entanglements with a much larger and more serious enemy, the Chinese, who were disturbed by Burmese expansion into the Shan states, Chiang Mai and Laos which bordered their southwestern province of Yunnan. Hsinbyushin's final years were marked by few accomplishments and he died in 1776, only to be succeeded by his son Singu Min who ordered the withdrawal of Burmese armies from Siamese territory.

Singu Min ruled until 1781 when he was assassinated. His successor Maung Maung fared even worse, surviving for only seven days before King Bodawpaya (1782-1819), the fourth son of Alaungpaya, seized power. Believing himself to be the Buddha reincarnated, Bodawpaya had all his rivals massacred, including the royal family, and was responsible for the construction of both the extraordinary Mingun Pagoda and the vast Mingun Bell. He conquered the Kingdom of Arakan and established a new capital at Amarapura (near Mandalay) in Upper Burma.

The megalomaniac Bodawpaya's harsh policies in Arakan, including the drafting of thousands for forced labour in Upper Burma, drove large numbers of refugees across the Naaf River into what was by that time British territory. Rebels used the Bengal side of this loosely defined border as a staging area for raids on Burmese garrisons in Arakan. The Burmese, claiming the right to cross the Naaf in hot pursuit of insurgents, caused increasing apprehension in the British and Burmese-British relations steadily deteriorated.

Bodawpaya died in 1819 and was succeeded by his grandson Bagyidaw. Like his grandfather, Bagyidaw continued to rile the British by pursuing aggressive policies both in the Kingdoms of Assam and Manipur and on the Bengal border. Burmese forces marched into Assam, intervening in a succession struggle, which placed the British in a delicate position since both pretenders to the throne sought protection on British soil and organised resistance movements. Manipur was also invaded because its raja was reluctant to become a vassal of the new Burmese king. Beset by refugees from Manipur, the raja of yet another state, Cachar, fled to British Indian territory. In 1823 the British declared Cachar and a neighbouring state Jaintia protectorates. On the India-Arakan border, Burmese troops seized East India Company personnel and an island in the Naaf River claimed by the British.

In January 1824 Burmese forces marched into Cachar and fought British troops, and warring resumed on the Naaf River. Worried by the Burmese attempts to seize Bengal, the British governor general Lord Amherst ordered his forces by sea to Lower Burma, and captured Rangoon on May 10. The Burmese were thus obliged to forsake Arakan and return to Upper Burma.

The first Anglo-Burmese War lasted from 1824-26, until peace was restored with the signing of the Treaty of Yandabo on February 24 1826, providing for the cession of the territories of Arakan and Tenasserim to the British, an end to Burmese suzerainty over the Indian hill states of Assam and Manipur, an indemnity of £1 million to be paid to the British for the costs of the war, and the exchange of diplomatic representatives between Burma and British India. British troops left Rangoon in December 1826 after full payment of the indemnity; the treaty, however, was a shattering blow to Burmese pride. When representatives were exchanged, Bagyidaw tried to negotiate the return of Tenasserim, but in vain.

In 1837 Bagyidaw, growing increasingly insane and incompetent, was overthrown by his brother Tharrawaddy, but political stability was further undermined by revolts among the Shans in Lower Burma during the period of 1838-40. Tharrawaddy reneged on the Treaty of Yandabo and in 1839 formal diplomatic relations were severed. The king died seven years later, to be succeeded by his son Pagan Min, a wholly ineffective and corrupt monarch. Government in both Upper and Lower Burma steadily began to crumble, whilst unrest continued apace in the Shan states.

In 1852 the second Anglo-Burmese War broke out over a dispute involving two British merchants who had been arrested by the Burmese governor of Rangoon for evading customs duties. Britain, keen at this time to extend her empire and to put down what they deemed to be 'inferior natives', sent an armed naval escort to Rangoon to demand compensation and the removal of the Rangoon governor. The British further insisted that an indemnity of £100,000 be paid and that the king himself should apologise personally. By October, the British had seized Rangoon, Martaban, Bassein, Pegu and Prome. On December 20 1852, it was announced that Lower Burma would be annexed as a province of British India.

Following a revolt by his half-brother Mindon Min at Shwebo in December 1852, Pagan Min was deposed and forced into retirement in February 1853. The new King Mindon refused to recognise the annexation of Lower Burma, but did not resume hostilities.

A peaceful, intellectual ruler and devout Buddhist, King Mindon exercised a conciliatory attitude towards the British and extended diplomatic contacts with other Western countries. Like the monarchs before him, he also moved his capital, this time from Amarapura to a site a few miles away at Mandalay Hill. In 1861 he constructed a teak palace enclosed by square walls 2km long on each side.

King Mindon died on October 1 1878 and was succeeded by his 19-year-old son Thibaw. A weakling, he was shrewdly manipulated by his 'secondary queen' Supayalat, the Central Palace queen's second daughter. She ousted her elder sister as Thibaw's chief queen and even undermined the position of her mother.

Thibaw's fatal blunder, however, was to seek an alliance with the French (already at that time involved in a war with China over Vietnam whilst extending her influence into Laos) as a counterbalance to the British. Consequently a strong French presence in Upper Burma was perceived as a strategic threat to India, which the British could not tolerate. Britain, herself, was eager to annex Upper Burma for that would open up the supposedly rich markets of southwestern China. And so eventually British forces sailed from Thayetmyo further up the Irrawaddy in a flotilla of steamboats on November 17 1885. The Third, and final, Anglo-Burmese War had begun. The capital Mandalay fell on November 28 and an armistice was hastily drawn up. King Thibaw and Queen Supayalat refused to flee and were exiled to India, never to see their native country again. In February 1886 Burma became a directly administered province of British India.

By 1890 there were some 60,000 British troops and police in Burma, their responsibility being to suppress the large numbers of armed bandits and insurgents in the land. There was unrest throughout the country, exacerbated by the fact that the British recruited Karens to fight Burmans. By 1889 the Shan states were brought under British rule.

During this period, however, swift economic progress was taking place: the development of efficient steamship transportation, the opening of the Suez Canal in 1869 and the construction of railways (reaching Mandalay by 1889, Myitkyina by 1898 and Lashio by 1902) all drew the country more tightly into the international economic system in ways that would have as far-reaching consequences as had the extinction of the Konbaung Kingdom in 1886. Between 1870 and 1926-27 the value of exports increased 20 times and the value of imports 15 times. Modern, large-scale Western enterprise was firmly established: teak, rice, mining (rubies), tin, tungsten and petroleum were all exploited to the full. Land under cultivation grew by 145,300 hectares between 1861 and 1870 and between 1890 and 1900 rice land increased by 943,900 hectares. In the early 1870s the annual average of rice exported was 732,000 tons: by 1900 this had become 2.5 million, by 1920 3.6 million.

All this required extra labour and though there was some Chinese immigration after 1852, the vast majority of immigrants during the late 19th and early 20th Centuries came from the regions of Bengal and Madras in India. Indeed by the end of the 19th Century, India was supplying most of the workers for Lower Burma's rice-mills and dockyards and for the other burgeoning industries. The total was further swelled by natural disasters in Madras and Bengal which drove more and more immigrants into Burma. The Indian population of Lower Burma increased from 297,000 in 1901 to 583,000 30 years later. By 1918 around 300,000 labourers had come to Rangoon: 13 years later the city's population consisted of 50% Indian, but only 36% Burmese, with lower percentages of Chinese, Indo-Burmese, Eurasians and Europeans. English and Indian, rather than Burmese, were the languages most often spoken in the streets and offices.

All the while, however, resentment on behalf of the Burmese was growing, mainly over nationalist issues but also over economic hardship. By 1930 there were mounting communal tensions as Burmese cultivators found themselves at the mercy of Chettiar money-lenders and also as labourers in the port cities competed with Indian immigrants for jobs which were becoming increasingly scarce. In May 1930 there was a riot in Rangoon involving Burmese and Indian dockworkers, and indeed throughout the 30s there were sporadic outbreaks of violence against the Indian and Chinese communities. In July 1938 renegade Buddhist monks led Burmese mobs through Rangoon on a rampage of killing which resulted in the deaths of around 200 Indians.

Further unrest amongst the Burmese stemmed from a variety of causes, but essentially it was the desire to rid themselves of British colonial rule. This had been fomenting ever since the annexation of

Upper Burma, particularly in the rural areas where a 'saviour king', or Setkya Min, had promised to liberate the people from the colonialists. The most widespread of these movements first appeared in 1930, when in October of that year Saya San, a doctor and member of an organisation called the General Council of Burmese Associations (GCBA), formed in 1919-20, proclaimed himself king, setting up a palace with royal insignia in Tharrawaddy District north of Rangoon. The rebels, however, armed with just spears and swords, were no match for the superior British forces and the uprising was subdued by 1932.

During the 1930s nationalists were divided as to whether Burma should continue to remain part of India. Those against separation argued that a separate Burma would not be able to profit from further political reforms taking place in India unless it were granted self-governing dominion status, which the British were not prepared to accord. The British Parliament, however, voted for separation and approved a new constitution for Burma in 1935 over the spirited opposition of many nationalists. Under the new system a British governor of Burma still retained extensive powers, though a nine-member cabinet was appointed by the governor in consultation with an elected House of Representatives. Elections were held in 1936, and when the new constitution was implemented the following year, Dr Ba Maw, leader of the *Sinyetha* (Poor Man's) Party, was chosen Prime Minister by a coalition of parties.

The *Dobama Asiayone* (We Burmans Association) had emerged in 1930-31 during the Saya San rebellion in part as an urban response to what was essentially a village phenomenon. Its members drew attention to themselves by calling each other *thakin* or master. This was taboo in polite colonial society, because the word was customarily used by Burmese as a respectful term of address to the British, like the term *sahib* in India. The founders of the society claimed that the Burmese must develop a 'master mentality' as opposed to the 'slave mentality' which the British had imposed. Their choice of the term *thakin* was viewed as a first step in this direction, and they were soon known to the general public as Thakins, gaining national prominence through the medium of Rangoon University.

In the autumn of 1935, two men of strong political persuasions, Maung Nu and Aung San, were elected President and Secretary respectively of the Rangoon University Student Union (RUSU). Both men, however, got into trouble for publishing an article in the union's newspaper calling for the dismissal of a Burmese member of the faculty for alleged moral improprieties, and were expelled. This provoked a student strike in February 1936, which swiftly assumed a wider political significance. Strike headquarters were set up at the Shwedagon Pagoda and demonstrations forced the closure of the campus. The RUSU gained the support of Rangoon-area high school students through the All-Burma Student Union. Thakin Nu and Thakin Aung San (as they were now called) were readmitted to the university but by this time had already committed themselves to full-time political careers.

The Thakins, who had no single, consistent political ideology, succeeded in having two of their members elected to the legislature in the 1936 election and organised a number of strikes in 1938 and 1939. They were among the first groups to force the issue of outright independence, expressed by the rural followers of Saya San, into the urban and university arena. And in particular it was Aung San who proposed independence in terms of *Burmese* rather than *Burman* nationalism.

In February 1939 Ba Maw was replaced as Prime Minister by Tharrawaddy U Pu. In September of that year, as war broke out in Europe, Ba Maw's *Sinyetha* Party joined forces with the Burma Revolutionary Party, a Thakin group formed by Kodaw Hmaing (a former Buddhist monk and writer and one of the founders of the *Dobama Asiayone*) and Aung San, to form the Freedom Bloc, a coalition committed to total independence. In September 1940 U Pu's government was replaced by one formed by U Saw, head of the *Myochit* (Patriot) Party, who attempted to suppress the Freedom Bloc and to persuade the British to grant Burma full self-governing or dominion status.

Increasing Japanese interest in Burma at this time stemmed not only from the fact that the country was rich in strategic resources (such as oil), but also because the Burma Road provided a route through which the Allies could supply the Chiang Kai-shek government in Chongqing. Its severance would hasten a successful conclusion of the war with China. In 1939 Japanese agents contacted Ba Maw who, the following year, discussed the possibility of obtaining Japanese support for independence with his ally Aung San. In August 1940 Aung San and a fellow Thakin were smuggled out of Burma on a ship bound for Amoy, subsequently reaching Tokyo, to lay the groundwork for the armed struggle against the British in concert with Japanese advances into Southeast Asia.

An intelligence organisation, the *Minami Kikan*, was set up by the Japanese military to coordinate operations in Burma. Aung San returned home, contacted the Thakins and arranged to smuggle 28 men out of the country. These men, together with Aung San, comprised the 'Thirty Comrades', who received military training from the Japanese on Hainan Island off the south coast of China. They formed the core of the Burma Independence Army (BIA), established in Bangkok in late December 1941, whilst underground movements were being organised within Burma itself.

When Japanese forces began the invasion of the Tenasserim area along the Andaman Sea and other parts of Lower Burma in January 1942, the BIA aided their advance, occasionally engaging retreating British forces in combat. One of the 'Thirty Comrades', Thakin Shu Maung, infiltrated Rangoon in early February and organised sabotage activities. This man, who had started his career as a humble postal clerk, was to become better known by his *nom de guerre* Ne Win (meaning 'brilliant like the sun'). Rangoon fell in March 1942, British troops evacuated Mandalay, and the Burma Road was cut off in May.

When most of Burma was in Japanese hands, Ba Maw was made Prime Minister (in August 1942) and Aung San commander of the 4,000-strong Burma Defence Army, the successor of the BIA. In January 1943 Japanese Prime Minister Tōjō Hideki annnounced that independence would be granted by the end of the year. In August Ba Maw was proclaimed head of state in a ceremony at Rangoon that recalled the traditions of Burmese kingship. *Bogyoke* (General) Aung San was appointed Minister of Defence and Commander of the new Burma National Army (BNA), and Thakin Nu, Minister of Foreign Affairs. In reality Ba Maw's government had very little actual power: nominally independent, Burma was seen by Tokyo as an economic and strategic component of its all-out war effort, a fact of which Aung San was fully aware. All the while he was secretly organising resistance plans against the Japanese, incorporating, amongst others, such diverse groups as the Karen National Organisation, the Japanese-sponsored East Asia Youth League, former associates from *Dobama Asiayone* days, and the leftists.

Lord Mountbatten, head of the South-East Asia Command, agreed to cooperate with Aung San. The 1944 Japanese offensive into India through Manipur had failed, and by the end of January 1945 Allied troops had reopened the Burma Road and captured Myitkyina. On March 27 Aung San, receiving a signal from Mountbatten, led a revolt of the BNA, which began attacking Japanese units. Rangoon was captured in early May, though hostilities continued in various parts of the country up to and even after the Japanese surrender on August 15 1945. At the end of May 1945 the BNA was officially recognised as a component of Allied forces and renamed the Patriotic Burmese Forces (PBF).

But if in return for aiding the British, General Aung San was to expect the immediate granting of Burmese independence, he was to be disappointed. On May 17 1945, the Churchill Government issued a white paper proclaiming a very conservative programme: the 1937 constitution, with its elective Prime Minister, was to be suspended and the governor, appointed by London, would retain all authority. Although what the British called 'Burma Proper' (a term used by the colonialists to describe the central region of the country), where the population was predominantly Burman, would be given 'full self-government within the Commonwealth' after 1948, the Shan states and the other border regions inhabited by non-Burman minorities would remain under British rule indefinitely. Thus in essence it granted Burma less than the Japanese had, even though Ba Maw himself had only been a puppet leader.

Aung San initiated a campaign against the white paper at a mass meeting in Rangoon on August 19 1945, demanding that independence be granted immediately. There was universal discontent: a general strike broke out in September 1946 and the country rapidly degenerated into chaos. The British governor, Hubert Rance, with few troops at his disposal, was forced to comply with Aung San's demands. A new executive council was formed; Aung San served as Deputy Chairman, and six of its 11 members were supporters of the Anti-Fascist People's Freedom League (AFPFL). The general strike ended on October 2 1946. In December of that year, Labour Prime Minster Clement Attlee invited Aung San and other political leaders to London. On January 27 1947, Attlee and Aung San signed an agreement calling for full independence within a year, elections for a constituent assembly within four months, continued British aid, British sponsorship of Burma to membership of international organisations and, most significantly, the promise that the border areas would be included within the boundaries of the new nation.

In April 1947 elections were held for the Constituent Assembly. There were a total of 255 seats, Burma Proper being allotted 210, of which 24 were reserved for the Karens and four for Anglo-Burmans, and the border areas were apportioned 45. The AFPFL won an overwhelming victory, returning 248 representatives, most of whom were socialists or members of the People's Volunteer Organisation (PVO), which was in effect the private army of the AFPFL. The assembly met on June 9, and Thakin Nu was chosen as its president.

On the morning of July 19 1947, a mere 40 days later, gunmen entered the Secretariat building in central Rangoon and assassinated Aung San and seven of his ministers. U Saw, left out of the political process after the January 1947 Attlee-Aung San agreement, had plotted the murders, apparently nurturing the desperate hope that with Aung San out of the way, the British governor would turn to him to lead the country. Possibly he was also planning a takeover by force. But the crime was carelessly conceived: the assassins were traced to U Saw's house by the police, and U Saw and his accomplices were immediately arrested.

The sudden, violent death of Aung San, the architect of Burma's independence, at the age of just 32 stunned the nation. All that had been carefully constructed now seemed on the verge of collapse. Governor Hubert Rance, however, wisely showed no inclination to use the assassination as a pretext to delay the independence process. He appointed Thakin Nu, President of the Constituent Assembly and Vice-President of the AFPFL, Prime Minister forthwith. In May 1948 U Saw and his associates were duly executed.

On September 24 1947, the Constituent Assembly approved the constitution of the independent Union of Burma. It provided for a parliamentary system of government and a bicameral legislature. The Upper House, the Chamber of Nationalities, had strong minority representation (72 out of 125 members were non-Burman); the Lower House, the Chamber of Deputies, was elected from geographical constituencies defined by population. It nominated the Prime Minister, who in turn was responsible to it, whereas the President of the Union of Burma had only formal powers as Head of State. Shortly afterwards there followed the creation of the Shan and Kachin States and later also the Karenni (Kayah) State. The Chins of the western border were not granted a state, but a Chin Special Division was established. Although a Karen State was not set up, a referendum on this issue was promised and the Karen Affairs Council was created to 'aid and advise the Union Government on matters relating to the Karens'.

On October 17 1947, Prime Ministers U Nu and Clement Attlee signed a treaty formally recognising the independence of the Union of Burma. The British agreed to cancel a £15 million debt and provide a military mission. The Burmese government claimed the right to expropriate British properties, though with adequate compensation for the firms involved. On December 10 1947, the British Parliament (despite spirited opposition from Churchill's

Conservative Party) passed the Burma Independence Act and January 4 of the following year was set as the date for the transfer of power.

Taking full advantage of Burma's newly-created independence, various factions began to stir up trouble throughout the country: communists, Muslim rebels, Karen leaders (embittered by what they perceived as British desertion of their people and disillusioned with the non-creation of a Karen State) and Kachin commanders attempting to suppress the communists in central Burma, all instigated disorder. By 1951 a government minister actually admitted that less than half the country was under effective state control, and in many areas its authority was limited to the daylight hours. To compound matters, a new threat had surfaced in 1949 as the Chinese Civil War spilled over onto Burmese territory. After Yunnan Province in southern China was taken over by the communist People's Liberation Army, Nationalist (Kuomintang) forces crossed the border into Burma and began using the frontier area as a base from which to attack the communist forces. Before long these troops (numbering as many as 12,000 by 1953 and known as the Chinese Irregular Forces, the CIF) had entrenched themselves in Shan State. From fighting the communists, they turned their attention to establishing a lucrative opium export business, extending their control over most of the eastern part of Shan State. Here a system of 'war-lordism' flourished which gradually spread into western Laos and northern Thailand, creating the infamous 'Golden Triangle'. By 1953 over 80% of the Burma Army was occupied in fighting CIF groups, which they were never to succeed in dislodging from their Shan State stronghold.

For ten years from the granting of independence, Burmese politics was dominated by the AFPFL, whose popular support was assured through its historical role as the party of *Bogyoke* Aung San, though it remained a coalition of diverse individuals and groups. U Nu's chief economic policies consisted essentially of land reform, nationalisation and the establishment of a socialist welfare state, but these were never going to be easy goals to achieve. The government found itself increasingly dependent on foreign aid (such as Japanese war reparations, the equivalent of some US$250 million, grants from the United States and long-term loans from the World Bank); even the Soviet Union and other communist countries donated gifts and loans and agreed to purchase surplus Burmese rice. By 1960 many sectors of the economy had not even returned to pre-war levels: petroleum and teak exports, for example, were down to 52% and 39% of pre-war levels. Burma's position in the international economic system was rapidly deteriorating, necessitating the government to change tack and to emphasise instead the development of the economy through encouragement of the private sector. This notion, proposed in the 'Four-Year-Plan' of 1962, was to have dire consequences, for it aroused the discontent of those military officers (most notably Ne Win) committed to a socialist policy. Ne Win, in fact, had previously served as caretaker Prime Minister (proposed, ironically as it turned out, by U Nu himself) from October 1958 until February 1960, since U Nu, desperate to resolve an increasingly worsening situation, had requested the army to assume temporary control.

In February 1960 Ne Win began the process of reinstating a civilian government by holding elections for parliament. For the first time in Burma's history more than half the electorate (59%) turned out to vote and U Nu won a landslide victory. U Nu reorganised his party and renamed it the *Pyidaungsu* (Union League) Party, but not even a change of name could bolster the party's internal divisions and U Nu was forced to relinquish his post as party president. Both the effectiveness of the government and the economy were on the wane: the time was ripe for Ne Win to step in once again. On March 2 1962 the man who had re-named himself 'brilliant like the sun' seized power in a military coup. The 1947 constitution was suspended, parliament dissolved and several eminent political figures, including U Nu, were arrested.

The date of April 30 1962 is one remembered with trepidation by many Burmese, for it was the day that Ne Win's newly formed Revolutionary Council (consisting of high-ranking military officers) announced 'The Burmese Way to Socialism'. For, far from becoming the 'socialist union' which Ne Win allegedly intended, Burma rapidly began to tear itself asunder.

For 12 years Burma faltered, languished and declined. In April 1972 Ne Win and 20 other military leaders resigned their commissions, though Ne Win remained as Prime Minister and Head of the Burma Socialist Programme Party (BSPP). A new constitution was announced on January 3 1974; two months later the Revolutionary Council (Ne Win's 'flagship') dissolved itself and power was transferred to the newly elected People's Assembly (*Pyithu Hluttaw*). Ne Win proclaimed himself President and the 'new' Socialist Republic of the Union of Burma was created.

For seven years, from 1974-81, Ne Win's continued 'reign' was dominated by strikes, student unrest, insurgency, massive inflation, declining exports, smuggling, opium trafficking, and complete isolation from the outside world.

In August 1981 at the Fourth Congress of the BSPP, Ne Win stunned the Burmese nation by announcing his intention to retire as President following the October elections to the People's Assembly. In November he was succeeded by San Yu, the former BSPP General Secretary, though he retained his post as leader of the BSPP. A complex and unpredictable character, Ne Win differed from other modern-day dictators (like Ceaucescu or Honecker, for example) by consistently and single-mindedly placing enormous emphasis on astrology and numerology. For years Ne Win hid himself away in a luxurious, heavily guarded villa by Inya Lake in Rangoon; on the other side of the lake on University Avenue, as irony would have it, lay the home of Daw Khin Kyi, widow of Burma's independence hero *Bogyoke* Aung San and mother of Daw Aung San Suu Kyi.

Daw Aung San Suu Kyi was barely two years old when her father died, yet, despite spending much of her early life out of the country, she never forgot her background and heritage. Cultured, elegant, svelte, and quite remarkably charismatic — and always 'Burmese' — Suu received her education at St Hugh's College, Oxford, where, perhaps somewhat surprisingly in the light of subsequent events, she rarely took an active role in politics. And yet before her marriage to British Tibetologist Michael Aris in 1972, she was known to have remarked: 'The day might come when my country may need me as it had needed my father.'

Maybe it was fate, then, that brought Daw Aung San Suu Kyi back to Burma in April 1988, though the actual reason was for Suu to tend her dying mother Daw Khin Kyi, who had suffered a severe stroke (and who was to die just eight months later on December 27). The country by now was in deep decline and on the verge of ripping itself apart. Ne Win's idiosyncratic management of the economy had resulted in dire financial consequences, the final, damning indictment of which came on December 11 1987 when Burma was granted the UN-afforded status of Least Developed Country (LDC). Foreign debt had reached a massive US$3.5 billion at the same time as foreign exchange reserves had shrunk to US$20-30 million. Burma's per capita income had slipped to below US$200, manufacturing was at less than 10% of the GDP and yet, remarkably perhaps, the country's literacy rate stood as high as 81%.

It had been a sorry degeneration into poverty and civil discontent, but not wholly unpredictable if one examines Burma's turbulent past.

Nonetheless, Ne Win's rule *was* characterised by bizarre moves and punctuated with singular, seemingly illogical acts. On September 5 1987, for example, Sein Lwin (Secretary of the State Council) decreed that all 25, 35 and 75 kyat banknotes were to be demonetised without compensation (the 75 kyat note had been introduced by Ne Win himself to celebrate his 75th birthday). In a trice, 80% of the country's money in circulation was wiped out, and many students found themselves penniless. Instead of bolstering the economy, this action had exactly the opposite effect: it created massive inflation, increased still further the already rampant (and illegal) black market activity and instilled profound resentment and distrust amongst the student population.

This latest economic move was too much for the students to take: over 500 spilled out onto the streets of Rangoon destroying government vehicles in a Bacchanalian rampage. The state responded by immediately closing all the universities and colleges. In another bizarre twist the following month, new banknotes were issued in the denomination of 45 and 90 kyat. In reality this was quite typical of Ne Win: both 45 and 90 added up to and were divisible by nine, Ne Win's lucky number.

The year 1988 began just as 1987 had ended, with a floundering economy and massive discontent amongst the student population. On March 13 students clashed with the *Lon Htein* (riot police); three days later the scenes became even uglier. The *Lon Htein* gunned down a number of students in cold blood: one of the most brutal periods in Burma's history was just dawning. The following day at least 1,000 students were arrested and taken to Insein Jail, north of Rangoon.

On March 18 ('Bloody Friday') thousands of students converged on the Sule Pagoda. Under the command of Sein Lwin, thereafter known as the 'Butcher of Rangoon', the *Lon Htein* and *Tatmadaw* moved in and scores of demonstrators were murdered.

Two months later, on June 20, over 5,000 students staged a peaceful protest in Rangoon; the following day hordes of students marched towards central Rangoon chanting slogans. Once again the *Lon Htein* intervened and around 80 protesters were massacred. The state responded by announcing a 60-day ban on public gatherings and imposing a 6pm to 6am curfew in Rangoon. However, on June 23 the students established a strike centre at the Shwedagon Pagoda. In Pegu, meanwhile, 80km northeast of the capital, there were further bloody clashes and at least 70 people were shot.

Exactly one month later, the Burma Socialist Programme Party (the

BSPP) convened a special session which was attended by over 1,000 delegates. Ne Win appeared, closely shadowed by his most loyal subject Khin Nyunt, and began a 30 minute address. To the surprise of those present, Ne Win put forward a proposal for a new parliament and for the creation of a multi-party system (thus, in theory anyway, making Burma the first so-called 'socialist' country to permit a multi-party system; but, as time was to show, little would come of the motion). It was, though, what Ne Win *didn't* say that caused more consternation — or rather what was announced on his behalf by Htwe Han, the BSPP Central Committee Headquarters Secretary. Since he (Ne Win) felt in some small measure responsible for the tragic events of the previous two months and since he was now advancing in years, he had decided to quit as Party Chairman and Party Member. More was to follow: not only would Ne Win resign, but so too would San Yu, the BSPP's Vice Chairman and State President, BSPP General Secretary Aye Ko, Defence Minister Kyaw Htin, Finance Minister Tun Tin, and Joint Secretary General Sein Lwin. Indeed the very core of Burma's military leadership was apparently resigning *en masse*. In reality, Ne Win had absolutely no intention of relinquishing power (most political observers agree that he *never* has had).

Three days later the Central Committee of the BSPP held a meeting, choosing Sein Lwin as Ne Win's successor. The following day Sein Lwin was elected Chairman of the Council of State. No move could have been better calculated to enrage the students, for Sein Lwin (a subordinate of Ne Win in the Fourth Burma Rifles), had, of course, acquired the nickname the 'Butcher of Rangoon' for ordering the *Lon Htein* to cut down the demonstrators in the spring. In fact, Sein Lwin's record of anti-student violence stretched back over a quarter of a century as he had also been responsible for the student killings at the hands of the military and the dynamiting of the Rangoon University Student Union building in 1962, as well as brutally suppressing the student demonstrations in 1974 against the military's handling of the funeral and burial site of former UN Secretary General U Thant.

July 28, one of the holiest days in Burma's calendar, was the Full Moon Day of *Waso*, the beginning of the Buddhist Lent and a number of students and anti-government protesters congregated at the Shwedagon, Rangoon's most sacred pagoda. Four days later an underground student organisation, the All-Burma Students' Union (*ba ka tha*) brazenly distributed leaflets calling for a national strike on August 8, which was a highly auspicious day in the Burmese calendar (8s were said to be lucky for the opposition, whereas 9s were favourable to Ne Win and this was 8/8/88). Symbolically, it was also the date of the fall of the Ava Dynasty according to the Burmese era, 888 BE). On August 3 the government declared martial law; 10,000 demonstrators defied the ban, however, and marched through the centre of Rangoon. From August 3 until the proposed day of the general strike, hundreds of protesters were arrested for flouting martial law.

At precisely eight minutes past 8am on the morning of August 8 1988, the dockworkers in the port of Rangoon walked out. The strike was on. Monks, women, students, people from all ethnic groups marched through the city waving portraits of Aung San, demanding democracy and economic reform. All over the land they demonstrated: from Mandalay, Sagaing and Shwebo in the north to Bassein in the Irrawaddy Delta, from Pegu, Toungoo, Pyinmana and Mindu in the central plains to the towns of Yenangyaung and Chauk along the Irrawaddy River, from Moulmein, Mergui and Tavoy in the southeast to Taunggyi, capital of Shan State, even as far north as Myitkyina, the capital of the northern Kachin State.

In Rangoon, meanwhile, the *Tatmadaw*, anxious and unsure, waited in the wings. At 5.30pm Rangoon's commander Myo Nyunt ordered the crowds to disperse or face the consequences. Instead, more people joined in and the throngs swelled. At 11pm hordes of demonstrators still remained outside the Sule Pagoda; all of a sudden, trucks of *Tatmadaw* appeared from behind the City Hall. Monks, women, children, schoolgirls and students fled, terrified, in every direction as they tried to escape the wanton bursts of gun-fire. No one knows the exact number who perished, nor how many were massacred in pagoda-studded Sagaing the following day where countless unrecognisable bodies were dumped into the Irrawaddy River. As one eye-witness recorded:

'And then like lightning, army units appeared. They fired right into the crowds, shooting anybody. It was insane. When unarmed demonstrators got on their knees to peacefully resist the rows of soldiers, they were shot dead. The pavement turned red ... Soldiers ... bayonetted children, shot Red Cross workers as they attempted to aid the wounded and opened fire in front of Rangoon General Hospital, killing doctors and nurses ... The gravely injured were left to die in the streets ... soldiers threw bodies of the dead and injured into trucks and took them to the cemetery, where the living and dead were cremated together.'

It was now four months since Daw Aung San Suu Kyi had returned to Burma to care for her ailing mother. No longer could she bear to watch her countrymen and women suffer: it was time for her to assume the mantle of her late father Aung San. On August 26 a large crowd, many of them merely curious, turned up at the hallowed Shwedagon Pagoda. They had come to catch their first glimpse of the daughter of *Bogyoke* Aung San, whose huge portrait had been placed above the stage where she was to speak, alongside a resistance flag of World War II.

> 'A number of people are saying that since I've spent most of my life abroad and am married to a foreigner, I could not be familiar with the ramifications of this country's politics. I wish to speak out very frankly and openly. It's true that I've lived abroad. It is also true that I am married to a foreigner. But these facts have never, and will never, interfere with or lessen my love and devotion for my country by any measure or degree. People have been saying that I know nothing of Burmese politics. The trouble is I know too much. My family knows better than any how devious Burmese politics can be and how much my father had to suffer on this account ... The present crisis is the concern of the entire nation. I could not, as my father's daughter, remain indifferent to all that was going on. This national crisis could, in fact, be called the second struggle for independence.'

With these words, delivered in flawless Burmese, Daw Aung San Suu Kyi won over the hearts of the people, and at the same time set herself on a fateful collision course with Ne Win.

Burma remained in a state of chaotic uncertainty until, at 4pm on September 18, the music programme of the BBS (Burma Broadcasting Service) was interrupted with the following announcement:

> 'In order to bring a timely halt to the deteriorating conditions on all sides all over the country and in the interests of the people, the defence forces have assumed all power in the state with effect from today.'

This was the birth of the 'State Law and Order Restoration Council' (the 'SLORC'), another of Ne Win's madcap political babies. Ostensibly under the command of Saw Maung, one of Ne Win's staunchest allies, the SLORC imposed a curfew on Rangoon from 8pm to 4am and banned all gatherings of more than five people.

On September 20 Saw Maung pronounced himself Prime Minister, Foreign Minister and Defence Minister all at the same time. But both he and the so-called 'State Law and Order Restoration Council' were soon to realise (most reluctantly) that the Burmese people would and *could* never accept or tolerate a one-party state. Concessions would have to be made to save the country from plunging even further into the abyss of bankruptcy and civil unrest. And thus four days later Aung Gyi (who had twice been imprisoned for his opposition to Ne Win), Tin U (likewise) and Daw Aung San Suu Kyi set up the National League for Democracy (NLD), which was registered as a political party on September 27.

Daw Aung San Suu Kyi, determined to carry on her father's struggle for freedom, threw herself wholeheartedly into the political fray. Tirelessly she toured the country, drawing vast crowds wherever she went. On one occasion, within a period of 13 days, she visited more than 50 towns and villages in Pegu, Magwe, Sagaing and Mandalay Divisions, as well as the Shan, Kayah and Karen States. Wherever she travelled, she was harassed and provoked by the SLORC and the *Tatmadaw* and vilified in the state-run national press. Not once, however, did she flinch nor weary in her struggle to win democracy, respect and reforms for the Burmese people.

Eventually on February 16 1989 the BBS announced that elections would be held the following spring. Saw Maung was desperate to prevent further unrest and was convinced that the outcome of any election would reveal a hopelessly splintered opposition. But Daw Aung San Suu Kyi continued her campaigning throughout the land, constantly flouting the authorities, until finally, as far as the SLORC was concerned, she overstepped the mark. Her outspokenness and honesty proved her undoing in June that year.

'U Ne Win', she daringly proclaimed 'is one of those that caused this nation to suffer for 26 years, U Ne Win is the one who lowered the prestige of the armed forces. Officials from the armed forces and officials from SLORC, I call upon you to be loyal to the state. Be loyal to the people, you don't have to be loyal to U Ne Win.'

Fearful and timorous, both the *Tatmadaw* and the SLORC remained loyal to Ne Win and on July 20, Daw Aung San Suu Kyi was placed under house arrest.

Elections did eventually take place on May 27 the following year (the numbers of that date, of course, adding up to and being divisible by nine). The previous January, however, Rangoon's Elections Commission had banned Daw Aung San Suu Kyi from standing for election. Not that it made a jot of difference either to the result or to the SLORC's subsequent reaction to the outcome. Daw Aung San Suu Kyi's National League for Democracy captured 392 out of the 485 seats contested (81%) in the 492-member assembly (elections in seven of the constituencies were postponed for 'security reasons'). The National Unity Party (NUP), formerly Ne Win's Burma Socialist Programme Party, won a meagre ten seats.

SLORC never handed over power to the people of Burma, claiming, amongst other things, that since Daw Aung San Suu Kyi was married to a foreigner, state secrets were at risk; instead they simply wiped out all the opposition. According to *Amnesty International* and Burmese political commentators, the SLORC continued to wage war on the country's ethnic groups and minorities, sold logging concesssions to the Thais (thereby permitting the wholesale destruction of the world's last remaining teak forests, and amassing some US$1 billion in hard currency with which to purchase arms), peddled jade and gems, and accumulated vast sums out of opium trafficking. They continued to spend 40% of the nation's annual budget on defence, acquiring tanks, aircraft and military supplies from Poland, Yugoslavia, China, Singapore, Pakistan and Portugal (amongst other countries) to suppress their own people. They used chemical weapons against the Kachin, persecuted the Muslim Rohingyas of Arakan State and forced thousands to flee their own homeland. They raided Buddhist monasteries in Mandalay and, in scenes reminiscent of the Khmer Rouge in the days of Pol Pot, forcibly relocated hundreds of thousands of people from the towns to the countryside in order to disperse dissenters. According to a report by the UN Human Rights Commission, there have been more than 1,000 allegations of abduction, forced labour, murder, rape, torture and arbitrary arrest. Other reports state that at least 40,000 citizens have been press-ganged into working as unpaid porters for the SLORC.

'It has been explained patiently time and again that Myanmar has no political detainees, and those politicians who happen to be under restriction are so because they have broken the existing laws of the country they call their own, and not for their political persuasions ... in Myanmar, all religions flourish freely'.

*Working People's Daily*, December 30 1992.

Meanwhile, the West tut-tutted in mild disapproval, whilst ASEAN (The Association of Southeast Asian Nations, namely Brunei, Indonesia, Malaysia, Philippines, Singapore and Thailand) merely responded with what it referred to as 'constructive engagement'. The universities — the very future of Burma — opened and closed sporadically, the students, without work, study or hope, hung around the streets, temples and coffee-shops and the Military Intelligence (MI) maintained an evil eye on all. Talking to foreigners was deemed an act of treason.

> 'Even as the State Law and Order Restoration Council has been endeavouring to bring about resurgence of patriotism and raise the spirit of national consolidation among the people, some powerful neo-colonialist nations, the organizations under their influence and the news agencies and media organizations under their authority have been using all methods synchronously in propagating all kinds of rumours, making false allegations, spreading the evil taint of agitation and incitement as well as carrying out myriad destructive activities so as to cause deterioration of national solidarity and to weaken the spirit of patriotism among the nationalities.'
>
> (Speech by Khin Nyunt at the opening ceremony of the Special Training Course No 5 for Doctors at the Central Institute of Public Services at Phaunggyi, quoted in the *Working People's Daily*, March 12 1993).

In December 1990 opposition politicians took to the jungle to evade capture and torture, and set up a provisional National Coalition Government of the Union of Burma at Manerplaw in the eastern border area of the country under control of the Karen Liberation Army, who had themselves been waging a 40-year-old guerilla war against the Burmese authorities. At the beginning of December 1991 Saw Maung suffered a nervous breakdown and was replaced on April 23 1992 by Than Shwe, yet as a foreign diplomat remarked:

> 'Ne Win still pulls the strings. The military chiefs run things day by day but go to him before making any important decisions. He appointed them all and they owe their loyalty to him. He is the ultimate arbiter of power.'

On July 10 1991 Daw Aung San Suu Kyi received the Sakharov Prize for 'Freedom of Thought'; on October 14 she was awarded the Nobel Peace Prize, on May 14 1992 her son Alexander accepted a human rights award on her behalf from the International Human Rights Law Group in Washington, and on June 30 1992 she received UNESCO's Simon Bolivar Prize for her contributions towards 'freedom, independence and dignity of peoples'.

On July 30, shortly after beginning her fourth year under house arrest, she received an honorary political science degree from

Thailand's Thammasat University. She has since been awarded four more prizes, including Copenhagen's prestigious Rose Prize. Isolated from the outside world, like the country she tried to rescue, Daw Aung San Suu Kyi is today only allowed to read, write and play the piano in her house on University Avenue. The SLORC ignores all pleas for her release; in 1992 U Aye, of Burma's Foreign Ministry, was known to remark 'You can forget about that individual, she's finished', whilst Kyaw Win, deputy director of the MI, commented 'We cannot release her ... because we are afraid that some unscrupulous elements might manipulate her and destabilise the situation.'

Eventually in 1992 Michael Aris and his two children were twice permitted to visit Daw Aung San Suu Kyi (and, at the time of writing, once — in April 1993 — with his youngest son). Subsequently the SLORC made two further 'concessions' in an attempt to finally silence its Western critics. On September 11 1992 the following announcement appeared in the *Working People's Daily*:

> 'In view of the fact that the security, prevalence of Law and Order and regional peace and tranquillity of the State have improved, the State Law and Order Restoration Council hereby deletes the prohibition 'No one shall go into the streets from 23:00 hours (11 pm) to 04:00 hours (4 am) without specific permission to do so' of Order No. 4/90 of 10th October, 1990 which was the latest amendment of paragraph 1, sub-paragraph (a) of Order No. 2/88 of 18th September, 1988, with effect from this day.'

On September 27 1992, the *Working People's Daily* issued another decree from Khin Nyunt, Chief of the Military Intelligence (MI) and referred to in the *Bangkok Post* as the 'Prince of Evil' and the 'Prince of Darkness':

> 'In consideration of the improvement and stability of the general situation in the State and in view of the interest of the people, the State Law and Order Restoration Council hereby revokes the following Martial Law Orders with effect from this day:
>
> (1) Martial Law Order No 1/89 dated 17th July, 1989, of the State Law and Order Restoration Council issued in respect of the conferring of executive and judicial Martial Law powers to be exercised by certain Military Commanders within their respective Military regions;
> (2) Martial Law Order No 2/89, dated 18th July, 1989, of the State Law and Order Restoration Council issued in respect of the procedure to be followed in administering justice by the Military Tribunals.'

Those *au courant* with Burmese politics believe these 'changes' to be purely cosmetic — particularly in light of the fact that in a subsequent government shake-up, all the top posts of the new 18-man constitutional commission went to senior figures in the armed forces. In addition few Burmese commentators have taken seriously the so-called (and hitherto long drawn-out) National Convention, assembled in January 1993 and chaired by Myo Nyunt.

'For genuine party democracy to flourish in Burma,' announced Myo Nyunt, 'it will be necessary to work hand-in-hand with the military. To put it frankly, the maintenance of national stability, peace and tranquility without the participation of the *Tatmadaw* is extremely risky and dangerous'.

In no way do these words differ in substance from the regular contents of the *Working People's Daily*, of TV and Radio Myanmar or from remarks made by Saw Maung when Chairman of the SLORC:

'I tell you if anyone wants to enjoy the human rights they have in the USA, England or India, provided that country accepts (them), I will permit them to leave. But in Myanmar, I can only grant rights suitable for the Myanmar people. In our military science there is no such thing as dialogue, someone might say 'look friend, please don't shoot', well that is not the way it works.'

In February 1993 the SLORC denied visas to a group of Nobel Peace laureates who had planned to visit Southeast Asia in an attempt to press the military into releasing Daw Aung San Suu Kyi. Edward Broadbent, President of the Montreal-based International Centre for Human Rights and Democratic Development, the group organising the mission to Burma, commented:

'We have recently received refusal for visas (for the group) on grounds that (we) support the government in opposition ... the party led by Aung San Suu Kyi. This is an extraordinary revelation by this government that it would deny visas to people who have been recognised globally ... as committed to non-violence and peace.'

The mission, which was set to include up to seven Nobel Peace Prize winners including former Costa Rican President Oscar Arias, Archbishop Desmond Tutu of South Africa and the Dalai Lama of Tibet, would have been the first of its kind to travel together to push for a non-violent change to peace.

'... the hooked-nosed colonialists who aggressed against, annexed and reduced the Myanmar Naing-Ngan to servitude, with the intention of retaining their grip on the country for a long time, carried out their blatant policy of divide and rule. They sowed distrust and suspicion among our national brethren, they used all stratagems, incitements and agitations to breed inter-racial hatred, encouraged a sense of separatism and secessionism to the extent that all such activities have been clearly documented in historical records so much so that they cannot deny or hide these malicious activities.

These people are past masters at this kind of thing in which they can even make cockerels of the same coop appear to be enemies to one another. Today too, the BBC continues with skilful cunning to maintain this tradition to encourage mistrust, suspicion and division and thereby create Kayin-Bamar hatred. And in addition to that, a group of 'Nobels' too smart for their own good, joined in and interfered in our internal affairs. And what about those who were responsible for accepting these meddling 'Nobels'? Such an individual can be likened to a person who hires out rooms for questionable purposes. And what this person has done in the matter of the meddling 'Nobels' interfering in the internal affairs of Myanmar amounts to adding fuel to the fire.'

Aung Min, *Burma Working People's Daily*, March 9 1993.

It would undoubtedly seem, then, that the SLORC's repeated pledge of a transition to democratic and civilian rule is unlikely to be honoured in the forseeable future.

# PRESS, TV and PROPAGANDA

The military-run Burmese media offers practically no news or information to either locals or tourists, but provides plenty of unintentional light-hearted entertainment. Fortunately most Burmese can tune into the BBC's World Service so they are well aware of developments both at home and in the world outside, from which the SLORC tries so desperately to cut them off.

The state's English flagship is the *Working People's Daily* which in many ways resembles the daily newspaper that used to be published in the former German Democratic Republic. All the items about the West concern either disasters (such as plane crashes) or trivia (in the style of the British tabloids); local news revolves around the great achievements of the military. The front page used to be headed by the following so-called 'Noble Desire':

'Although the State Law and Order Restoration Council has had to take over, due to unavoidable circumstances, the sovereign power of the State to prevent the Union from disintegration and for ensuring the safety and security of the lives, homes and property of the people, it wishes to retransfer State power to the people, in whom it was initially vested, through democratic means within the shortest time possible.

Therefore, the entire people are urged to give all their co-operation to ensure the rule of law and for prevalence of peace and tranquility.' The *Tatmadaw*.

Similar proclamations appear throughout every edition: 'Only when the people are able to enjoy convenient and easy livelihood would they be physically and mentally at peace. The *Tatmadaw* is carrying out this duty and all nationalities of the Union are urged to give all co-operation and assistance in this great task'.

Burmese headlines include: 'Onion Cultivators Co-operative Societies formed in Magway Division', 'Minister for Forestry Lt-Gen Chit Swe inspects the No 93 saw mill, Paungde,' and on December 20 1992 'Chairman of State Law and Order Restoration Council General Than Shwe takes part in State Law and Order Restoration Council Chairman's Bowl Golf'. Foreign headlines are even more informative: two stories which dominated the issue of July 23 1992, for example, were: 'Hippo who mourned brother's death killed by lightning' and 'Man kills neighbour because dog wet on newspaper'. 'Keep up with the latest world news! READ WORKING PEOPLE'S DAILY THE CHOICE OF DECISION-MAKERS.'

(Incidentally, no private Burmese publication can be printed unless it contains at least three of the SLORC's slogans).

**TV Myanmar:**
6.30pm
1.      Marching Songs
        Military Songs
2.      Song Variety
7.00pm
3.      Plant Vegetables
        Breed Livestock
7.30pm
4.      A Special Programme to Uphold: 'National Spirit'
7.40pm
5.      Song Variety
8.00pm
6.      News and Weather Report
7.      International News

8.      The Police Story 'Country Boy'
9.      National News
10.     The Next Day's Programme

**Radio Myanmar:**
08.30  News
08.40  Slogans
        Music Now To Nine
13.30  News
13.40  Slogans
        Lunchtime Music
21.00  Music in Latin Mood
21.10  Editorial
21.15  News
21.30  Radio Magazine
22.00  Portfolio for Easy Listening
('News', incidentally, consists solely of the daily diaries of Secretaries 1 and 2).

# Press

If possible, try and obtain a copy of a book entitled 'Rangoon', which was printed in Calcutta in the 50s (when it was priced at just K2): 'Mingaladon Airport, 11 miles out of Rangoon', it proudly proclaims, 'bids fair to become the Clapham Junction of airways in South and South East Asia' and asserts that 'the Rangoon Turf Club, whose race-course is reputedly the finest in Asia'. Advertisements encourage you to 'get the finest on Pan American' or maybe try 'SAS' for 'only SAS flies today the airways of tomorrow'; tourists are advised to 'Look in at The Burma Cold Stores Ltd where your money buys most: the finest array of foreign provisions, liquors, toilets and cold meats.' A language section includes such essential expressions as: 'Please ask the butler to put in fresh bathing water', 'Please get the water closet cleaned up', 'Let the sweeper clean the room properly', 'How much do I have to tip the butler?', 'I want my tea', and 'Is there any fishing in Rangoon?'.

This publication compares favourably with a small brown book entitled 'Burma Guide' published by Chalermnit in Thailand in 1987. The 'Little Guide to Burma' informs the reader in wonderfully idiosyncratic Thai-English that 'Buses although cheap are not recommended because of delays and a lot of waitings, never in time', suggests places to 'satay' in Mandalay, and, most embarrassingly, refers to one of Mandalay's finest pagodas as the 'Kunthodaw'. Well, what do you expect for 50 baht?

Another Indian publication, 'Burmese Self-Taught', which first appeared in 1936, contains such useful phrases as 'He says he cannot find the horse', 'Is it a man or a woman?', 'Must I boil the egg?', 'Lend me a piece of blotting-paper', 'There are plenty of hog deer in the jungle and sometimes one finds hares and pigs', 'You have hit a red deer, Sir', 'You cannot hunt tigers without elephants', 'Come here with your hoe', and 'White ants do not eat iron-wood or teak'. Reprinted in 1991 and priced at 90 rupees, this book is clearly essential reading for visitors to Burma in 1993.

Regarding propaganda, other than the Press and TV, tourists in the past could scarcely have failed to notice the huge red signs all over the country. Formerly written both in Burmese and English, they proclaimed such pearls of wisdom as: 'THE TATMADAW WILL NEVER BETRAY THE NATIONAL CAUSE', 'ONLY WHEN THERE IS DISCIPLINE WILL THERE BE PROGRESS', 'CRUSH ALL DESTRUCTIVE ELEMENTS', 'NEVER HESITATING, ALWAYS READY TO SACRIFICE BLOOD AND SWEAT IS THE TATMADAW', 'TATMADAW AND THE PEOPLE CO-OPERATE AND CRUSH ALL THOSE HARMING THE UNION', 'ANYONE WHO GETS RIOTOUS AND UNRULY IS OUR ENEMY', 'BEWARE OF ABOVEGROUND AND UNDERGROUND DESTRUCTIVE ELEMENTS', and most wryly, right outside the American Embassy in Rangoon, 'DOWN WITH MINIONS OF COLONIALISM'. The most amusing of all, perhaps, was the one which stood beside a football field in Pyinmana and proudly declared: 'MYANMAR SPORTS MUST OVERWHELM THE WORLD'. However, with the SLORC anxious to improve its image and with January 1993's National Convention in mind, these hoardings now appear almost exclusively in Burmese, the English translations having been painted over.

Burmese propaganda starts at an early age: tests for primary school children consist of questions like: 'Soldiers fight ... our country' (fill in the blank). A Burmese friend remarked sardonically that the obvious answer was 'against' and certainly not 'for'.

# ECONOMY

In terms of natural resources, Burma is potentially one of the richest countries in Asia. Gems (mainly rubies and sapphires from Mogok, 70 miles northeast of Mandalay), jade (from Mogaung in the Kachin State, west of Myitkyina), gold, silver, zinc, tin, lead, antimony, petroleum (though recent drilling results have proved disappointing and Shell, amongst other firms, has decided to pull out: see below), natural gas (Burma recently signed a multi-million dollar contract with the French company Total to develop a huge gas well in the Gulf of Martaban), prolific land resources (rice, fruit, sesame, pulses, beans, ground-nuts, cotton, maize, sugarcane, wheat, sunflower, rubber, tobacco, jute), a multitude of fruits, teak, hardwood and vast unexploited fisheries and sea-food should all, in theory, add up to a healthy and vibrant economy. However due to the government's ineptitude and the fact that most of the profits from the country's wealth merely fund the 300,000-strong *Tatmadaw*, purchasing arms and military aircraft, Burma is bankrupt. The former 'Golden Land' (*Shwe Pyidaw*) now ranks as the fifth poorest nation in the world and survives solely by means of widespread yet illegal black market trading and opium trafficking (opium production in 1991 stood at 2,350 metric tons, twice the output of 1988 when the SLORC took over and enough to supply 60% of the world market).

Border trade with Thailand provides funds for the smugglers and the SLORC with the six major crossings being at Mae Sai, Mae Hong Son, Mae Sariang, Mae Sot, Kra Buri and Ranong. Figures are naturally imprecise, but in 1982/83 it was estimated that some K920 million (or 51%) of all black market goods were smuggled through the Thai border. Thailand provides textiles, plastic products, medicines, machinery and spare parts, chemicals, electrical goods, foodstuffs and watches, whilst in return Burma trades timber (as a result of these massive teak and logging concessions to the Thais, Burma now has the fifth highest deforestation rate in the world), gems, jade, gold, tin, tungsten, livestock, opium and heroin, marine products, rice, rubber, industrial art objects and antiques. All this is known euphemistically as Burma's 'Informal Trade'.

As far as 'Formal Trade' is concerned, Burma's economy continues to rely heavily on agriculture which contributes 35 to 45% of the GDP and provides employment for 60 to 70% of the labour force. Rice is vital to the country's economy and rice cultivation is a way of life for about 70% of the population. It contributes 40 to 50% of export earnings and provides employment to about 65% of the labour force. Indeed, rice takes up nearly half the total cultivated area of 25 million acres. Prior to World War II Burma was the largest rice exporter in the world, contributing roughly half of the world's total rice exports, but this figure has dropped steadily: today Burmese rice is of very poor quality, fetching prices much lower than those prevailing in the world market. It is simply not possible anymore to process high quality rice owing to the old and outdated rice mills from the pre-war days. Nor is it possible to increase rice exports because of Burma's growing population and the lower level of resources allocated to the agricultural sector.

Oil exploration, though strategically important and financially essential to the SLORC, has proved almost fruitless to foreign enterprises. However, oil companies remain Burma's biggest investors, having provided some 65% of foreign investment since 1988. Over US$400 million have been ploughed into oil exploration in the past five years, from which the SLORC takes between 70-90% of the profits. Prospects, however, do not look good, as a recent report in the *Bangkok Post* confirmed:

'FOREIGN oil companies took on guerillas, jungle and some of the hardest rock there is, only to find that Burma's Golden Land held no riches for them.

Three years after descending on the country, most are now packing their bags to leave.

'We came on the assumption this could be the next great oil play in the world ... We've drilled all the potential elephants (big projects). $400 million and not a nickel to show for it.'

But though wildcat wells in 10 on-shore blocks were nearly all dry, two companies recently found deposits in the Andaman Sea. The discovery keeps alive the hopes of Burma's military government that an energy boom will fuel an economic recovery ... The state-run Myanmar Oil and Gas Enterprise, meanwhile, is still toiling away with 47 veteran wells to draw about 13,800 barrels per day ...'.

'Burma's oil exploration has now gone full scale after years of fits and starts. Foreign businesses were nationalised in 1962. The government allowed four foreign oil companies between 1974-76, including Total, but they were not successful.

Another attempt in 1985 was abandoned when oil prices tumbled. Officials say they know their country has large reserves of oil.

Now they are also complaining of high dock handling charges and difficult logistics in insurgency areas. Add the nightmare of poor communication facilities, say the companies, and they are paying more than anticipated in having to build roads and bridges in remote parts. Oil companies have spent more than $400 million, boosting

Burma's scarce foreign exchange reserves.' *Bangkok Post*, November 26 1992.

In a recent publication entitled 'Myanmar: The Golden Land', the SLORC, eager to woo foreign investors, list the so-called 'Eligible Economic Activities' opened for foreign investment under the alluring banner: 'Myanmar: Golden Opportunities'. These 'activities' consist of:

Agriculture, Livestock and Fishery, Forestry, Mining, Industry (Foodstuff, Textile, Personal Goods, Household Goods, Leather Products and the likes, Transport Equipment, Building Materials, Pulp and Paper, Chemicals, Chemical Products and Pharmaceuticals, Iron and Steel, Machinery and Plant), Construction, Transport and Communications and Trade.

The following twelve economic activities are restricted to be carried out solely by State-owned Economic Enterprises, but allowance can be made by the Government for the participation of any other persons or enterprises subject to conditions as prescribed in the procedures relating to the State-owned Economic Enterprises Law:

1. Extraction of teak and sale of the same in the country and abroad;
2. Cultivation and conservation of forest plantation with the exception of village-owned fire-wood plantations cultivated by the villagers for their personal use;
3. Exploration, extraction and sale of petroleum and natural gas and production and products of the same;
4. Exploration and extraction of pearls, jade and precious stones and export of the same;
5. Breeding and production of fish and prawns in fisheries which have been reserved for research by the Government;
6. Postal and Telecommunications service;
7. Air Transport service and Railway Transport service;
8. Banking service and Insurance service;
9. Broadcasting service and Television service;
10. Exploration and extraction of metals and export of the same;
11. Electricity generating services other than those permitted by law to private and co-operative electricity generating services;
12. Manufacturing of products relating to security and defence which the Government has, from time to time, prescribed by notification.

If proposals for economic activities not specified in the above are submitted, they will be considered individually by the Union of Myanmar Foreign Investment Commission.'

A foreign investor can set himself up in business alone by bringing in 100% foreign capital. If he wishes to enter into a partnership with a Burmese company: 'the foreign capital to be brought in must be at a minimum 35 percent of the total equity capital. The minimum amount of foreign capital to be brought in is US$100,000 at present.'

One of Burma's most valuable assets are the forests which cover 57% of the total land and produce about 75% of the world's teak resources. Fish and fishery products also have a high export potential, but have been badly mismanaged over the years, whilst beans and pulses (which form the third largest group in terms of export earnings after rice and timber), and oil cakes (eg sesame cakes, groundnut cakes, cotton cakes and coconut cakes) are other major earners.

In 1990 when Thailand attracted some five million tourists, Burma amassed a paltry 8,968, raising a mere K130 million for its flailing economy. With the SLORC desperate for foreign currency and eager (superficially at least) to improve its reputation in the West, a Ministry of Hotels and Tourism has been set up, according to the *Working People's Daily*, to 'raise the momentum of hotel and tourism services'. New destinations have been opened up, private hotels and travel agents have been established and individual travel once again permitted. Whether this new Ministry will actually achieve anything remains to be seen: needless to say it is headed by an army officer who goes under the name of Maj-Gen Kyaw Ba. One thing's for certain, Burma needs desperately to improve its economic standing: the kyat has lost 76% of its value within the past four years, inflation is running wild (official figures of 28.7% look extremely dubious), it has a foreign debt of US$4.8 billion and a deficit of US$659 million. All in all, Burma hardly qualifies as one of Southeast Asia's new brand of 'Tiger Cubs', more like a bedraggled Siamese kitten.

# POPULATION & PEOPLE: THE ETHNIC GROUPS

'There is in Burma this extraordinary profusion of races, all hugger-mugger, many of them divided into sub-tribes, and many of them on top of each other.'

There has been no recent census in Burma so one can only give a rough estimate of the population. Some sources quote 35 million, others 45 million. The precise figure is thought to be nearer 41.6 million. The capital Rangoon (and its vicinity) is home to around 3.2 million Burmese, the second largest city Mandalay approximately 450,000. The country is a veritable hodgepodge of different ethnic groups (possibly as many as 135) of which around two-thirds are Burman. The other main groups are:

**Shan**: around five million, they are Buddhist and have the same origins as the Thais (from Yunnan province). At the collapse of the Pagan Dynasty at the end of the 13th Century, a wave of Shan immigrants flooded into Burma and for the next 250 years they were the dominant race in the land. They have their own written script and a history and literature dating back centuries.

**Arakanese**: about four million who live in Arakan State on the west coast and bordering Bangladesh. They are roughly 30% Muslim and are of Tibeto-Burman ethnicity.

**Karen**: around two and a half million, comprising at least 11 different tribes and groups including the **Kayah**, **Karenni**, **Pa-O**, **Padaung** (the so-called 'giraffe-necked' women) and **Kayaw**, though they are generally divided into three groups: **Pwo**, **Sgaw** and **Bwe**. In fact, the Karenni (Red Karen or Kayah) are ethnically and linguistically distinct from the Karen. Their small state, adjoining the southern Shan State, retained its autonomy even during British rule, and only became part of Burma after independence (the KNPP, the Karenni National Progress Party, was founded in 1948 in protest at being coerced into joining the Union of Burma). The Karen are 80% Buddhist (animist; animism being the attribution of living souls to plants, inanimate objects and natural phenomena, belief in spirits. See the following section on religion) and 20% Christian (Baptist).

**Kachin**: around two million of Tibeto-Burman ethnicity. They are

Christian or animist. The original name of the race was *Jinghpaw* or *Singhpo*, which was of Tibetan origin, being derived from the Tibetan term *sin-po* meaning cannibal. The Kachins, who possessed no written language until the end of the 19th Century, have always insisted that they descended from the Tibetan Plateau about 1,250 years ago and entered what is now northern Burma. However, the complete lack of any written history makes it extremely difficult to associate any time factor with this descent but tradition, handed down from generation to generation, maintains that the descent took place some 50 or 60 generations ago.

**Mon**: around one million. Of Mon-Khmer descent, they are linguistically closer to the Khmer and are Buddhist. Formerly referred to as the Talaings, their main settlement areas are around the port of Moulmein and the former capital of Pegu.

Other ethnic groups include Chinese, Indian, Chin (Nagas), Lahu, Wa, Akha, Lisu and hilltribes such as Danu, Palaung and Taungyo who inhabit Shan State. Roughly 70,000 Intha live in and around Inle Lake, including the famous 'leg-rowers'.

# RELIGION, PAGODAS AND TEMPLES

'Burmese Buddhism ... is a world strange for the most part to Western perceptions ... one almost from another planet ... one of karma, merit, endless rebirths, *nats*, and pagodas.'

Theravada Buddhism (the original or 'pure' school of Buddhism) is the dominant faith, practised by over 80% of the population. Known as the 'Doctrine of the Elders', it is the oldest form of the Buddha's teachings, handed down by means of the Pali language. According to tradition, its name is derived from the fact of having been fixed by 500 holy Elders of the Order, soon after the death of the Buddha. Theravada Buddhism is sometimes referred to as Southern Buddhism or Pali Buddhism and is also practised in Sri Lanka, Cambodia, Laos and Thailand.

'He (the traveller) finds no god in Rangoon, but only the placid, unwinking, half-smiling image of Gautama Buddha, who, five hundred years before Christ, attained to Nirvana, and whose image is to-day worshipped by one-third of the human race.'

Burmese Buddhists are followers of Siddhartha Gautama, the Buddha (though not the first), who lived in North India in the 6th Century BC. The Buddha was concerned with the amount of suffering that he saw around him and was determined to find its cause. After much searching amongst the religious and philosophical sects of his day, he attained Enlightenment under the Bo (Bodhi) tree at Bodh Gaya, when he recognised that the cause of suffering was desire and attachment.

You can eliminate desire, lust and attachment by following the eight-fold path of right belief, right aim, right speech, right action, right livelihood, right effort, right mindfulness and right contemplation.

The five great commands of the Buddha are:
1. To kill no living thing.
2. Not to steal another's property.
3. Not to commit any sexual crime.
4. Not to speak what is untrue.
5. Not to drink intoxicating drinks.

The highest and ultimate goal of all Buddhists is to achieve nirvana (*nibbana*), which literally means 'extinction' or 'freedom from desire'.

In Buddhist terminology, this constitutes the absolute extinction of that life-affirming will manifested as 'Greed', 'Hate' and 'Delusion', and convulsively clinging to existence; and therewith also the ultimate and absolute deliverance from all future rebirth, old age, disease and death, from all suffering and misery. 'Extinction of greed, extinction of hate, extinction of delusion: this is called Nibbana', or, to put it another way, 'the absence of hatred, greed, delusion, suffering, and narrow individualized existence'.

Every Burmese Buddhist boy is expected to become a monk for a period (the ordination ceremony, a grand event where the head is shaved, robes given and vows taken, is known in Burmese as *shinpyu*), which may vary in length from a few days to a whole lifetime. In a similar ceremony, little girls (would-be nuns) have their ears pierced.

Hinduism and Islam also have substantial numbers of followers, the latter particularly in the Arakan State. Many Karens, Chins and Kachins are Christian and animist beliefs persist in certain areas, mainly amongst the hilltribes who still cling to their ancestral gods. The nature of their beliefs and the form in which they express them are of great importance, for these beliefs (animism) exert a powerful influence over their day-to-day lives. In all animist areas the spirits are deemed to have the same characteristics as human beings, the same tendency to be good to those they like and to frustrate and pester those who earn their displeasure. Acting on the logical assumption that these spirits are just as amenable to threats and flattery as their human counterparts, animists, through their religious ritual and sacrifices, do what they can to appease and placate the spirits.

The most celebrated group worshipped by the Burmese are the *nats*, a bizarre collection of mischievous spirits, and there are *nat* shrines throughout the country. There are 37 'inner *nats*' (those allowed into the precinct of the pagoda) and images of the 37 can be seen at the Shwezigon Pagoda in Nyaung-U, near Pagan. There are hundreds of 'outer *nats*'. The most important place for *nat* worship is Mount Popa, 50km southeast of Pagan.

*Nats* are supposed to have supernormal powers, but it does not follow that all are good — goodness and power do not always go hand in hand in the world of *nats* as anywhere else. Nor are they immortal, though their life span is much longer than a human being's. They, too, are on the journey of birth and rebirth; they, too, are subject to death, decay and misery.

Alongside *nat*-worship, stand astrology and fortune-telling. Many a pagoda precinct is home to a Burmese astrologer, numerologist, palm-reader or fortune-teller. Pious Buddhists would not think of undertaking any important business without consulting their horoscopes or an astrologer to determine the most auspicious occasion. Indeed Burma's Independence Day was set only after careful astrological calculations.

> 'In Burma, graceful, slender pagodas, often encrusted thickly with gold leaf, and rising from fifty to three hundred feet in the air, are seen; and everywhere, in every stately pagoda and every little jewelled shrine, the same image, calm, unseeing, immovable to earthly joys or sorrows, Gautama, as he attained the long-sought Nirvana.'

Pagodas consist mainly of two types. The first is a bell-shaped stupa of solid brickwork raised on a series of receding terraces and crowned by a finial. The term *zedi* which is derived from the Pali word *cetiya* is applied to such structures. They were erected either to enshrine some relics of the Buddha, of a Buddhist saint or else to commemorate a sacred spot. Each has, therefore, a sealed-up chamber, often in the basement and sometimes in the *dhatugabbha* (meaning a shrine for relics) which lies between the bell-shaped section and the finial. The second type is a hollow vaulted temple mainly for enshrining the Buddha image. It is square in plan sometimes with projecting porches or vestibules. A series of receding roofs rise above the chapel and finally a bell-shaped stupa or a curvilinear finial tops the structure. On these general types are evolved various forms of pagodas and temples by introducing different architectural and decorative features. Pagodas are not merely places of religious worship and rituals, they are also centres of social activities. Every pagoda has an annual festival, which serves as both a trade fair and a clan gathering. Traders and pilgrims contribute voluntary funds to the pagoda; in this way, good business is done and at the same time, merit is made.

The various structures can be divided into nine categories (see Chapter Seven on Pagan for specific examples):
1. Stupa whose dome is modelled on a reliquary (a receptacle for relics).
2. Stupa whose dome is modelled on a tumulus (ancient sepulchral mound).
3. Sinhalese-type stupa.
4. Temple based on North Indian model.
5. Temple based on Central Indian model.

6. Temple based on South Indian model.
7. Cave temple based on Indian model.
8. Ordination hall.
9. Library.

Most of the pagodas are built of brick and stucco while some are of stone. The images of the Buddha themselves are either of marble, alabaster, bronze or even of bricks and mortar. The smaller ones are sometimes made of gold and silver.

Generally in Burma there are four conventionally accepted postures of the Buddha image: seated (two postures), standing and recumbent (reclining). The first posture of the seated image represents the Buddha in meditation, with the hands one upon the other resting near the navel, and the second, Enlightenment, with the Buddha seen cross-legged and the left hand open on the lap and the right hand on the right knee, the fingers pointing downwards. The standing image represents the Buddha teaching, with the right hand raised; the recumbent (reclining) posture is that of the Buddha at the time of entering nirvana, lying on his right side, the head in the right hand and the left arm lying on the left leg.

*Buddha image in the posture of Enlightenment.*

# FESTIVALS

Some Burmese festivals (known as *pwe*) have fixed dates; others vary from year to year according to the full moon days.

## January

Independence Day (Jan 4), marked by parades, fairs, theatrical plays and dancing, is a major public holiday and there is a week-long fair at the Royal Lake in Rangoon.

## February

Union Day (Feb 12) is when Burma's various ethnic groups parade through the streets of Rangoon in traditional costume. In the capital itself there is a grand week-long government exhibition and carnival; in other towns there are fairs, dancing and theatrical performances.

The full moon (in the lunar month of *Tabodwe*) is the time of the rice-harvesting festival *Htamane*, when food of the same name, consisting of sticky rice mixed with sesame, peanuts, ginger and coconut, is offered. It also marks the enshrinement of eight sacred hair-relics of Buddha in the Shwedagon Pagoda more than 2,500 years ago.

## March

Peasants' Day (March 2) and Armed Forces' (Defence Services') Day (March 27) are marked by parades and firework displays. The full moon day is *Taboung* when there are special alms offerings to monks, and fairs are held at the temples.

## April

Burma's Buddhist New Year *Thingyan*, celebrated over three days around the middle of the month, is a joyous and exceedingly wet occasion. Buddha images are ceremonially bathed and monks are lavishly entertained. The word *Thingyan* is derived from a Sanskrit word meaning the entry of the Sun to any of the Twelve Signs of the Zodiac.

## May

The full moon day of *Kason* honours the day on which, in different years, the Buddha was born, achieved Enlightenment and died. Processions are held in temples, Buddhists pour water on the sacred banyan tree and rituals are enacted at the Shwedagon and other pagodas. The annual Festival of Spirits takes place some time during May-June. May 1, May Day, is also celebrated as the Workers' Day.

## June

On the full moon day of *Nayon* Buddhist students are examined on their knowledge of the *Tripitaka* religious texts.

## July

The full moon day of *Waso* marks the beginning of the three-month period of Buddhist Lent, a time monks spend in retreat in their monasteries. Gifts of everyday necessities and robes are offered to help them through their spell of deprivation. During Lent there are no weddings, no courtships and no Burmese would even contemplate moving home. This is the most common period for young men to enter the monkhood temporarily. Martyr's Day (July 19) is dedicated to the memory of *Bogyoke* Aung San, Burma's independence hero. Wreaths are laid at the Martyrs' Mausoleum near the north entrance of the Shwedagon Pagoda.

## August

Towards the end of August a week-long festival, sometimes known as the 'Spirit Festival', is held at Taungbyon, 32km north of Mandalay, to propitiate the *nats*. Throughout the land, the full moon day of *Wagaung* is an auspicious occasion for offering alms and merit-making.

## September/October

September and October (the height of the rainy season) are the months when boat races are held on rivers and lakes throughout Burma. The most spectacular festival takes place in October at the Phaung-Daw-Oo Pagoda on Inle Lake. At this splendid event four of the five Buddha images, originally of sandalwood, but now covered so thickly by gold leaf applied by pilgrims that they appear to be rather shapeless objects of pure gold (the fifth image is left to take care of the monastery) are placed on the Royal Barge, the *Karaweik*, and a procession takes place around the lake, stopping at each large monastery and village. There they spend the night before moving on the following morning to the next village (these visits represent those made by King Alaungsithu several centuries ago). At Yaunghwe they spend three nights and then they return to the pagoda via the right hand side of the river. On the last day of the festival, which lasts nearly three weeks, there is a boat race. This consists of long boats, three at time, each containing around 100 people who row with their legs (on both sides).

The Buddhist Lent ends on the full moon day of *Thadingyut* and the Buddha's return from Heaven is celebrated with the 'Festival of Lights', involving all manner of lights, lamps, candles and fireworks. The poorest Burmese have some candles burning, even if they cannot afford paper lanterns or electric lamps. Dancing and various forms of entertainment take place and as with most festivals, people gather at pagodas all over the land.

## November

The full moon day of *Tazaungmone* is also an occasion for a festival of lights (best witnessed in the Shan State), as well as a Weaving Festival in which young girls engage in weaving competitions, making new robes for the monks by the light of the full moon. At the Shwedagon there is an all-night weaving-contest, the results of which are donated to the monks.

## December

The *Nadaw* full moon is a time for honouring the spirit world and *nat* festivals (*nat-pwe*) are held in many parts of the country. Christmas Day is also a public holiday.

Finally, there is another kind of festival which does not really fall within the usual confines of the term 'festival' but which marks the death of a *Sayadaw*, the abbot of a monastery, and is known as a *Phongyi-byan*. More accurately it is a funeral festival lasting a number of days. Having gone from *Phongyi* to *Sayadaw*, the abbot has earned the right of nirvana, the cherished goal of all Buddhists. The body is generally embalmed and lies in state for three days. There are two catafalques, specially erected, one in which the body actually lies in state and another duplicate token one. At the latter, professional mourners extol the virtues of the late *Sayadaw* in song and word. On the actual day of the cremation, which takes place on a lavishly and colourfully decorated pyre, thousands of devout men, women and children gather to pay homage, an occasion which bears all the hallmarks of a pagoda festival.

# LANGUAGE

Burma boasts over 80 different languages, divided into the three linguistic classes of Tibeto-Burman, Mon-Khmer and Thai-Chinese. The national language is Burmese, though many of the ethnic and tribal minorities speak their own tongue or dialect. As you would expect of a former British colony, the older generation of Burmese speaks English; however, as a result of the government's isolationist and xenophobic policies, the majority of the youth can manage little English. Tourist guides and trishaw drivers, though, speak English and often French and German.

Burmese (*Bama zaga*) is the official language of Burma, and is spoken (*bama-lou*, in the Burmese fashion) by at least two-thirds of the population. The most important regional tongues are Arakanese, Shan, Kachin, Karen and Mon. Hindi, Bengali and several Chinese dialects are also spoken among the various communities found mostly in the large towns and border areas adjoining India, Bangladesh and China.

Signboards of shops, restaurants, hotels, banks and government offices are written in Burmese, though some appear in English as well. Written Burmese, which to the outsider looks like a series of bubbles and circles from which various lines emanate, is based on a modified version of the old Mon alphabet which, in turn, is derived from South Indian alphabets. Street and town names, as well as the names of railway stations, are often written only in Burmese.

Burmese is monosyllabic and agglutinative (which means it combines simple words without a change of form in order to express compound ideas): it has neither conjugation nor declension, so that, in almost every instance, its composite words can be taken to pieces and the power of each part clearly shown. Burmese has three tones: an ordinary (unmarked) tone, an abrupt tone and a prolonged heavy tone. It has 32 consonants which only occur at the beginning of a syllable (no consonants occur after the vowel), eight vowels and four diphthongs. Only 25 of the consonants are used in Burmese words, but all 32 are required for words borrowed from Pali. Verbs come at the end of the sentence, each noun has one form (though there are three classes of noun: simple, abstract and compound) and there is no article. The Burmese alphabet consists of 44 letters and the script is written and read from left to right, top to bottom, though there is little use for punctuation as the sentences punctuate themselves. Below are a number of useful expressions, followed by a word list. There is no standard transliteration, so try your best. It will certainly be appreciated.

The book *Burmese self-taught* published in 1936 gives the following advice when addressing a Burman: — Do not raise the voice or shout, and speak slowly and distinctly. Be careful not to drop the aspirate. There is a great difference between p and hp, t and ht, but no practical difference between b and hb, d and hd. Be very careful to differentiate the sounds ay and eh; for instance ... ah-may is *mother* and ... ah-meh is *game* ... hlay *canoe* and ... hleh *a cart* ...'

## Useful phrases

| | |
|---|---|
| Hello | *Mingala ba* (for the polite form, men add *khin mya* and women *shin*) |
| How are you? | *Ne gao la?* |
| I am fine | *Ne gaombadeh* |
| Thank you | *Chezu tinbada* (there is no word for 'you're welcome'). |
| I'm sorry | *Thaung-bahmbah-deh* |
| How much? | *Be-lao lay?* |
| How much is that one? | *Da be-lao lay?* |
| What is that? | *Da ba leh?* |
| Too expensive | *Zeh mee-arday* |
| I'm going now | *Twa ba-oon meh* |
| Goodbye | *No sett-bar-day* |
| What is your name? | *Nammeh beloo kor-de-leh?* |
| My name is ... | *Chinnor (chimmah* for ladies) *nammeh* |
| How old are you? | *Ah-thay be-lao she be-lay?* |
| I am ... old | *Chinnor ah-thay ...* |
| Where do you come from? | *Beh ga la the-lay?* |
| I come from Mandalay | *Chinnor Mandalay ga* |
| Where are you going? | *Beh twa malay?* |
| I am going to the market/room/hotel/temple | *Ze/akah/hotel/paya twa meh* |
| I don't understand | *Nah mah lay boo* |
| I don't speak Burmese | *Chinnor myanmar loh nah mar lay boo* |
| Do you speak English? | *Khin mya ingelay loh pyor tah telar?* |
| No problem/never mind | *Kay sah mishibu* |
| Don't have | *Mishibu* |

# Word List

## Terms of address, people

| | | | |
|---|---|---|---|
| Mister (older) | *U* | Man | *Yaojar* |
| Mister (similar age) | *Ko* | Woman | *Main-ma* |
| | | Boy | *Yaojarlay* |
| Mister (younger) | *Maung* | Girl | *Main-ka-lay* |
| Mrs/madam | *Daw* | Student | *Tjaon-dha* |
| Little/young girl | *Ma* | Teacher | *Hsaya* |

## Accommodation, etc

| | | | |
|---|---|---|---|
| Hotel | *Hotel* | Shower | *Yeh cho* |
| Guest house | *Teh-kho-gan* | Soap | *Sahpyar* |
| House | *Ain* | Toothpaste | *Twah-dye-say* |
| Apartment | *Ain-gan* | Shampoo | *Gaon-shaw-yay* |
| Manager | *Man-neija* | | |
| Luggage | *Tit-har* | Chair | *Kalatyne* |
| Room | *Akan* | Table | *Sabweh* |
| Sleep | *Ay-dte* | Telephone | |
| Tired | *Mor-de* | (noun) | *Teh-li-poun* |
| Key | *Tho* | Telephone | |
| Lock | *Tho-khat* | (verb) | *Pohn-kaw* |
| Bed | *Eh-ya* | Television | *Ti-vi* |
| Pillow | *Gao-ohn* | Radio | *Ray-dee-o* |
| Sheet | *Eh-ya kin* | Cassette player | *Keq-s'eq* |
| Air conditioner | *Leh-eh set* | Cassette tape | *Keq-s'eq-k'we* |
| Fan | *Panka* | Typewriter | *Leq-hneiq-seq* |
| Bathroom | *Yay cho-gun* | Mosquito net | *Chin dtao* |
| Towel | *Myeh natohpawa* | Mosquito | *Chin* |
| | | Candle | *Pe-yaung-daing* |
| Toilet | *Ain-dha* | | |
| Toilet paper | *Ain-dha thone set-koo* | | |

## Travel, etc

| | | | |
|---|---|---|---|
| Go | *Twa* | Trishaw | *Side-car* |
| Come | *La-de* | Horse-cart | *Mien-lay* |
| Arrive | *Yao-teh* | Bicycle | *Sa-bay* |
| Motor car | *Car* | Train | *Mee-yahta* |
| Taxi | *Taxi* | | |
| Petrol | *Da-hsi* | | |

| | | | |
|---|---|---|---|
| Train station | *Boo-dar* | Riverboat | *Thin-bo* |
| Platform | *Bpa-le-paung* | Riverboat jetty | *Thin-bo-zay* |
| Bus | *Bus-gar* | Map | *Myay-pone* |
| Bus station | *Gar-gay* | Ticket | *Letma* |
| Aeroplane | *Lay-yen-pyan* | Ticket office | *Letma-yaon* |
| Airport | *Lay-zay* | | |

## Necessities, emergencies, etc

| | | | |
|---|---|---|---|
| Police station | *Yeh sa khan* | Pharmacy | *Say-sine* |
| Police | *Yeh* | Medicine | *Say* |
| Embassy | *Than-yong* | Sick | *Pyarday* |
| Passport | *Nigh-gan-gu-leh-mut* | Pain | *Na-deh* |
| | | Headache | *Gaon-kai* |
| Customs | *Ah-kao-khaun* | Fever | *Hpyah-nah* |
| Post office | *Sa-daiq* | Malaria | *Hngeh-pya* |
| Post box | *Sa-daiq-baon* | Stomach-ache | *Bai-nah-de* |
| Bank | *Bandai* | Diarrhoea | *Wun-guy-day* |
| Change money | *Le-de* | Aspirin | *Eh-sah-payin* |
| Hospital | *Say yon* | Dirty | *Nyi-pah-tay* |
| Doctor | *Say yah-wun* | Fire | *Mee* |
| Dentist | *Thwa say yah-wun* | Lose (mislay) | *Pyao-dte* |

## General items, etc

| | | | |
|---|---|---|---|
| Book | *Sa-ouq* | Stamp | *Dah-zay-gaun* |
| Dictionary | *Abidan* | Address | *Lay-sah* |
| Paper | *Set-koo* | Send | *Poh-de* |
| Newspaper | *Thadin-za* | Photograph | *Daq-pone* |
| Magazine | *Me-gazin* | Camera | *Kin-mara* |
| Ballpoint pen | *Baw-pin* | Lighter | *Mi-jiq* |
| Letter | *Sa* | Cigarette | *Si-gar-ret* |
| Envelope | *Sa-ay* | Umbrella | *Hti (tee)* |
| Postcard | *Poska* | | |

## Eating, food, etc

| | | | |
|---|---|---|---|
| Eat | *Sa-de* | Bread | *Pow mont* |
| Taste | *Myi-de* | Toast | *Pow mont mee kin* |
| Food | *A-sar* | | |
| Restaurant | *Sah-tao-syne* | Butter | *Htaw bat* |

| | | | |
|---|---|---|---|
| Menu | *Hinsayin* | Jam | *Yo* |
| Bill | *(Burmese just say 'be-lao lay?': 'How much?')* | Cake | *Cake-mont* |
| | | Sugar | *Tha-ja* |
| | | Salt | *Hsa* |
| | | Rice | *Tar-min* |
| Cook | *Che-dte* | Fried rice | *Tar-min-jo* |
| Breakfast | *Mah-nessa* | Noodles | *Kao-hswe* |
| Lunch | *Neh-leh-za* | Curry | *Hin* |
| Supper | *Nyaza* | Soup | *Hincho* |
| Plate | *Pa-gan* | Chillies | *Nga-you-tea* |
| Fork | *Kay-yin* | Spicy | *Sa-teh* |
| Spoon | *Zoon* | Fish | *Nga* |
| Knife | *Dah* | Prawns | *Bpazun* |
| Water | *Yay* | Meat | *A-thar* |
| Drinking water | *Thow yay* | Chicken | *Jet* |
| Soda water | *Soda* | Duck | *Wanbeh* |
| Ice | *Yay-geh* | Beef | *Ah-may-tha* |
| Milk | *Noh* | Pork | *Wet* |
| Tea | *La pay yay* | Eggs | *Jet-oo* |
| Coffee | *Kah-fee* | Fruit | *A-thie* |
| Beer | *Biya* | Pineapple | *Na-na thie* |
| Bottle | *Pah-lin* | Mango | *Tha-yet thie* |
| Glass | *Pan-gweh* | Banana | *Hnget pyaw thie* |
| Cup | *Kwe* | | |
| Lemon | *Showk-thie* | Vegetables | *Hin-thee hin-ywet* |
| Orange | *Lay-mor-thie* | | |
| Tomato | *Kay-yan-chin-dee* | Potatoes | *Alu* |
| | | Mushroom | *Hmou* |

## Around town, directions, etc

| | | | |
|---|---|---|---|
| City/town | *Myo* | Lake | *Kan* |
| Village | *Ywa* | Island | *Tjun (kyun)* |
| Farm | *Lay* | River | *Myit* |
| Countryside/ jungle | *Taw* | Sea | *Pin lair* |
| | | East | *A-shay* |
| Road | *Lan* | West | *A-na* |
| Market | *Ze* | North | *Myah* |
| School | *Tjaon (kyaung)* | South | *Town* |
| | | Left | *Beh-beh* |
| University | *Tahk-ah-tho* | Right | *Nya-beh* |
| Bridge | *Da-dah* | Straight | *Teh-deh* |

## Shopping, entertainment, etc

| | | | |
|---|---|---|---|
| Buy | *We-de* | Silver | *Ng-way* |
| Sell | *Yaun-de* | Diamond | *Sane* |
| Pay | *Bpeigh-de* | Emerald | *Mya* |
| Price | *Ze-no* | Ruby | *Bah-da-mya* |
| Cheap | *Bpo-de* | Sapphire | *Neelah* |
| Expensive | *Zeh mee-arday* | Burmese | |
| Money | *Ng-way* | make-up | *Thanakha* |
| Kyat | *Chat* | Burmese sarong | *Longyi* |
| Dollar | *Daw-la* | Glasses | *Myeh-mahn* |
| Pound | *Paun* | Shop | *Sine* |
| Carving | *Pa bu* | Teashop/café | *La-pet yay sine* |
| Silk | *Poh* | Bookshop | *Sa-ouq sine* |
| Ring | *Let-tsoot* | Cinema | *Yoh-shin-yoh* |
| Jade | *Jao-sayn* | Museum | *Paya-daiq* |
| Lacquer | *Yung-dte* | Closed | *Bpay-teh* |
| Gold | *Shwe* | Open | *Pwin-de* |

## Temples, religion, etc

| | | | |
|---|---|---|---|
| Pagoda/temple | *Paya* | Monk | *Phongyi* |
| Stupa | *Zedi* | Abbot | *Sayadaw* |
| Monastery | *Phongyi-tjaon* | Monkhood | *Sangha* |
| | *(kyaung)* | Festival | *Pwe* |
| Buddhism | *Bouda badha* | Temple festival | *Pwedo* |
| Novice monk | *Shin* | *Nat* festival | *Nat-pwe* |

## For the tourist

| | | | |
|---|---|---|---|
| Tourist | *Kabba-leh-kay-yee-thay* | Shwedagon Pagoda | *Shwe-dagon Paya* |
| Traveller | *Kay-yee-thay* | Bogyoke | |
| Foreigner | *Nine-gun-jar-tha* | Market | *Bo-jouq-zay* |
| Guide | *Lanbya* | Sule Pagoda | *Su-lay Paya* |
| Guide-book | *Lanbya sa-ouq* | National | *Amyo-dha-* |
| Translate | *Badha-bpyan-de* | Museum | *pya-daiq* |
| | | Inya Lake | *Inyakan* |
| Understand | *Na-leh-de* | Royal Lake | *Kandawggyi* |
| Thailand | *You-dee-ya* | Palace | *Nando* |
| | | England | *Ingelan* |

**Everyday terms**

| | | | |
|---|---|---|---|
| No | *Mah-hoh-poo* | Cold | *Aye-deh* |
| Yes | *Hohk-dtay* | Hot | *Bpu-deh* |
| Same | *Ah-dtudu* | Dry | *Chow* |
| Good | *Gaung day* | Wet | *Soh-de* |
| Bad | *Mah gaung boo* | Rain | *Mo* |
| | | It is raining | *Mo ywa-de* |
| Big | *Chee* | Sun | *Nay* |
| Small | *Ngeh* | Near | *Nee-de* |
| A little | *Ne-ne* | Far | *Weigh-de* |
| Nothing | *Bama* | Inside | *A-teh* |
| Fast | *Myan-de* | Outside | *A-bpyin-hma* |
| Slow | *Hneigh-de* | This | *Dee-har* |
| Early | *Sozoh* | That | *Ho-har* |
| Late | *Now-tja-de* | Who? | *Ba-doo-lay?* |
| Soon | *Matjami* | Which? | *Bay-har-lay?* |
| What? | *Ba-lay?* | How? | *Below-le?* |
| Where? | *Baymarlay?* | Here | *Dee-mar* |
| Why? | *Badjaolay?* | There | *Ho-mar* |

**Numbers**

| | | | |
|---|---|---|---|
| Zero | *Tow-nya* | Nine | *Koh* |
| One | *Tit* | Ten | *Tah-say* |
| Two | *Hnit* | Eleven | *Say-tit* |
| Three | *Tohn* | Twelve | *Say-hnit* |
| Four | *Lay* | Twenty | *Hnit-say* |
| Five | *Ngar* | Fifty | *Ngar-say* |
| Six | *Chah* | Hundred | *Taya* |
| Seven | *Koh* | Thousand | *Ta-taun* |
| Eight | *Shit* | | |

**Days of the week, time**

| | | | |
|---|---|---|---|
| Sunday | *Tanin-ganwe-ne* | Friday | *Tao-jar-ne* |
| | | Saturday | *Sah-ne-ne* |
| Monday | *Ta-nin-lar-ne* | Minute | *Mi-niq* |
| Tuesday | *In-ga-ne* | Hour | *Na-yi* |
| Wednesday | *Bo-tar-hoo-ne* | Day | *Ne* |
| Thursday | *Char-tha-ba-day-ne* | Week | *Ta-bah* |
| | | Month | *Lah* |

| Year | *Hniq* | Morning | *Mar-net* |
|------|--------|---------|-----------|
| Today | *Dee-nay* | Midday | *Nay-lair* |
| Tomorrow | *Ma nay pyan* | Evening | *Nyar-nay* |
| Yesterday | *Ma nay ga* | Night | *Nyar* |

For months of the year, use the English words; you're unlikely to be familiar with the Burmese calendar.

# FOOD AND DRINK

'Almost the worst thing in Burma, the filthy, monotonous food.'
*Burmese Days*, George Orwell

Well perhaps Orwell *was* being a little harsh, though most first-time visitors to Burma (particularly the vast majority who have come directly from Thailand) are disappointed with Burmese cuisine which lacks the style, variety, elaborateness and sheer splendour that are the hallmarks of Thai food. But, given a suitable opportunity (say a sampling of traditional Burmese home cooking or at festival-time, for example), the foreigner may well be pleasantly surprised.

Plenty of good food is available in the markets: meat, fish, seafood (squid, dried octopus), eggs (including turtle's and quail's), vegetables, fruits, herbs and spices, but little of it seems to find its way into the restaurants of the government-run hotels. There, the staff remain intent on serving bland (and invariably lukewarm) Sino-Burmese cuisine. And their attempts at Western food are even more of a culinary disaster. The most sensible idea is to wander off to a restaurant, whether it be Burmese, Chinese (of which there appear to be vast numbers and many different varieties) or Indian. Or better still, get invited to the home of a resident Burmese. For there you'll sample authentic Burmese cooking which, in truth, is nowhere near as bad as Orwell described. Burmese tend to eat with their hands, but you'll be given a spoon and fork. Finally, try and avoid the stir-fried grasshoppers and beetles if you're at all squeamish.

Burmese cuisine has been influenced by its neighbours China, Bangladesh, India and Thailand, of which China and India have had the strongest impact. Curries, soups, noodle-dishes, rice and raw or cooked vegetables form the basis of most meals. The omnipresent curry can be made from chicken, duck, beef, pork, mutton, sea-food or fish (in the Inle Lake region there is a particularly wide variety: catfish, eel, mudfish, feather-back, mugel and small shrimps) or, for the vegetarians, there is egg curry or a wide selection of omelettes. Common spices include chillies (though the food is less hot than in Thailand), coriander, turmeric, cumin, ginger, galangal, lemon-grass, tamarind and garlic. Vegetables include onions, spring onions, aubergines, courgettes, mange-tout, potatoes, beans, maize, cauliflowers, cucumbers and tomatoes. There is also a wide diversity of fruit: numerous types of bananas, pineapples (which can be bought for just K8 in Taunggyi), custard-apples from Prome, mangoes, mangosteens, oranges, lemons, limes, watermelons, rambutans, lychees, durians, avocados, coconuts, papayas, apples, pears, pomelos from Moulmein and even strawberries from Maymyo.

Burma's 'national dish' is *mohinga*, a curry-flavoured fish soup. Traditionally this is eaten with noodles and garnished with chopped onion, extra chillies, lemon or lime wedges or crispy fritters. Another popular dish, which emphasises the Chinese connection, is Shan noodles (Shan *kau'hswe*) stir-fried with pork, spices, onion, tomato, strips of omelette and topped with a few chopped chives and a squeeze of lime. The Southeast Asian influence is evident in the use of *ngapi*, Burmese fermented fish paste.

*Lepet* is a peculiarly Burmese 'dish', regularly offered to guests (when it will often be presented in a lacquer box). Shredded fresh ginger is mixed into fermented green tea-leaves and is served with peanuts and deep-fried dried beans. A multitude of other ingredients can also accompany *lepet*: deep-fried crisp onion, garlic, toasted sesame seeds and dried shrimps. Typical Burmese fare includes *hincho* (clear soup with powdered shrimp and vegetables), *hsan byoke* (a boiled rice dish), *oh-no kau'hswe* (curried chicken with noodles), *wet-thani* (reddish pork curry), *taung-bho-hmou* (Burmese mushrooms), and *nga lethok* (fish salad). Particularly appetising dishes are *bpazunasayjaw* (prawns with vegetables), *gananhin* (crab curry; a speciality from Arakan State), *mot-tee*, Arakan-style *mohinga*, *charzanhinga* (special chicken bone soup with mushrooms and glass noodles), *chinzorga* (a delicious lime dip with chillies and salt), *amedatownjaw* (minced pork with onions and chillies) and *ngapijaw* (fish paste with chillies, garlic and onions). A celebrated Burmese dessert is *san win ma kin*, a semolina-based pudding, made with coconut milk and baked in a large, shallow, stainless steel dish. When the top becomes golden brown, it is served onto a glossy banana leaf and neatly folded into a parcel.

# Drink

Orwell's colonialists seemed more than content with their liquor. These days, however, Mandalay Beer, a tradition since 1886, keeps most tourists going (when it's available), though there are a variety of stronger alcoholic beverages, notably Mandalay Rum. Inevitably, Johnny Walker Whisky is to be found in most places.

Bottled water, soda water (with bizarre, copied logos such as 'Singapore Mineral Water Rangoon' with a logo of Singapore Airlines on the oft re-used bottle), orange and lemon pop ('lemon sparkling'), both sickeningly sweet, 'Vimto' (a throw-back from the colonial days), sugar-cane juice (*chanyay*), Chinese, Burmese and 'English' tea are all to be found. The last-named is even sweeter than the notorious 'Vimto' or dreaded lemon barley, as it's made with condensed milk heaped thick with spoonfuls of sugar. Perhaps the best choice, then, is *ziphawyay*, plum juice, served with heaps of ice (if you're brave enough), which is very refreshing.

A recent hoarding in Rangoon proudly proclaims 'PEPSI AND 7 UP THE CHOICE OF A NEW GENERATION (PEPSI-COLA PRODUCTS MYANMAR LTD)', so decadent colonialism has finally made it to Burma.

Chinese tea is offered free of charge in restaurants, tea- and coffee-shops, while bottled water and soft drinks vary from K6 up to K65 (depending on the whim of the vendor) and beer anything up to K80 (including imported beers such as Heineken and Tiger). 'English' tea retails at just around K4. Under no circumstances drink the tap water.

# CONDUCT AND TABOOS

'The Burman's ready kindliness to the stranger is remarkable'.
                                              Norman Lewis, *Golden Earth*.

Since Burma, like its neighbour Thailand, is essentially a Buddhist
country, similar codes of behaviour apply. The Burmese, however,
tend to be more respectful and less aggressive than the Thais. They
will cheerfully strike up conversation with you or, if their English isn't
up to it, just smile. Always be courteous and polite and try to keep
smiling too. It's very easy to lose your temper in Burma: after all, it
can be the most bureaucratic and frustrating land in the world. If you
do raise your voice or lose your temper, you will achieve precisely
the opposite of what you intend. Burma is one of the most destitute
nations on earth, so planes, buses and trains will be late, the air-
conditioning won't work, there'll be no hot water and the restaurant
will run out of Mandalay Beer. The answer to many of your requests
will invariably be '*Mishibu*', 'No have', and the response to your
question 'How far is the town/market/pagoda/temple?' will most likely
be the imprecise and frustrating '*Ma we bu*, 'It's not far.'
    As with other Buddhist lands, the head is the most sacred part of
the body and the foot the lowest. Don't touch anyone on the head
(don't, for example, pat a little child on the head) and under no
circumstances point your foot at anybody, particularly at any statues
of Buddha. All images must be shown the utmost respect. If you
walk past someone of a higher status, eg a monk, or an older
gentleman, lower your head as a mark of deference.
    FOOT WEARING IS STRICTLY PROHIBITED is a sign you'll come
across constantly in this golden land of pagodas. So it's shoes and
socks off, in spite of the fact that the ground is often scorching hot.
Don't wear shorts in the temple grounds (or even on the streets): it's
discourteous and considered 'low class'. The Burmese are too polite
to criticise or pass comment, but they'd prefer if you were smartly
dressed, even when it's over 40° centigrade and you're only half-way
up the 1,729 steps of Mandalay Hill (see comments below).
    Never cause anybody to 'lose face' but instead smile, flatter and
be respectful, and you'll get along fine. You'll soon notice that in
order to save face and out of deference to you, the Burmese will
rarely say 'no': instead they'll beat about the bush, grin or even say
'yes' when they do actually mean 'no'.
    Never treat so-called 'status-inferiors' (like trishaw drivers or hotel
staff) as servants. They may be desperately poor, but they are

*Mural from the Jataka Tales, Mahawizayazedi Pagoda, Rangoon, depicting scenes from the life of Buddha.*

*Novice monks on Ngapali beach, near Sandoway.*

*BURMESE BELIEFS: THE SPIRITUAL LIFE*
*(Top left) ogre; (top right) nat; (centre) Sehtatgyi Pagoda, Prome; (bottom) Buddha*
*on the way to enlightenment, Meilamu Pagoda, Rangoon.*

*Shwedagon Pagoda, Rangoon.*

*Sweeping the pagoda precinct, thereby acquiring merit on the way to nirvana.*

'Chinthes' at Sagaing and elephants at Monywa. These are the all-powerful guardians of Burmese pagodas and temples.

exceptionally friendly, eager to help and to practise their English (they'll be even more delighted and amused if you can speak any Burmese). If you can only manage '*mingala ba*' ('hello'), they'll be ecstatic and compliment you on your perfect command of the Burmese language.

If a Burmese invites you to his or her home, always accept, bring a small gift, take off your shoes before entering and eat or drink whatever you're offered. You will find, when a Burmese hands something to you, he or she will do it with their right hand, supported at the elbow by the left hand. Try and follow suit. If you invite a Burmese for dinner, you must pay. Never 'go Dutch'. Always refer to an older man as '*U*' and an older/similarly aged lady as '*Daw*'. Always ask before taking a photograph: they'll be flattered and rarely say no (though some of the hilltribes won't let you photo them).

As in Thailand, members of the same sex will often be seen walking hand in hand, but nothing should be read into that. Indeed the Burmese are nowhere near as broad-minded and liberal as the Thais (nor are they as promiscuous) and homosexuality, for example, is frowned upon. Burmese men are far less effeminate than the Thais, and neither *ladyboys* (*katoeys* as the Thais call them or *mein-ma-shar* in Burmese) nor prostitutes (*pah*) throng the streets of Rangoon and Mandalay, as they do Bangkok and most towns across the border.

When shopping, bargaining is a must: the general rule is to look flabbergasted at the vendor's first offer and suggest half the price. Eventually you'll reach a compromise: you can always walk away if you're not satisfied with the price. But always keep the bargaining good-natured and never get angry or abusive. You'll only lose face.

Burmese men (except for the richer Shan who tend to wear jeans or trousers) wear *longyi* or sarongs (a wraparound garment folded and tucked in at the waist), which they frequently tie and untie. Traditionally the *longyi* is worn with a collar-less shirt (*eingyi*), a short jacket (*taik-pone*) and a shoulder-bag, the design of which varies from state to state. On formal occasions, a type of turban called a *gaung-baung* is also added. Burmese ladies dress smartly in *eingyi* and *hta-mein* (a lady's sarong) and, despite the heat, somehow always manage to look elegant. For formal occasions, they will also put on a light scarf (*pawar*).

For tourists, the following advice is given: 'Dress in Myanmar is casual. Formal attire is only required for formal occasions or when paying courtesy calls on government officials. Light clothing is recommended all year round. A light sweater will be useful during the cool season (November to February in Yangon) and a heavy sweater when travelling to the northern or hilly areas. An umbrella is useful during the rainy season (mid-May to mid-October). Footwear must be removed before entering religious buildings and homes.'

All over Burma women wear *thanaka* bark powder on their faces. Sometimes it is applied in a circle or square shapes over the cheeks, with more on the forehead, frequently it is smoothed thinly all over the face. It serves as protection against the sun as well as softening and cooling the skin and enhancing the beauty. The *thanaka* is a hardwood tree from Upper Burma and the powder is made from the bark by rubbing on a flat stone (*kyaukpyin*) with a little water which results in a pale yellow paste. This collects in a groove round the edge of a stone. Nowadays it can be bought in powder or cake form. Burmese kids and men will also apply *thanaka*.

In his poem *Mandalay*, Kipling remarked 'An' I seed her first a-smokin' of a whackin' white cheroot'. However, as Mi Mi Khaing observed in her marvellous book entitled *The World of Burmese Women*:

'The 'whacking great cheroot' of Kipling's day is rarely seen these days though it was part of my childhood background as our closest, favourite maiden aunt used to smoke one, usually one that she had rolled. Nowadays, it can be found in some delta towns. It was a 10-inch long cylinder with a diameter of about one inch and packed so loosely that its common accompaniment is a full sized enamel plate held under it by the smoking lady.

'The Burmese distinction between a cheroot and a cigar is quite different from the English dictionary meaning which gives a cheroot as a cigar with an end (the smoking one) open and a cigar as having both ends pointed (and sealed). The Burmese 'cigars', a welcome present to connoisseur friends abroad, are in Burmese distinguished from cheroots simply by their *hsay-pyin* and *hsay-paw*, strong and weak. The strong are smoked by men, and the weak, the manufacture of which vastly predominates over the manufacture of the strong, this 'weak tobacco' is the pervading article in the female world's culture, and smoked by men and women alike.'

Along with cheroots, betel, referred to as *kun-yar* in Burmese, is the image most readily associated with the Burmese. In fact, betel has a long tradition in Burmese history and fulfils an important role in society as Mi Mi Khaing explains:

'Betel was a highly relished, symbolically cherished, stimulating chew. Its trade, monopolized by women, was an extensive business.

Female purveyors, sellers, and servers of betel provided quids not only to court, monks and public, but also laid them before images and scriptures, by the thousand daily in some cases ... It was an elaborate culture, with buildings donated specially for chewing betel, with jewelled silver or lacquered betel containers, with gourd or gold phials for lime paste to go with it. Quids required a variety of products, which presumably the women had to procure and assemble: areca nut for astringence, grown mostly in wet regions south; green betel-leaf also from wet regions for fresh tang and aroma; burnt and slaked lime to smear on the leaf and blend the taste of the two; cutch, boiled from heart-wood of *Acacia catechu* grown in their own dry region, to cool down the lime; and tiny bits of spices to heighten fragrance.'

Finally (but most importantly) Burmese bureaucracy — indeed society itself — functions and survives through rampant, but technically illegal, black market activity and massive currency swindling. Burmese society is wholly corrupt, from the military brass at the very top to the poorest peasant in the land, and it's just something you'll have to come to terms with. Bribery is an essential part of everyday life, whether it be with dollars, kyat, cigarettes or Johnny Walker Whisky. If you can help it, don't discuss politics: Burma's Military Intelligence (MI), run by the 'Prince of Darkness' Khin Nyunt, is as ruthlessly efficient as Erich Honecker's was in former East Germany, and talking to a foreigner is, for a Burmese, theoretically an act of treason. Above all, be discreet: if you can't desist, refer to Daw Aung San Suu Kyi as the 'Lady' and to Ne Win as the 'Old Man', 'Number One' or 'Him' but *never* by name.

'They should never have assumed that things in Burma are like any other place.'

U Win Tin.

Chapter Two

# Before you go

## VISAS

Tourist visas are valid for a stay of 14 days and extensions are not permitted. However, there is no limit to the number of times you can re-enter the country, provided you have a valid visa obtainable from one of the Embassies or Consulates listed below. For the two-week trip to Burma virtually all tourists arrive at Rangoon's Mingaladon Airport, and this will continue to be the case unless Lanna Air Tours' charter flights from Chiang Mai to Pagan start up again, or Thai or Bangkok Airways initiates flights between Bangkok/Mae Hong Son and Mandalay. Since October 1 1992 the border between Mae Sai and Tachilek has been open (though it was officially opened by the Chiang Rai and Kengtung governors five days later), with a possible tour extension up to Kengtung 120 miles away (167 km). Just to visit Tachilek, a one-day pass is issued at Mae Sai for K400 or the equivalent in US dollars, while a three-day visa to visit Kengtung is issued for 400 baht at the Burmese Embassy in Bangkok. Entry by overland route is also allowed for package tours from Ruili and Wantin in Yunnan province (China) to Lashio via Muse and Kyukoke. The Burmese authorities in Myawaddy (opposite Mae Sot in Thailand) no longer permit non-Thai tourists to cross the border: foreigners used to be able to cross over for a US$10 admission fee, with an additional charge of US$5 for a camera and US$10 for a video camera. Apparently tourists arriving at Myawaddy complained of extortion by so-called tourist guides.

Business visas are available upon production of a letter of introduction from any 'acceptable' Burmese organisation. These are valid for one month, and can be extended for up to three months after arrival in Rangoon.

At present Burma has Embassies or Consulates in the following cities: Bangkok, Beijing, Belgrade, Bonn, Cairo, Canberra, Colombo, Dhaka, Geneva, Hanoi, Hong Kong, Islamabad, Jakarta, Kathmandu, Kuala Lumpur, London, Manila, Moscow, New Delhi, New York, Ottawa, Paris, Prague, Rome, Seoul, Singapore, Tel Aviv, Tokyo, Vientiane and Washington.

## Major embassies

The following Burmese embassies issue the speediest visas:

**Bangkok**: 132 Sathorn Nua Road (corner of Thanon Pan), Bangkok 10500. Tel 233 7250, 234 4698, Fax 236 6898, Telex 20971.
**Hong Kong**: Myanmar Consulate General, Room 2424, Sun Hung Kai Centre, 30 Harbour Road, Wanchai. Tel 827 7929, 827 9843, Fax 827 6497, Telex 74373.
**Jakarta**: 109 Jalan Haji Agus Salim. Tel 320 440  Fax 327 204, Telex 61295.
**Singapore**: 15 St Martin's Drive, Singapore 1025. Tel 235 8763, 235 8704, Fax 235 5963, Telex 21467.

The address of the London embassy is: 19A Charles Street, London W1X 8ER. Tel 071-629 6966, Fax 071-629 4169, Telex 267609.

---

*Responsible travellers always contact the*

# BURMA
### Action Group
Working for human rights, democracy and the health and safety of all the peoples of Burma

*84 Long Lane, London SE1 4AU Tel: 071 403 6303*

# INOCULATIONS AND HEALTH PROBLEMS

The following immunisations are recommended by the British Airways Travel Clinic in London:

POLIO: Within 10 years.

TETANUS: Within 10 years.

TYPHOID FEVER: Within three years. Probably unnecessary if over 35 and had four past regular boosters.

HEPATITIS A: Significant risk if antibody negative. There is now a new jab called *Havrix* which has replaced the old and not wholly effective gamma globulin. You require three shots within the space of a year to give ten years' protection.

The following may be considered optional but you should take into account the comments in reaching a decision with your doctor:

RABIES: Within one to three years depending on exposure to risk. Beware of rabid Burmese dogs and don't be fooled by the friendliness of the celebrated Burmese cats, which were actually bred in Thailand (typical!).

HEPATITIS B: Transmission is through sex or contact with contaminated blood, needles and syringes. The vaccine is available on private prescription or through British Airways Travel Clinics (Tel 071 831 5333).

TB: Children should be immunised at any age; less important for adults. A skin test (Tine) is available if you are in doubt about your immune status.

## Seasonal Diseases

Seasonal diseases normally only occur during the months shown below. The requirement for immunisation depends on the areas you visit and your living conditions.

**JAPANESE ENCEPHALITIS**: From June to September. Immunisation should be considered if travelling during these months, though the risk is confined to rural areas where the mosquito vector breeds in rice fields.

**DENGUE FEVER**: From June to October. This viral disease is endemic in many areas and is spread by day-time biting mosquitoes (*aedes aegypti*) which breed, for example, in water-storage containers, flower vases, etc. Prevention entails avoidance of mosquito bites. At present there is no vaccine available, though, according to a recent report issued by the World Health Organisation, Thai doctors have developed a vaccine known as 'attenuated tetravalent vaccine'. Although proven to be safe and effective for humans, the vaccine has yet to be tested in children under actual field conditions.

**MALARIA**: Malaria is a risk throughout Burma except in Rangoon and areas above 1,000m. It is most intense during the months of March through to December, though is present all year round. The recommended prophylactic is proguanil (*Paludrine*) 100mg twice daily and chloroquine (*Nivaquine/* Avloclor) 150mg (base) twice weekly. Tablets should be started one week before entering a malarial zone and continued regularly for at least four weeks after leaving the last zone. An alternative for journeys of less than three months is mefloquine (*Lariam*) 250mg once a week. If you intend taking mefloquine, go and see your GP: it's only available on prescription and can have serious side-effects. Unfortunately, some strains of malaria are proving resistant to all drugs; so prevention (mosquito nets, coils and repellents and clothing which covers all the body) is strongly recommended.

For up to date information on malaria (a recorded message) phone the Malaria Reference Laboratory in London, tel 071-636 7921.

Burma's political upheavals have pushed thousands of refugees across the Thai border in recent decades, and their constant movement makes malaria control well nigh impossible. Some 15,000 new cases (70% involving *Plasmodium falciparum*, the most serious strain of the disease) occur annually among the 30,000 Karen tribespeople living along the frontier and in many villages infant-mortality rates approach 30%.

Burma remains one of the countries where *Plasmodium falciparum* has become multi-resistant to anti-malaria drugs. Exposure to the risk of malaria infection is almost unavoidable in areas where vector mosquitoes are difficult to control, such as valleys with *Anopheles minimus* breeding in streams and forests, with *Anopheles dirus* breeding in shaded pools and wells (in Mudon and the vicinity of Moulmein, for example), and coastal marshes with *Anopheles sundaicus* and DDT-resistant *Anopheles annularis*.

Owing to the AIDS explosion, pharmaceutical companies (with the notable exception of the French firm Rhone Poulenc Rorer) are turning away from investing in malaria research for, quite simply, (and some may say, cynically) AIDS effects the so-called civilised Western societies in far greater numbers than malaria. And so, malariologists are finding their funds for research being severely curtailed (many are having to rely solely on funding from the World Health Organisation). Indeed experts are now resorting to the 2,000-year old Chinese herbal medicine *Qinghaosu* and its derivatives, despite the fact that this drug has not been rigorously tested and may well have toxic side-effects. A recent report from San Francisco asserting that Colombian and Spanish scientists have developed the first successful vaccine against malaria has yet to be substantiated.

The best advice for travellers to Burma who think they may have malaria at present is as follows: if a measured fever of 38°C or greater develops, seven days or more after arriving in a malarious area, immediate medical help should be sought. If suitable help is unavailable (as is likely to be the case in Burma) or your condition deteriorates, self treat with *Halfan* (or quinine plus *Fansidar*, 500mg sulfadoxine and 25mg pyrimethamine) without further delay and get to a doctor (preferably in Thailand or Singapore) as soon as possible. For *Halfan* (halofantrine hydrochloride): take two tablets six hourly for three doses and repeat one week later. As these tablets may be difficult to obtain abroad (impossible in Burma), ask your clinic doctor for a supply to take with you.

Malaria is transmitted by mosquito bite, so:

1. Cover exposed skin after dusk when at greatest risk or use repellent.

2. Return before dusk from country areas where mosquitoes are most active.

3. Sleep in screened rooms or use a mosquito net (remember to tuck in the edges and spray inside with repellent).

4. Air conditioning, vapour pads and smoke coils deter mosquitoes but are by no means 100% guaranteed to scare off all.

5. 'Buzzers' (sold in pharmacies and supermarkets all over the world) are useless.

**AIDS**: Unofficial reports indicate that 1.26% of people tested (an estimated 2,700 cases) were found to be HIV positive, with the Chinese border areas (Bhamo, in Kachin State) worst affected. Only 14 official AIDS cases have been reported in Burma. This is clearly a gross (and tragic) under-estimation: many prostitutes are being 'sent' to work in Thailand and, according to reports, those who test HIV positive are returned to Burma where they are executed with potassium cyanide injections by the SLORC's security forces. Over 50 Burmese prostitutes were rescued last year from a brothel in Ranong Province in Thailand.

Despite no comment on the subject from the SLORC, Burma, already wallowing in a mire of latent prostitution, is also on the verge of a major AIDS crisis. According to the *Burma Action Group*'s report entitled *Burma and the United Nations: A Proposal for Constructive Involvement*:

'Rampant inflation and low wages make it impossible for many families to feed their children, resulting in a dramatic increase in child labor and the trafficking of children, especially young girls, across the border into Thailand and slavery in brothels and other businesses.

This traffic has become the second most important source of increased HIV infection in Burma, the first being intravenous drug use that is growing out of control among ethnic minorities and urban youth. A report by the UN World Health Organization predicts an impending AIDS epidemic in Burma unless immediate steps are taken to contain the disease. Burma is already thought to have, along with Thailand and India, the highest rate of HIV infection in Asia. One Burmese government study reportedly found that more than 80 percent of prison inmates in several different prisons were HIV positive.'

## General health precautions

Because Burma is much less developed than Thailand, Malaysia or Singapore, take extra care. Don't drink tap water, avoid ice and ice-cream, unpeeled fruit, raw vegetables and salads and be careful in some of the restaurants. The food has often been hanging around all day (just as it has been in the markets) pestered by flies. It can get swelteringly hot in Burma (particularly in Prome, Pagan and Mandalay) so take precautions against the sun. Around some of the temples and pagodas, you'll occasionally see a snake, but nowhere near as often as some people imagine. Otherwise, the worst thing you'll probably contract is diarrhoea or possibly dysentery. If you're worried, seek treatment in Bangkok or Singapore. (Fear not, the situation is certainly better than it was in 1935 (according to a Burmese pamphlet published in 1946 and entitled *Burma Facts and Figures*: 'In 1935 the numbers of deaths were:—88,426 due to Fevers (including 60,000 from Malaria); 11,954 from Respiratory Diseases; 6,858 from Cholera; 2,733 from Accidents; 2,261 from

Snake-Bites or wounds by Wild Animals; 1,321 from Plague; 1,262 from Small Pox; 222 by Suicide; 213 from Rabies; and 125,528 from other causes.').

# CURRENCY, BLACK MARKET

The Burmese unit of currency is the kyat (pronounced 'chat'), divided into 100 pyas. The official (ie government, bank, or state-run hotel) rate is approximately US$1: K5.93 (traveller's cheques, K6.15). However, the actual (ie black market) rate varies from K70-120 depending on where you are (the best rate is in Rangoon, the worst up-country). So, if you buy a Pepsi on the streets at K30, say, it'll cost you 30 cents at the black market rate, yet US$5.06 at the official rate.

On arrival at Rangoon's Mingaladon Airport, you are asked to complete a Foreign Exchange Declaration Form (FED Form, which has replaced the old FEC 1 form) which you must retain throughout your stay. You have to write down the exact denominations of the notes you have brought into the country. You are supposed to declare all your foreign currency on this form and each time you change money officially, the balance will be deducted. When you leave, you should have in your possession your final total: ie say you declare US$200 and officially change US$150, you will be expected (in theory, at least) to show the remaining US$50 on your departure. Naturally, if you did change US$150 at the official rate you'd only receive K889, whereas on the black market (ie the 'true' value) you'd get K15,000.

(NB: FITs — Foreign Independent Travellers — who have not pre-booked a tour of any description *must* change the stipulated US$200 immediately after arrival at Mingaladon Airport. If they fail to do so and have had any contact with a private travel agent in Burma, that travel agent will have his operator's licence taken away. If you are travelling on your own in Burma but *have* pre-booked a tour, make sure that the Embassy staff does not stamp FIT in your passport — or you, too, will be obliged to change a minimum of US$200 at the official rate).

In practice, you can declare very little (say US$30) and officially change around US$10 for which you'll receive about K59 (don't forget to have your FED form stamped by the official every time you change money 'legally' or, for example, when you pay your US$5 entrance fee at the Shwedagon Pagoda), and subsequently acquire some K19,000 (US$190) on the black market. In order to appease the currency officials at the airport, you may change *some* money at one of the government institutions. In any case, there are other, legal ways of acquiring kyats.

Ideally, find a Burmese friend to pay for everything, and settle up with him discretely either in dollars or with gifts. Failing that, most regular visitors to Burma follow the age-old tradition of bringing in cigarettes, whisky and presents and selling them off during their stay. '555' are the preferred brand of cigarettes (though any foreign make will do) and Johnny Walker Black Label is the most sought-after whisky. It's better to trade whisky than cigarettes; anyway a bottle of Johnny Walker Black Label should go for anything up to K1,350, while Red Label can be sold off for K1,200. A carton of '555' fetches around K700-800. Other items that can easily be traded in Burma are: T-shirts, counterfeit Thai watches, lighters, ballpoint pens, shampoo, soap, lipstick and make-up (bring a supply of all these in any case to give away as presents to the Burmese you happen to befriend). Obviously if you bring your full complement of cigarettes (400) and whisky (two litres), plus a sizeable collection of gifts, you won't have to bring anywhere near as many dollars. As with foreign currency, you are supposed to declare all your valuables on arrival on your 'Customs Department Myanmar Passenger's Declaration' form — 'valuables' in this instance include 'refrigerator, air conditioner, tools, equipments and articles for exhibition'!

Unless the SLORC demonetises the currency again, the present kyat bills in service are: K200, 90, 45, 15, 10, 5 and 1. Converting left-over kyat back into dollars on departure is an arduous and risky proposition, and you're not allowed either to bring in or take out any kyat with you (it may be possible to illegally acquire kyat in Thailand, Malaysia or Singapore, however, prior to your arrival, if you think it's a chance worth taking). Traveller's cheques can only be changed at the official outlets — so there's little point in bringing any of them with you — and, whilst other currencies are acceptable (eg Thai baht and Singapore dollars), the US dollar, as ever, is the most sought after foreign currency. Don't bother with credit cards: they can also only be used at official places. Finally, don't forget to retain US$6 for your Rangoon Airport departure tax.

NB: The following article by Chit Tun appeared on January 28 1993 under the heading 'Burma's Central Bank to issue Forex Certificates':

'Burma's Central Bank is to issue US dollar foreign exchange certificates from next week in what it said is a move to boost the country's foreign currency earnings and serve the convenience of foreign tourists.

In a statement issued on Wednesday January 27, the Bank said it would issue certificates for denominations of US$1, 5 and 10 from February 4th.

It said the certificates will be freely convertible into other currencies but can be used only in Burma.

They can be exchanged with US dollars at par — one unit of the certificate (or one Burmese dollar) for one US dollar.

If they are exchanged for pounds sterling, the exchange rate will be the daily gross rate of the banks.

The certificates can be bought at three state-owned banks, at state-owned hotels and at airports.

Every foreign traveller will be required to buy at least $200 worth of the certificates, and any Burmese citizen can accept the certificates as payment, the Bank said.

It said Burmese citizens who have received the certificates can hold them for deposit in foreign currency accounts.

Under existing rules, no Burmese citizen can hold foreign currency except under a licence from foreign exchange authorities, with the result that anyone without such a licence who has come by foreign currency has no option but to sell it in the currency black market.

Since under the new arrangement Burmese citizens can legally hold foreign exchange certificates, the black market is expected to disappear.

Also, as holders of the certificates are given the chance to open foreign currency accounts, they will now have the means to buy certain high-class imported goods such as cars and television sets which can be bought only with foreign currency.'

Foreign Exchange Certificates (FECs) are issued in three denominations: US$10, $5 and $1 and are exchangeable with US dollars or pounds sterling. Various traveller's cheques (eg American Express, National Westminster Bank Ltd, etc) and Visa Card are acceptable for purchasing FECs, but the exchange rate is as unfavourable as that available at the various government outlets.

*'Chinthes' standing guard outside Syriam's Kyaikkauk Pagoda.*

Chapter Three

# Getting There and Away

## TOURS AVAILABLE: WHERE AND HOW TO BOOK THEM, COSTS

Although employees at some of the Burmese Embassies around the world might not know it (nor those who work for the state-run travel agency Myanmar Travels & Tours), independent travel to Burma was officially permitted from October 10 1992. The Burmese Embassy in Bangkok stipulates that individuals can apply for 14-day tourist visas (which are to be issued within 24 hours) at a cost of 400 baht but they must officially change at least US$200 (or other equivalent acceptable currency) during their stay. However, if individuals book a tour (of even just one person) there is no need to change any money officially, though the Embassy staff may well tell you otherwise. You must, however, have written confirmation stating that you have pre-booked (and paid for) a tour and then 'Package tour' will be stamped on your visa. If you apply for a visa as an individual having pre-booked a tour *without* written confirmation from the travel company concerned, the Burmese Embassy will stamp 'FIT' (Foreign Independent Traveller) in your passport and you will then be obliged to change the mandatory US$200 at the official rate.

The SLORC, it goes without saying, are in dire need of foreign currency, and naturally they would prefer foreigners to travel with their own disorganised Myanmar Travels & Tours (MTT; formerly known as Tourist Burma), but so eager are they for foreign currency that they are granting licences to private travel agents in Rangoon with almost reckless abandon (the 1992/93 Rangoon 'Yellow Pages' lists 23 travel agents, though now there are actually many more in existence). Likewise, non-governmental hotels and guest houses are springing up in all the major destinations as the SLORC predicts 500,000 tourists will visit Burma in 1993, an increase from around 10,000 in previous years — rather a shot in the dark, it would appear, on the military's behalf.

## BRITAIN

It is certainly possible to make all your travel arrangements in the UK, though there are at present only a handful of companies organising trips to Burma. In past years, all tour agencies were obliged to book through the state-run Myanmar Travels & Tours and consequently their programmes were both heavily restricted and hugely expensive. However, since the October 1992 easing of restraints, UK travel companies are now able to offer a variety of flexible itineraries arranged via private Rangoon-based travel agents. Below is a list of UK-based agencies who can arrange tours to Burma:

Andrew Brock Travel Ltd, 54 High Street East, Uppingham, Rutland LE15 9PZ, Tel 0572 821330, Fax 0572 821072.

Explore Worldwide Ltd, 1 Frederick Street, Aldershot, Hants GU11 1LQ, Tel 0252 344161, 319448, 333031, Fax 0252 343170.

Pettitt's India, 14 Lonsdale Gardens, Tunbridge Wells, Kent TN1 1NU, Tel 0892 515966, Fax 0892 515951. Formerly specialising in tours to India, Nepal and Pakistan, they are now expanding into Burma.

Right Now Books and Tours (Burma), 36c Sisters Avenue, London SW11 5SQ, Tel/Fax 071 223 8987. Specialists in all aspects of travel both to and within Burma.

The Travel Alternative Ltd, 27 Park End Street, Oxford OX1 1HU, Tel 0865 791636, Fax 0865 791732.

Trans Indus Limited, Northumberland House, 11 The Pavement, Popes Lane, Ealing, London W5 4NG, Tel 081 566 2729, Fax 081 566 1903. Formerly specialists in the Indian subcontinent, they, too, are now expanding into Burma.

## SOUTHEAST ASIA

The majority of travellers choose to deal with travel agents in Bangkok or, to a lesser extent, Singapore. Tour companies in Thailand and Singapore tend to have more up-to-date information on Burma and, in any case, most flights to Rangoon come in from Bangkok or, increasingly, Singapore. Now that private Burmese tour companies are mushrooming in Rangoon, it is perfectly feasible (and cheaper) to make direct contact yourself, organise your itinerary with them, book your own air ticket and pick up the visa at the Burmese Embassy of your choice (as previously mentioned, Burmese Embassies around the world are now under instruction from the SLORC to issue tourist visas — including individual or so-called 'FIT', Foreign Independent Traveller — within 24 hours; sometimes even quicker).

NB: Recently a circulation was sent round all the private tour operators in Burma 'advising' them not to handle FITs (Foreign Independent Travellers) who do not change US$200. Private firms dealing with FITs who have not changed US$200 at an official (ie government) outlet, will have their licences revoked.

# Bangkok

The vast majority of tours to Burma are organised via the government-run Myanmar Travels & Tours in Rangoon and they are not cheap. Bangkok's appointed representative is Skyline Travel Service Co. Ltd, but now that there are licensed non-governmental agencies in Rangoon, there is absolutely no need to go through Skyline who are overpriced, inefficient and trying desperately to cling on to their monopoly of travel to Burma. One last (and major) disincentive for not using their services is that Skyline (and by extension Myanmar Travels & Tours) will only take you to places of their choosing, and certainly nowhere off the beaten track or off their list of so-called 'approved areas'.

Numerous other companies in Bangkok operate tours to Burma and advertise all over the place, eg Diethelm, MK Ways, Exotissimo Travel (who seem particularly rude and unhelpful), Siam Wings, Asian Lines Travel, Katsha International Travel Service, etc, but they too make their reservations either via Skyline in Bangkok or Myanmar Travels & Tours in Rangoon, and are expensive. So, unless you are in a hurry or want everything handed to you on a plate, make your own arrangements directly with Rangoon either before leaving home or after arriving in Southeast Asia, or contact the non-governmental Swiss-Thai Travel Co., Ltd in Bangkok (see next page).

For the sake of information and comparison, Skyline offers tours starting from five days/four nights (taking in Rangoon, Pagan and Mandalay) up to the maximum 15 days/14 nights. Tours of six days/five nights, eight days/seven nights and 13 days/12 nights are also possible: these all include Rangoon, Pagan and Mandalay but add on Taunggyi (for the six-day tour), Kalaw (eight-day tour), Pindaya, Inle Lake and Thazi (13 days), whilst the full two weeks also encompasses Maymyo and Pegu.

Costs are high: the five-day tour comes to US$1,280 (plus US$130 single supplement), six days, US$1,500 (US$150 single supplement) and eight days US$1,650 (US$200 single supplement). Now these tours are by plane (from mid-October to April) and by ground transportation (during May, June, July, September and early October). I say 'by plane', that, of course, depends on whether Myanma Airways still has any planes left: as a Burmese friend once remarked to me lugubriously on learning of yet another Myanma Airways disaster: 'Ah, one more plane fall from sky'.

Skyline's eight, 13 and 15-day tours all use ground transportation (sedate 'express' trains, antique coaches and archaic buses): the eight-day tour costs US$1,020 for full board (US$100 single supplement) or US$770 for just bed and breakfast; the 13-day tour comes to US$1,520 full board (US$175 single supplement), US$1,140 bed and breakfast, while the maximum stay (15 days/14 nights) costs US$1,780 (US$220 single supplement), or US$1,330 'B & B'. Since the food in the hotels tends to be bland and luke-warm, go for half-board. You can eat outside much better and much more cheaply. In addition to the above costs, you have to pay Skyline the following extras:

Airfare Bangkok/Rangoon/Bangkok on Thai Airways (TG): US$235 or 5,875 baht (which is a bit of a liberty as you can buy it yourself for 5,300 baht if you are prepared to shop around). The ticket costs between £148 and £161 if purchased in the UK. (Skyline will also sell you the BKK/RGN/BKK routing on Myanma Airways at US$180).

Burma visa fee: US$24, which is approximately equivalent to 600 baht (it's only 400 baht if you apply at the Embassy yourself).

Bangkok Airport Tax: US$8 (200 baht).

Rangoon Airport Tax: US$6 (this can only be paid in US dollars or in the new Foreign Exchange Certificate equivalent. You *must* remember to retain US$6 or you won't be able to leave the country).

Skyline requires a deposit of US$200 when booking and, though they state that they need three weeks to obtain the visa (particularly if you book from abroad), it can actually be processed in a couple of days in Bangkok. If you go to Skyline's office, you'll require your passport, three photographs and various application forms (which they supply). You are also obliged to sign a form asserting that you 'are not a journalist, reporter or freelance newspaperman'. If you are (and it says so in your passport) you have little chance of obtaining a visa. If you are a member of one of those 'dubious' professions and it doesn't mention it in your passport, sign the form regardless and lie about your occupation; in the meantime dream up as innocuous a profession as possible.

NB: Within the space of nine months, Skyline have, for some reason, seen fit to increase the prices of their tours by massive amounts. For example, in January 1992 the eight day/seven night tour on full board cost US$760, yet now Skyline are charging US$1,020, the 13 days/12 nights trip has gone up from US$1,230 to US$1,520 (full board) and the price of the maximum 15 days/14 nights tour has risen from US$1,420 (full board) to US$1,780. The itinerary, however, remains identical, the appalling ground transportation and surly service have not improved, nor has the standard of accommodation or meals.

## Travel agent (non-government)

Those who wish to travel to Burma independently from Bangkok or on a non-governmental tour (and have not organised a schedule beforehand) are advised to contact the helpful, efficient and English-speaking:

SWISS-THAI TRAVEL CO., LTD
Rajadamri Arcade Bldg,
95 Rajadamri Rd,
Pratumwan,
Bangkok 10330
Tel 251 9960, 251 7654, Fax 254 3571, Telex 22648.

You may have read that in late 1990, a Thai travel agency called Lanna Air Tours commenced so-called 'cultural tours' of Burma, flying from Chiang Mai to Pagan, on to Mandalay and back to Chiang Mai. Lanna Air Tours had signed a contract with Thailand's domestic carrier Bangkok Airways to use them as a charter company, having previously obtained special permission from the Burmese government. However, the Bangkok Airways flights had to be cancelled after barely 15 months: this was because Bangkok Airways decided to phase out their Indonesian-made Bandeirante aircraft, which they had originally used, in favour of the 32-seater Shorts. This change-over increased Lanna Air Tours' charter fee by 45%, which would have made the tour price much too expensive. However, it is still possible that if Lanna Air Tours can obtain a better deal with Bangkok Airways, these tours will be re-opened one day.

# Singapore

The travel agent in Singapore most geared up for tours to Burma is: TINA TRAVEL & AGENCIES SDN. BHD., #03-35 Golden Landmark, 390 Victoria Street, Singapore 0718, Tel 297 1778/9, 294 4782, Fax 292 5639, Telex 37378.

Another agent in Singapore which arranges programmes to Burma is German Asian Travels (Pte.) Ltd, 126 Telok Ayer Street, #02-01, Singapore 0106, Tel 221 5539, Fax 221 4220.

The advantage of travelling from Singapore is that you can now fly twice weekly direct to Rangoon on SilkAir (formerly Tradewinds), a subsidiary of Singapore Airlines and consequently one of the best airlines in Southeast Asia. The cheapest price for a return ticket is S$950 from Consolidated Tours Pte Ltd, 35 Selegie Road, #B1-03 Parklane Shopping Mall, Singapore 0718, Tel 336 3033, Fax 336 9889. Tickets for SilkAir direct can be purchased either at 77 Robinson Road, Ground Floor, SIA Building, Singapore 0106 or at 55 Airport Boulevard, 3rd Floor, SATS Building. For reservations and reconfirmations call 221 2221. Their Rangoon base is at 537 Merchant Street, Tel 84600, Fax 83872, while other Asian offices are in Indonesia, Philippines, Taiwan and Thailand. SilkAir also have agents in Austria, France, Germany, Italy, Switzerland, Hong Kong, Japan and Australia.

SilkAir's sole UK agent is: Travel 2 Limited, Hill House, Highgate Hill, London N19 5NA, Tel (071) 272 3090, 281 3991, 281 8558, Fax (071) 272 7540, 281 8105. A highly efficient company, specialising in airfares to Southeast Asia (but unfortunately not tours to Burma), Travel 2 also have offices in Manchester, Tel 061 832 1508, 061 839 5370, Fax 061 833 2791 and Glasgow, Tel 041 353 3300, Fax 041 353 3359. Their airfares for SIN/RGN are £165 (one way), £327 return. Prices for the routing LHR/SIN/RGN/SIN/LHR vary from £822 up to £878, for LHR/BKK/RGN/BKK/LHR from £645 to £932. Reservations, reconfirmation and ticketing can also be made at any Singapore Airlines (SIA) office throughout the world.

# Hong Kong

The company to contact in Hong Kong for private tours to Burma is:

PASSPORT TRAVEL MANAGEMENT (FE) LTD
Suites 1603-6, 16/F,
Polly Commercial Building,
21-23A Prat Avenue,
Tsimshatsui,
Kowloon,
Hong Kong
Tel (852) 722 1023, Fax (852) 369-9284, Telex 47886.

# Rangoon

Booking directly through one of the many recently-licensed Rangoon-based travel agents is clearly the cheapest (if not always easiest) way of arranging a trip to Burma. At this early stage it is difficult to say which agencies are reputable and which are not. For example, one company — Thuriya Tours and Travels — has already proved to be unreliable and others have strong MTT or government links. One agency, however, that can be recommended is:

EMPEROR TRAVELS & TOURS
No 47, Room 13, Bogalayzay St,
Rangoon
Tel (95-1) 71168, Fax (95-1) 89960/89961 (609, marked for the attention of 'Emperor Travels & Tours'), Telex 21201, 21236 BM/UKA 1666.

   Emperor's tours (all payable in US dollars) vary according to the size of the group. Prices start at US$126 for a group of 10-15 on a two day/three night visit to Rangoon with accommodation at the Thamada Hotel (room only), whereas an individual traveller would pay US$215. A four day/three night tour of Rangoon starts at US$196 (room only); if you include Pegu, the price is actually cheaper: US$189. An eight day/seven night tour of Rangoon, Meiktila, Pagan (Thiripyitsaya Hotel) and Mandalay (Mandalay Hotel) starts at US$549 for groups of 10-15 (room only), going up to

US$999 for an individual (US$1,149 for full board). A similar ten day/nine night trip starts at US$629 on a room only basis, whilst a single traveller would pay US$1,149 (US$1,396 for full board).

The 12 day/11 night tour takes in Rangoon, Meiktila, Pagan, Taunggyi, Inle Lake and Mandalay and prices here vary from US$777 for a group of 10+ (on a room only basis) to US$1,879 for an individual on full board. An individual on 'B & B' would pay US$1,699. The 14 day/13 night programme adds on Pindaya, Kalaw, Mount Popa and Pegu and prices vary from US$860 to US$2,099. The 15 day/14 night highly comprehensive tour encompasses Rangoon, Meiktila, Mandalay (Amarapura and Sagaing), Mingun, Monywa, Pagan, Mount Popa, Meiktila, Prome, Pegu, and Shwedaung: prices vary from US$870-US$2,099.

Since Rangoon has very few fax machines (most companies appear to share the same number), the best way of making contact is either via telex or by express mail.

Booking is fairly straightforward (and avoids middlemen and travel agents' fees): send a fax, telex or letter to Rangoon (see above) requesting your tour or suggesting an itinerary of your own choosing, and transfer the necessary funds to the relevant account at the Myanmar Foreign Trade Bank. Emperor will then send immediate confirmation by fax, telex or letter and you can apply for your visa at any Burmese Embassy around the world. Remember, though, that the prices do not include air fares, airport taxes, entrance and visa fees and insurance.

So-called 'business tours' are also available for a stay of up to two weeks. They cost US$90 a day per person (or US$70 for two) and include lunch and dinner at a Chinese restaurant, transportation throughout Rangoon, airport transfers and an English-speaking guide. Reservations should be made 14 days in advance by fax or telex with all the necessary details (full name, nationality, passport no., arrival and departure date, flight details and hotel name) and settlement should be by telex transfer as described above.

Finally, Emperor also offers many other competitively-priced itineraries to all the main destinations, as well as arranging visits to the newly-opened resorts like Ngapali, Sandoway and Bassein. Given sufficient notice, they can organise trips to (amongst other places) Chaungtha, Moulmein, Kyaiktiyo ('The Golden Rock Pagoda'), Lashio (in northern Shan State) and Akyab and Myohaung (in Arakan State).

# Airlines

The following airlines fly into Rangoon's Mingaladon Airport:

THAI AIRWAYS INTERNATIONAL (TG): Monday, Thursday, Saturday, Flight TG 305 on an Airbus 300, dep. BKK 1450, arr. RGN 1530. TG 306 departs the same days at 1630, arriving in Bangkok at 1810. The cost of the normal return fare is 5,850 baht; the cheapest available is 5,300 baht from World Express Limited, Chongkolnee Building, 56 Suriwong Road, Bangkok, Tel 233 7950, 237 8831, Fax 233 7954.

Outside Thailand, tickets can be purchased at any TG office: in the UK the price varies from between £148-161.

MYANMA AIRWAYS (UB): Monday, Thursday, Saturday, flight UB 222 on a Fokker 28, dep. BKK 1020, arr. RGN 1100 (this flight also goes on a Tuesday but is UB 226). Flight UB 222 departs on a Wednesday and Sunday at 1605, arriving at 1645, and on a Tuesday and Friday at 1805, arriving at 1845. Return flights are as follows: Monday, Thursday, Saturday UB 221 dep. RGN 0745, arr. BKK 0925 (UB 225 departs at the same time on a Tuesday); Wednesday and Sunday UB 221 dep. RGN 1330 arr. BKK 1510 and Tuesday and Friday UB 221 dep. RGN 1530 arr. BKK 1710.

From Singapore, UB flies twice weekly (on Thursday and Sunday, UB 244) dep. SIN 1755, arr. RGN 1925, but they are expected to add on a third flight every Tuesday, departing Singapore at 1755 and arriving Rangoon at 1940. Return flights are as follows: every Thursday and Sunday dep. RGN 0715 arr. SIN 1145 (UB 243). The additional flight will leave Rangoon every Tuesday at 1225, arriving Singapore at 1655.

Myanma Airways also offers irregular services (at present twice weekly) from Jakarta (via Singapore) and also two times a week from Hong Kong. Tickets for Myanma Airways' international routes should (and generally can) only be purchased in the countries they serve, eg Thailand, Singapore, Hong Kong and Indonesia (and Burma, of course). Their office in Bangkok is located at 48/5 Pan Road (Thanon Pan), just off Silom Road, not far from the Burmese Embassy (Tel 233 3052, 234 9692, Fax 238 3179).

SILKAIR(MI): Two weekly flights from Singapore on Mondays and Fridays: MI 512 dep. SIN 1250, arr. RGN 1410 (on a Boeing 737-300). The return leg, MI 511, leaves Rangoon at 1510 and arrives at Singapore at 1930. Available for a best priced S$950 return (from

Consolidated Tours Pte Ltd in Singapore) and £165 (one way) and £327 (return) from Travel 2 in the UK.

AIR CHINA (CA, the former CAAC): Once a week (Wednesday) from Kunming on a Boeing 737-300; CA 905 departs Kunming at 1140 and arrives at Rangoon at 1220. It then leaves Rangoon (CA 906) at 1300, reaching Kunming at 1620.

AEROFLOT (SU): Offers an infrequent service (at present once a month) to and from Moscow, via Vietnam and Laos on the way in and via Bombay on the way back on a Tupolev 154. According to the International Airline Timetable, flight SU 523 departs Moscow at 1940 and arrives at Rangoon at 1245 the next day. The return flight (SU 524) departs Rangoon at 1755 and arrives at either 0355 or 0455 (the following morning), depending on which day you leave.

BIMAN BANGLADESH (BG): Offers an irregular and unreliable seasonal service between Bangkok and Rangoon.

NB: Thai Airways International are still toying with the idea of flying from Bangkok to Mandalay, whilst both TG and Thailand's private domestic carrier Bangkok Airways (PG) are working on possible links between Mae Hong Son in Northern Thailand and Mandalay. Future plans include extending this route to encompass Loikaw in Kayah State and Taunggyi in Shan State.

## ARRIVAL AND CUSTOMS

As soon as the doors of your aircraft open on the runway of Mingaladon Airport, Rangoon, and Myanma Airways' archaic steps are in place, make a dash for the bus. That way you'll be first in the queue for the ensuing battle with Burmese bureaucracy. Passport control is the initial obstacle in your path (head for the line bearing the sign 'TOURISTS'), who require your passport, visa and Thai-style pink arrival card. Then it's on to the newly-created 'Myanma Foreign Trade Bank Special Exchange Counter' called the 'Foreign Exchange Certificate Exchange Counter' (see above), where, unless you can prove you are part of a package tour or under 12 years of age, you will have to change at least US$200 at the government rate.

Then it's on to the Customs desk where officials check your customs and FED forms. You will need to complete two copies of the customs form (though on the flight coming over, they only ever hand out one). Next, remove your baggage from the squeaking conveyor belt, proceed through either the green 'Nothing to declare' or red 'Something to declare' channel, hand over one copy of your customs form and breathe a huge sigh of relief.

The whole process takes about an hour. You will then be besieged by hordes of smiling Burmese (eager to purchase your cigarettes and whisky and to carry your luggage) and hopefully greeted by your tour company guide who will reconfirm your return flight for you. In the sweltering heat, lug your bag (or get some kind Burmese to do it) all the way to the outside of the airport gates (vehicles are not permitted within the terminal compound), where either your private 'limousine' or antique MTT bus will (hopefully) be waiting to whisk you away. Relax, keep your cool, you're in Burma, you've overcome the first few bureaucratic hurdles and you're on your way to your 'luxury' hotel. Ah yes, there's no place quite like Burma.

# DEPARTURE

Leaving Burma normally entails the following eight formalities:

1. Pay your airport departure tax of US$6 or FEC $6.
2. Check in your luggage and obtain your boarding pass.
3. Immigration checks your pink Thai-style departure card and asks three questions: 'What is your occupation?' (Don't say 'journalist' or 'reporter'), 'What was your address in Yangon?' and 'Are you an FIT or on a package tour?' (this, of course, affects whether you have changed the mandatory US$200 as an FIT, or no money at all if you are on a package tour).
4. Customs checks your customs and FED forms.
5. The customs officer hands you over to another customs official who asks: 'Have you purchased any gems, jewellery, gold, jade or antiques?' and 'Have you any kyat left?'. (Burmese regulations state that gems can only be purchased at the 'Myanma Gems Shops and other Authorized Shops where you will be given a voucher with a permit for export'. If you have bought gems or jewellery 'illegally', either have them well concealed and smile innocently at the official, or better still have a packet of '555' handy. Kyat, too, are not in theory allowed to be exported; in any case, out of Burma they are only of value as a curiosity, particularly the 45 and 90 kyat notes, or as a souvenir).

6. Your hand-baggage is X-rayed: remember to remove your camera and films. The machine says 'FILM SAFE' but it isn't.
7. Final hand-baggage and body search.
8. Wait in the departure lounge where there are two overpriced souvenir shops, a duty-free shop and a grubby restaurant (only dollars accepted).

Chapter Four

# Getting Around

## MODES OF TRANSPORT

'There was a fair amount of traffic: we passed something every four or five miles, a rusty bus or lorry, or a jeep. The chassis and engines all dated from the war, but the upper works, as sailors would say, were all home-made and variously quaint. Only natural mechanics of genius could have kept such contraptions in working order; and they were by no means being nursed along, but driven flat out.'

*Return to Burma.*

Burma has a quite extraordinary array of vehicles, many quasi-prehistoric, on which tourists can travel quite legally. There are so-called 'limousines', taxis, local buses, jeeps, pick-up trucks, Burmese 'tuk-tuks', bicycles, trishaws (which hold two passengers, one facing the front, one the rear), rickshaws, horse-carts and a number of rickety river vessels. If you travel independently, you will have to bargain for the fare, whether it be in kyat, dollars, baht, whisky, cigarettes, T-shirts, or anything else you have available.

The collection of buses belonging to Myanmar Travels & Tours are ancient, tumbledown vehicles which trundle along lugubriously and frequently break down (as, in fact, do most of the other Burmese modes of transport). You'll just have to grin and bear it. Burmese trains hurtle along at speeds of up to 30 mph, turning the journey from Rangoon to Mandalay into a 14 hour ordeal. Again, just keep smiling; after all, you're not on Myanma Airways. Boat journeys are fun; at Pagan you can meander down the Irrawaddy taking in the pagodas, temples and monasteries en route, or from Mandalay 'sail' away to Mingun to see the famous bell and pagoda.

And finally, Myanma Airways. They operate a wholly unpredictable domestic schedule with their 'fleet' (a veritable misnomer) of obsolete 44-seater Fokker Friendships; this aircraft dates back to November 1958 and I think Myanma Airways (or UBA, Union of Burma Airways, as it was then known) must have been one of the very first customers.

Burma has a number of domestic airports including: Mandalay, Nyaung-U (for Pagan), Heho (for Taunggyi and the Inle Lake Region), Bhamo and Myitkyina (in Kachin State), Putao in the far north, Kalemyo (west of the Chindwin River towards the Bangladeshi border), Kyaukpyu (an island off Arakan State), Lashio (in northern Shan State), Loikaw (in Kayah State), Akyab (now referred to as Sittwe, in Arakan State) for Myohaung, Tachilek, Kengtung and Mong Hsat (across the border from Mae Sai in Thailand), Moulmein (in Mon State), Mergui and Tavoy (in Tenasserim Division) and Sandoway (for the beach resort of Ngapali). Tourists are generally only permitted to fly from Rangoon to Nyaung-U, Mandalay and Heho, though occasionally it is possible to fly to Sandoway's Mazin Airport (Thandwe) and up to Akyab (Sittwe).

If you choose to fly on Myanma Airways the following rules apply: all timetables are unpredictable (if not non-existent), tickets for domestic flights should not be purchased abroad as there is absolutely no guarantee that they will be honoured inside the country; confirmed flight reservations are forgotten or mysteriously disappear without explanation. There are no announcements to explain delays, nor any when (or, rather, if) a flight is about to depart, so keep a firm eye on your fellow passengers and chase after them if they appear to be heading towards an aeroplane. Finally, if at all possible, only travel on Myanma Airways with hand luggage; this eliminates the probability of discovering that your flight has eventually departed without your luggage. NB: foreigners on domestic flights are required to complete a disembarkation card or to register with immigration. Remember to keep your passport handy at all times.

Myanma Airways do claim to have an official domestic timetable, but no tourist has ever set eyes upon it. In any case, they never stick to it. As one UB employee expressed when I foolishly inquired what time my flight from Pagan to Mandalay was departing: 'Why you ask me? Ask the pilot'. Myanma Airways also states 'Passengers reporting after the stipulated time will be refused accommodation' and 'If there is any question of an aircraft being overloaded, the parties authorised by the carrier to supervise the loading of aircraft shall decide which persons or articles shall be carried.'

The so-called 'scheduled' route for tourists, when functioning, takes in the Rangoon-Pagan-Mandalay-Heho-Rangoon loop in the morning and then flies back the other way in the afternoon. The approximate departure and arrival times are as follows:

Rangoon dep. 06.45
Pagan (Nyaung-U) arr. 08.30
Pagan dep. 08.45
Mandalay arr. 9.15
Mandalay dep. 9.30
Heho arr. 10.00
Heho dep. 10.15
Rangoon arr. 11.30/12 noon

Rangoon dep. 1300
Heho arr. 14.25
Heho dep. 14.45
Mandalay arr. 15.15
Mandalay dep. 15.30
Pagan arr. 16.00
Pagan dep. 16.15
Rangoon arr. 17.30

There are other flights to Mandalay, Heho and Nyaung-U (Pagan) but the only way you will find out about them is either at Myanma Airways' swelteringly hot office (they have fans, but never switch them on) at 104 Strand Road (Tel 72911 or 84566), or via your guide and you will have to pay in dollars. First choice for tickets goes to members of the SLORC, second choice to VIPs, diplomats and government officials, third choice to foreign visitors, expatriates and tourists and fourth (and last) 'choice' to the Burmese people. If there are any tickets left for locals, these are drawn by lots, so you soon learn that it's impossible for a Burmese to plan his or her own schedule in advance. Thus, attempting to purchase an airline ticket for the average Burmese citizen can humorously be referred to as 'all day sight-seeing in Myanma Airways office'.

For the sake of information and for those with a keen interest in aviation, it may be worth noting that, according to *Airport Support's*

*Directory of Airports and Airport Equipment*, Burma has only four 'officially' recognised airports: Akyab (Sittwe), Mandalay (not yet approved by Thai Airways for international flights), Mergui and Rangoon. Rangoon's so-called International Airport (Mingaladon) is presently under renovation and is even more chaotic than usual (if that's possible).

The following notice is pinned to the wall of the British Embassy in Bangkok:

'Visitors are advised to avoid travelling by internal Myanma Airways flights due to their poor safety record.'

# TRAVEL RESTRICTIONS

If you have pre-booked a two-week tour with MTT, your schedule will in all probability take in Rangoon, Mandalay (and the surrounding towns), Maymyo, Pagan, Meiktila, Kalaw, Pindaya, Inle Lake, Taunggyi, Heho, Thazi and Pegu. The following extra destinations have recently been declared 'safe' by the SLORC: Htaukkyant, Syriam/Kyauktan, Twante, Monywa, Prome, Sandoway, Ngapali, Bassein, Chaungtha, Letkhokkon, Kengtung (Kyaing Tong), Muse and Kawthaung (at least according to the list published by Myanmar Travels & Tours). You can add to that: Kyaikto, Kyaiktiyo ('The Golden Rock Pagoda'), Yathetaung ('Hermit Mountain'), Mottama, Moulmein, Setse, Kyaikkami, Thanbyuzayat, Mudon, Thaton, Nyaungdoon, Pyu, Toungoo, Pyinmana, Shwedaung, and Tachilek. Lashio (in northern Shan State) and Akyab and Myohaung (in Arakan State) are occasionally accessible with special permission (see Chapter Ten).

# USEFUL ADDRESSES

MTT's main office is at the junction between Sule Pagoda Road and Maha Bandoola Street in Rangoon, near the Sule Pagoda (77/91 Sule Pagoda Road, Tel 80321, 82013, 73382, 78376, 75328, Fax 82535, 89588, Telex 21330). Their Mandalay office is located in the Mandalay Hotel (Tel 22499/22586): there are also offices in all the other officially approved areas: Pagan, Kalaw, Pindaya, Taunggyi and Inle Lake. There's even an 'office' in a hut just next to Thazi railway station where you wait for the train to Rangoon. The MTT office at Inle Lake is situated on the jetty; in Kalaw, Pindaya and

Taunggyi, it's in the government-run hotels (of which there is just one in each town). On October 1, Myanmar Travels & Tours opened its most recent branch office at the border town of Tachilek to deal with tourists arriving from Mae Sai in Thailand and travelling on to Kengtung for sight-seeing.

If you become seriously ill in Burma, get out quick and seek treatment in either Bangkok or Singapore. Out of desperation, there is the **Rangoon General Hospital** (Tel 72311) on Bogyoke Aung San Road, the Kandawgyi Clinic on Natmauk Road (Tel 50149) or the Lake View Clinic on Kan Yeiktha Road 6½ mile (Tel 30083). Mandalay's General Hospital is on the corner of 30th and 75th Streets.

The **British Embassy** is located at 80 Strand Road (Tel 81700), the **US Embassy** at 581 Merchant Street (Tel 82055) and the **Thai Embassy** at 91 Prome Road (Tel 21713). **Thai Airways** are at 441/445 Maha Bandoola Street (Tel 75167, Fax 89564), **Myanma Airways**' Head Office is located at 104 Strand Road, while **SilkAir** are at 537 Merchant Street (at the corner of Pansodan Street), Tel 84600, 82653, Fax 83872. **Myanma Railways** can (in theory) be contacted on 74027, **Immigration** on 86434, **Customs** on 84533, **Rangoon Airport** on 62675, the **Police** on 199 or 82511, the Fire Brigade on 74211 and the Ambulance service on 192 or 71111.

The **General Post Office** (Tel 85499) is just down from the Strand Hotel at 39 Bo Aung Kyaw Street and is open from 9.30am to 4.30pm Monday to Friday, though don't bank on your mail reaching its destination (air mail letters cost K5 to Europe). It used to be possible for holders of American Express Cards to receive mail at an office near the Sule Pagoda (quoting the AMEX number on the outside of the envelope), but that's a decidedly risky proposition. Overseas calls can be made from the **Central Telegraph Office** (Tel 81133) at the corner of Pansodan and Maha Bandoola Streets.

Other addresses which may be of interest/use are:

Ministry of Foreign Affairs
Prome Road
Rangoon
Tel 22844, Fax 22950, 21719, Telex 21313.

Myanmar Foreign Investment Commission
653/691 Merchant Street
Rangoon
Tel 82207, 82101, 82946, Telex 21368.

Ministry of Trade (International Trade Department)
228/240 Strand Road
Rangoon
Tel 84299, 83514, 83517, 83519, Fax 89578, Telex 21338.

Ministry of Trade
No 70, Pansodan
Rangoon
Tel 73869.

Myanmar Foreign Trade Bank
80/86 Maha Bandoola Garden Street
Rangoon
Tel 84911, Telex 21300, 21332.

Myanmar Investment and Commercial Bank
526/532 Merchant Street
P.O. Box 442
Tel 83419, 87330.

# ACCOMMODATION

'Outside Rangoon, hotels as Europeans understand them do not exist.'
                                                      Norman Lewis, 1951.

As with transportation, if you are on one of MTT's tours everything will be arranged for you, that's to say your accommodation will already have been pre-booked. Burma, alas, has a dreary collection of run-down hotels — very much like its fleet of Fokker Friendships; old, shabby and worn at the edges. Many date from colonial times, like the legendary Strand Hotel in Rangoon, which in days of yore went under the grandiose title of 'The Gateway To The Land of Pagodas'. The Strand, in fact, is under renovation and only a few of the 100 rooms are available at the moment. Refurbishments are expected to be completed in 1993: but 1993 in Burmese could mean 2003.

Rangoon's largest hotel (with 229 rooms) is the vast, amorphous Inya Lake Hotel, built by the Russians and wholly characterless. It is also badly located for downtown Rangoon.

Mandalay boasts two main hostelries: the colonial-style but inhospitable Mandalay Hotel and the friendly but less 'grand' Mya Mandala (with swimming pool!). Pagan, likewise: the famous Thiripyitsaya and the Irra Inn (now renamed the Ayeyar Hotel), which enjoy an idyllic location by the banks of the Irrawaddy River, but which are both in a state of disrepair.

Regarding value for money, Burmese hotels must surely rate as some of the worst in the world (if you calculate the cost on money changed at the official rate, that is). Take the Sakhantha (Railway) Hotel (Tel 82975) in Rangoon, for example: it's seedy, shady and the ceiling leaks. The noise of the Rangoon to Mandalay 'express' next door doesn't offer much in the way of solace, either. Yet the Sakhantha charges from US$42 up to US$81 (for that you could stay in a four-star hotel in Bangkok), though locals settle up in kyat. Rates for the Burmese vary from K270-450, which, at the black market rate, only comes to US$3/5 (the room's correct value). If you've already paid for your tour in full, there's little you can do about it. If, however, you have entered Burma as an 'FIT' *without* a booked tour, you'll just have to hope for an obliging receptionist. Finally, although non-government hotels and guest houses are now being granted licences to accommodate tourists, even they are only 'officially' allowed to accept US dollars, though there are stories of hotel staff taking both kyat (changed at the government rate) and even kyat obtained on the black market.

# NAMES: OLD AND NEW

On May 27 1989 the SLORC announced that it had changed the name of the country from Burma to Myanmar and the capital from Rangoon to Yangon. This was simply a reversion to Burmese names that had been anglicised during British colonial times. Since these changes were decreed by a government which had lost a democratic election and had refused to hand over power, they are not accepted in this book. They have also been rejected by the ethnic groups, since the SLORC have failed to recognise the ethnic composition of the country, and by the opposition groups who regard the changes as a crude attempt to forget the history of the country during the past 40 years of military rule. For the record, however, the name changes are as follows:

| | |
|---|---|
| Burma | Myanmar |
| Union of Burma | Union of Myanmar (Myanmar Naing-Ngan) |
| Burman | Myanmar |
| Rangoon | Yangon |
| Pagan | Bagan |
| Maymyo | Pyin U (or Oo) Lwin |
| Pegu | Bago |
| Ava | Inwa |
| Akyab | Sittwe |
| Bassein | Pathein |
| Mergui | Myait |
| Moulmein | Mawlamyine |
| Myohaung | Mrauk-U |
| Amherst | Kyaikkami |
| Sandoway | Thandwe |
| Prome | Pyay |
| Syriam | Tanyin |
| Tavoy | Dawei |
| Magwe | Magway |
| Arakan | Rakhine |
| Tenasserim | Tanintharyi |

| | |
|---|---|
| Chindwin River | Chindwinn River |
| Irrawaddy River | Ayeyarwady River |
| Salween River | Thanlwin River |
| Sittang River | Sittoung River |
| | |
| Burma Airways | Myanma (no 'r') Airways |
| Tourist Burma | Myanmar Travels and Tours |
| Hotel and Tourist Corporation | Myanmar Hotels and Tourism Services |
| Diplomatic Stores | Tourist Department Stores |
| Burmese | Bamar |
| Karen | Kayin |
| Arakanese | Rakhine |

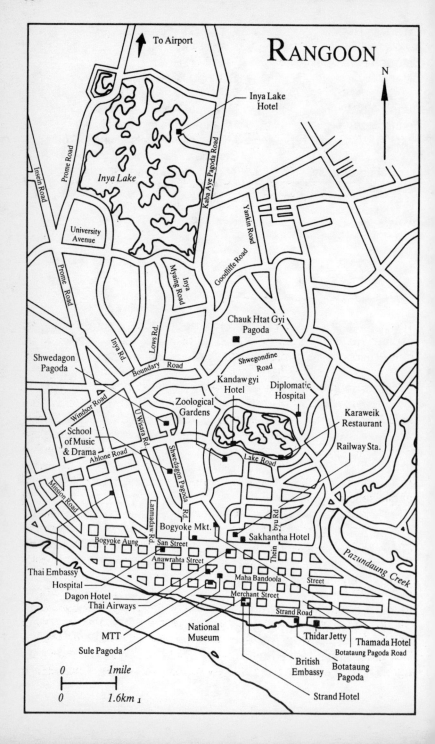

To Airport

# RANGOON

N

Inya Lake Hotel

Prome Road

Insein Road

Inya Lake

Kaba Aye Pagoda Road

Yankin Road

University Avenue

Prome Road

Inya Myang Road

Goodliffe Road

Inya Rd.

Lows Rd.

Chauk Htat Gyi Pagoda

Shwedagon Pagoda

Boundary Road

Shwegondine Road

Kandawgyi Hotel

Diplomatic Hospital

Windsor Road

Zoological Gardens

Karaweik Restaurant

U Wisara Rd.

School of Music & Drama

Ahlone Road

Shwedagon Pagoda Rd.

Lake Road

Railway Sta.

Mission Road

Lanmadaw Rd.

Bogyoke Mkt.

byu Rd

Sakhantha Hotel

Bogyoke Aung

San Street

Thein

Anawrahta Street

Pazundaung Creek

Thai Embassy

Hospital

Maha Bandoola Street

Dagon Hotel

Thai Airways

Merchant Street

Strand Road

MTT

National Museum

Thidar Jetty

Thamada Hotel

Botataung Pagoda Road

Sule Pagoda

British Embassy

Botataung Pagoda

Strand Hotel

0        1mile

0        1.6km

Chapter Five

# Rangoon and vicinity

## HISTORY AND GENERAL DESCRIPTION

The city of the stunning Shwedagon Pagoda, Rangoon is, as capitals go, comparatively new — in historical terms, that is. In all other respects it's a crumbling, decaying, Dickensian yet alluring metropolis. It is quite unlike any other place in Southeast Asia.

From the middle of the 18th Century, Rangoon steadily grew in importance, though it had no political status until after the annexation of Lower Burma by the British in 1852. Known as *Okkala* way back in the mists of time, and later *Dagon* (possibly from the Shwedagon Pagoda), it was renamed *Ran-kon* or *Yangon* meaning the 'End of Strife' after the conquest of Lower Burma by King Alaungpaya in 1755. The city then became Rangoon, an easy anglicisation of *Ran-kon*.

For a long time Rangoon was little more than an oversized village, even when King Alaungpaya made it the principal port in Burma in preference to Syriam (just across the river), which formerly held pride of place. Rangoon, then, was merely a riverside village with a total area of not more than one-eighth of a square mile and with a circumference of just a couple of miles. It was after the British chose to make it their administrative centre that the present chess-board pattern city, planned by their engineers, emerged: the cross streets being numbered in the American way. Heavily battered during World War II, Rangoon today remains very much as it did then, 50 years ago. There has been the odd lick of paint here and there plus a fortune (allegedly more than 350 million kyat) spent on the construction of a new pagoda. Known behind closed doors as the 'Socialist Pagoda', the Mahawizayazedi ('Great Conqueror') stands gleaming, in the shadow of the Shwedagon, subsidised by funds appropriated by Ne Win solely to make merit for himself and to appease the *nats*. The lavish pagoda, heavily gilded, glistens while the people, strolling by, wonder how the money might have been more wisely apportioned. As George Orwell remarked ironically in his novel *Burmese Days*: 'It was time now to be making ready for the next world — in short, to begin building pagodas.'

Rangoon today is threadbare and decrepit, the very antithesis of its neighbour Bangkok. It has no discos, no massage parlours, no traffic jams. In their place are the Shwedagon and Sule Pagodas and the delightful peoples of Burma.


# LOCAL TRANSPORT

You may well be ferried around Rangoon in one of MTT's ageing buses or, if you are on an independent tour, by chauffeur-driven 'limousine'. If, however, you decide to 'go it alone', you can travel by local bus or train, boat or ferry, taxi, pick-up truck, jeep, trishaw, rickshaw or even bicycle (the last-named is not recommended, as it will probably fall apart after a few hundred yards). Always agree the fare before setting out.


# PLACES TO STAY AND EAT

Prior to your arrival in Rangoon, your accommodation will already have been reserved (that's, of course, if you are on a pre-booked tour), so if there's anywhere you particularly want to stay (or avoid), let the travel agent know well in advance. Government hotels in the capital are universally dismal and grossly overpriced: the flagship, the old colonial masterpiece, the Strand (Tel 81530), once ranked alongside the Oriental in Bangkok and Raffles in Singapore, but that was many, many years ago. Today it languishes under 'renovation': nobody knows when it will be completed.

If you have any say in the matter, avoid the Russian-built Inya Lake Hotel (Tel 62857) at all costs. This elephantine construction (opened in 1961) is located, as the name suggests, near the Lake, but is more noted for its family of rats than for its service or style. Rates vary from US$55-350. Near the Royal Lake lies the Kandawgyi Hotel (Tel 82327), British-built, which offers luxurious bungalows, invariably reserved for the SLORC. You, most likely, will be accommodated in the main block (35 rooms), which is far from glamorous and priced from US$25-75. Situated in the vicinity of the main cinema is the Burmese-built Thamada Hotel (Tel 71499) at 5 Signal Pagoda Road, which was opened in 1972 and has been smartened up in recent months. Apart from the odd appearance of Burmese rodents of the genus *Rattus*, the Thamada (formerly known as the President Hotel) is not a bad place to stay. It has 58 spacious rooms with air-conditioning, though the bathrooms stink and the lift — surely the slowest in all of Southeast Asia — frequently gets stuck between floors. Rates here are: single room US$48, double US$72, twin US$78 (locals pay K210, K336 and K396 respectively). At the black market rate that comes to just US$4, which is quite normal by Rangoon standards. Nearby at 256 Sule Pagoda Road is the dreary Dagon Hotel (Tel 89354) which costs between US$15-25. The YMCA on 265 Maha Bandoola Street(Tel 71408) charges between US$15-40 and the Garden Hotel at 73/75 Sule Pagoda Road (Tel 71516) US$10-25. Notices pinned to the door or wardrobe in each government hotel room state:

'The attention of all guests is respectfully drawn to the following: Please do not entertain guests particularly opposite sex in your room. For reasons of security occasions may arise necessitating a search by the authorities concerned of the baggage belonging to a guest. If this happens your kind assistance, co-operation and understanding will be greatly appreciated. Kindly refrain from smoking while lying on the bed. Kindly refrain from any act which may be a source of disturbances to other guests. Thank you.'

The first non-government hotel to open was the View Kan Taw Yeik Hotel, No. 21-A, Natmauk Lane (2) (Tel 51313), located near the Kandawgyi Lake. Despite the fact that the owner's name is Daw Khin Nyunt, it is not SLORC property; consequently the service is much friendlier. However, a single room still costs US$35, a double US$40, plus US$8 for charges (whatever that means) and US$6 for breakfast which is optional. Another private establishment recently opened is the Kazoku Motel (Tel 50963) situated at No (1) Bogyoke Pya Taik Road. No doubt many more private hotels and guest houses will be appearing all over Rangoon, though it remains to be seen whether tourists can settle their bills at local rates and in kyat obtained on the black market.

Rangoon has a number of good restaurants so you can avoid the hotel cuisine, which, without exception, is grim. For Burmese cooking, try the Danubyu Restaurant, No 175, 29th Street (Tel 75397). I recommend the pork or beef curry and the sour vegetable soup, known in Burmese as *deezaungchingye*. The top Chinese restaurant in town is the Panda at No 205 Wadan Street (at the corner of Keighley Street and St John's Road, Tel 21152), while other excellent restaurants are Fu Sun at No 160, Kokkine, Kabaaye Pagoda Road, Holiday Restaurant, No. 51 Po Sein Road and Mya Kan Tha, No. 70, Natmauk Lanthwe (corner of Po Sein Road). If you fancy Indian cuisine, don't miss the New Delhi Restaurant, No 262 Anawrahta Road, between 29th and Shwebontha Streets. It serves great chapatis but I suggest you steer clear of the 'fighting balls'! A good snack bar is the Pearl at No. 5 York Road, while, amongst a plethora of coffee shops, I recommend the Aung Gyi Coffee Shop and the Pepsi Shop.

NB: Telephone numbers/calls in Rangoon and throughout Burma are unreliable, so don't be at all surprised if you can't get through to a hotel or restaurant, or if the line sounds as though you're speaking to Outer Mongolia.

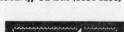

# ENTERTAINMENT/SHOPPING

Karaoke has predictably arrived in Rangoon, though under the SLORC's strict regulations:

1. No dancing allowed whatsoever.
2. Make no nuisance in the premises.
3. Refrain from causing disgraceful manners.
4. Don't exchange harsh words.
5. No annoyances to be caused.
6. Unbecoming behaviours are totally not entertained.
7. Actions infringing to the set rules of the state are not permitted.
8. No disturbances out of drunkeness or whatever.
9. Don't spit on the floor.
10. Please don't throw rubbish.
11. Staff members are strictly prohibited from participations.
12. Dress properly.

Mind you, nobody in their right mind comes to Rangoon specifically for entertainment: Bangkok's clearly the place for that. If you are interested, however, there are Burmese theatrical performances (*pwe*) at the Karaweik Restaurant on the eastern side of the Royal Lake (*Karaweik* is a legendary bird, traditionally carved on the prow of royal barges). It may also be possible (ask your guide) to pay a visit to the State School of Music and Drama, near the junction of Shwedagon Pagoda and U Wisara Roads. Puppet shows (*yoke thay pwe*) are also sometimes staged: there used to be famous shows in Pagan, until the puppeteers went on strike because of the SLORC. Again, ask your guide, friend, taxi or trishaw driver.

Burmese music is fun; it's quite different from anything you will have heard in the West. The musicians employ a bizarre collection of instruments, including the *pat saing* (a series of cylindrical drums), *kyi waing* (bell-metal gongs), Burmese harps (*soung*), zithers, clarions, *pattalar* (a Burmese xylophone), bamboo flutes, violins, bamboo clappers and cup-shaped bells.

If you're desperate, you could always try a Burmese movie ('Coolie Killer' being a recent example of this fine art), or take a stroll to the Zoological Gardens, located near the Kandawgyi Hotel. The Zoo is open daily from 8am to 6pm and the entrance fee is K4.

Bogyoke Aung San (formerly Scott) Market is the place to go for shopping; like so many Southeast Asian markets it's a vast, sprawling place selling the usual souvenirs plus goods smuggled in from Thailand, China and India. You will be approached to change money on the black market, but be discreet. Occasionally, you can purchase items in US dollars or Thai baht (again, if you want to, do it surreptitiously). Always bargain.

For sequinned tapestries, shoulder bags and hats, head for the Myanmar Handicrafts Store, No 119/120 Central Block; whilst for bronze wares, puppets, wood carvings and tribal handicrafts (many from Shan State) try Mr Slim's Tribal Souvenirs Shop, No 30 New Building Double Storey Ground Floor. For T-shirts of Burma, souvenirs, jewellery and silverware go to Zaw Winn Hlaing, No 7 Central Block, Bogyoke Aung San Market. Two charming ladies, Daw Khin Aye Myint and Ma Khin Hla Wai, will be delighted to serve you, but bargain hard. For a T-shirt of Burma, they'll ask K300, but you should be able to knock them down to K250, particularly with a bit of flattery.

Lacquerware is really best purchased in Pagan and sequinned tapestries (shoulder bags, hats, etc) in Mandalay. Umbrellas (best bought in Bassein), various wood and ivory carvings and jewellery (of dubious quality) can be found throughout Burma, so it's up to you whether you want to buy them in Rangoon or not. As for gems, jade and antiques, the safest advice is to forget it. Many are fake and in any case cannot 'officially' be exported unless purchased from a government outlet, such as the 'Diplomatic Stores' (the 'Tourist Department Stores'), where the prices are exorbitant and there's no worthwhile guarantee of authenticity. If you are absolutely determined to buy, I suggest you contact Taw Wyn Oo Jewellery, No 23 Bogyoke Aung San Market (Tel 83585); for gold, go to Zaw Winn Hlaing at No 73 Shwebontha St (Tel 76343).

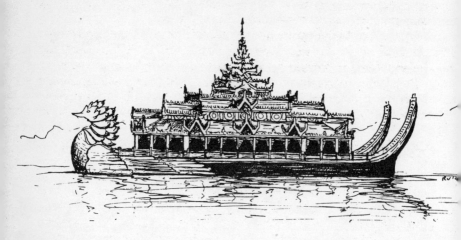

*Rangoon: the Royal Barge ('Karaweik') on Kandawgyi Lake.*

# SIGHTSEEING — IN RANGOON

## Shwedagon Pagoda

'A great golden spire rising over 300 feet from its platform atop a hill and surrounded by a village of smaller spires and temples ... Such colour — the shining gold of the central spire, the red and gold of the small spired shrines clustering about its foot; the intense greens, browns, and silvers of the gingerbready decorations on the tiered temple roofs; the glittering coloured-glass mosaic columns; the arresting orange splotches of the monks' robes. Such a multitude of images of the Buddha, big and little, lying and sitting, alabaster and plaster, plain and shining golden, crowded into Buddha halls by the dozen or seated each in a separate shrine building. And multitudinous other images of attendant beings of heavenly nature, of yellow-robed saints, guarding snarling lions (chinthes), and miscellaneous worshipping animals. So many shrines, all with their worshippers; and such devout worship of reverent kneeling, audibly fervent devotions, offerings of flowers, incense-sticks, and smaller paper umbrellas, washing of images, lighting of candles, and resounding gongs.'                                                    Winston King, 1958.

The most revered pagoda in Burma — if not in all of Southeast Asia — and the very spirit of Rangoon and the nation itself, the Shwedagon is one of the most awe-inspiring sights in the world. Early morning or particularly twilight are the best moments to admire this wonderful structure; or simply from afar from the Royal Lake. If time permits, visit twice or three times to fully appreciate the awesome splendour of the Shwedagon Pagoda.

'When I climbed up to the terrace of the monument, my eyes popped open in wonderment', wrote HRH Prince Damrong Rajanubhab of Thailand on his visit to the Shwedagon in 1936.

Believed to have been constructed in 585 BC, the Shwedagon was originally a mere 27 feet high, but was brought up to its present height of 326 feet in the 15th Century by Shin Sawbu, queen of Pegu. It commands veneration and worship not solely because it dates back 2,500 years, but because of the authenticity of its origin which finds support in Buddhist scriptures. It is thought that two Burmese traders, Tapussa and Bhallika of the Mon Kingdom of Okkala, who had journeyed to India by sea, met the Buddha and received a gift of eight hairs from his own hands. On their return, their sacred gift was enshrined by King Okkalapa in a golden pagoda on the Theinguttarra Hill, the most natural location for a temple. It is also believed that the sacred relics of the three preceding Buddhas, which had been enshrined on this hill — a staff, a water dipper (filter) and a bathing garment — were excavated and re-consecrated or re-enshrined along with the new relics, in effect giving the pagoda a four-fold religious significance. Kings, queens and commoners have, through the ages, bestowed gold, silver and a myriad of other gifts to embellish the pagoda. The gold-plating and the precious stones (rubies, sapphires and topaz) in the diamond bud and the vane and umbrella (*hti*) run into many millions of kyat.

There are four approaches to the Shwedagon with ascending flights of steps from all the four quarters: north, south, east and west, lined with vendors offering flowers, gold leaf, candles, books and an assortment of souvenirs. If you enter via the western approach from the U Wisara Road, you will find on reaching the platform a figure of the founder King Okkalapa himself on the wall towards the west-northwest corner.

The base of the pagoda is 2ft 3ins high with a perimeter of 1,420 feet. On the platform are 64 smaller pagodas with four large ones right in the centre of the four cardinal points. There are sphinxes, *chinthes* (leogryphs: half lion, half griffin), innumerable shrines, *tazaungs* (pavilions) and rest-houses which the Burmese refer to as *zayats*. The platform itself is paved with marble and, whichever way you turn, you will find superb woodcarvings, floral designs, mosaic-wrought pillars along with numerous Buddha images, cast in alabaster and brass. There are the famous bells: the *Maha Ghanta* Bell, 7ft high, 6⅔ft wide, one foot thick and weighing 16 tons, a gift by Singu Min in 1778, and the *Mahatisadda Ghanta* Bell which weighs 40 tons, is 8½ feet high, 7ft 8ins wide and one foot thick. This was a gift from King Tharrawaddy in 1841 and is the second largest bell in the land.

Entering by the southern stairway, you find two huge leogryphs, 30 feet high, and statues of ogres. Looking up, after the base, you will see three terraces called *piccayas*; the 64 small pagodas and the four big ones on the first terrace. After the next two terraces, you find the *Khaung Laung Pone* Bell which has a circumference of 442 feet at the base and 192 at the top, reaching a height of 70ft 4ins. Then comes the inverted begging bowl (*thabeik*), the twisted turban (*baung yit*) which takes you another 41 feet above; the lotus flower 31ft 5ins high; the plantain spire 52ft 11ins high, the *hti* (umbrella) going up another 33 feet (a donation of King Mindon, the penultimate king of Burma) and the vane tapering up and reaching towards the 76-carat diamond bud on top, a globe of gold, studded with precious stones.

At the foot of the hill, all around, lie many old and new monasteries, concealed by huge trees, palmyras and coconut palms. There are also a number of *zayats* (rest-houses) for pilgrims.

'The spot to which all travellers' paths converge in Rangoon is the Shwe Dagon Pagoda, the most sacred spot in all the Buddhist world. Up a long flight of stone we walk, on either side of which are chattering vendors of curious wares — silks and lace and gongs of brass, huge cheroots, eight or ten inches long, and as large round as your two thumbs, which contain tobacco enough for a family smoke, oranges, mangoes, jack-fruit and papaws, jade ornaments and tinsel jewels — indeed, almost anything that a Burman would want to eat or wear or bedeck himself with.

At the top of the steps a gorgeous, glittering sight indeed strikes the eye, for there rises a great and graceful column of gold, a hundred and fifty feet above the vast platform on which it is built, and which itself rises one hundred and seventy feet from the ground. The pagoda is very wide at the base, and tapers gradually to a ball-shaped top, on which is a crown of solid gold and jewels alone worth a round half-million dollars.

All around are little pagodas, or shrines, clustering close to the base of the parent, and each vying with all the others to show itself the richest and most bejewelled.

In the great pagoda is a huge Buddha, so covered with gold and gems that the covetous public is kept away from it by strong iron bars, while all the lesser shrines have other images of the placid saint, and some of them many, but all with exactly the same expression of ineffable content.'

Dr. Francis E. Clark, 1910.

Tourists who visit the Shwedagon alone have to pay an entrance fee of US$5 (don't forget to bring along your Foreign Currency form to be stamped) and are also occasionally asked for K5 to take photos. If you come as part of an MTT tour, the entrance fee is included. You must remove your shoes and socks at the bottom. There are two lifts to take you to the raised platform of the stupa, one for foreigners and one for Burmese. And, if the 'Old Man' has his way, (to paraphrase Kipling) 'never the twain shall meet'. (What Kipling actually stated was that 'East was East and West was West and never the twain should meet'. *The Ballad of East and West*, 1889).

'So, the great Shwedagon Pagoda stands today looking down on the country's turbulent history. Like a lotus blossom, it rises above the swamp and mire drinking in the cool crystal waters. It is never apart from human activities and its glory never tarnishes even though once trod by sacrilegious foreign boots and pillaged by thieving hands. It is a source

of spiritual strength and it has shared the joys and sorrows of people
throughout centuries.'

Khin Myo Chit, 1984.

## Sule Pagoda

Prounced 'Sue-lay', this pagoda is inevitably overshadowed by the
Shwedagon, but is wonderful nonetheless. Located in the centre of
Rangoon, near the office of MTT and surrounded by shops, the
eight-sided Sule Pagoda reaches 157 feet and, as Burmese shrines
go, is relatively small and compact. In some ways it has a more
intimate atmosphere than the awesome Shwedagon.

There are two accounts of the origin of the Sule Pagoda, which
dates back more than 2,200 years. One is that the Venerable
Mahinda went to Sri Lanka (Ceylon) 236 years after the nirvana of
the Buddha. As a compliment in return, three years later, the then
king of Sri Lanka sent an eight-man delegation to Burma. The
delegation, gifts and Buddha relics brought were received by Bhoga
Sena, king of what is now Syriam. The construction of the present
day Sule Pagoda was entrusted by the king to his minister Athoke.
In those days the pagoda was known as *Kyaik Kathoke* or *Kyaik Sura*
(*Sura* meaning a 'hero' and Athoke was a celebrated hero). In due
course, the pagoda became known as 'Sule'.

The other tale relates that, during the lifetime of the Buddha
himself, people congregated at the spot on which the pagoda was
subsequently built (*Su* means a gathering) to confer and to locate
the site for the building of the Shwedagon.

# National Museum

The National Museum was first inaugurated in June 1952 at the Jubilee Hall, Shwedagon Road and subsequently shifted to its present site, formerly the Bank of India, in February 1970. It has a rich collection of antiques, cultural objects, arts and handicrafts of indigenous races, royal regalia, musical instruments, decorative arts and an art gallery. The artifacts are displayed in different showrooms in what is in truth a rather gloomy three-storey building.

On the ground floor, the first object that strikes you — and indeed the main attraction of the museum itself — is the *Thiharthana Palin* (Lion Throne) which was presented by Lord Mountbatten in 1948. Built in 1816, during the reign of King Padon, it is the sole remaining throne of nine which were constructed: the other eight were destroyed by fire during World War II. Carved out of yamenay hard wood and finely gilded, it is flanked by royal regalia (all solid gold, including gold betel cups and vessels), silverware, artifacts, photographs, models and paintings of Mandalay Palace. You can also see various ceremonial robes, head-dresses, garments, girdles, divans and couches belonging to past members of the Burmese monarchy, even King Thibaw's state attire and ivory chair and Queen Supayalat's dressing table are on display.

There are opium weights, hilltribe costumes, paintings, woodcarvings, Buddha images from the Pagan period and tools dating back to neolithic times. Many of these displays are on the second and third floors of the museum which are easily missed. The entrance fee (if you come on your own) is US$4 and it is open from 10am to 3pm Monday to Friday.

*National Museum, Rangoon: hintha betel container.*

# Other attractions

Situated near the Rangoon River waterfront, east of the Strand Hotel and at the intersection of the Strand and Botataung Roads, is the **Botataung Pagoda** (meaning 'Pagoda of a Thousand Officers'). Legend has it that 1,000 officers brought two hairs of the Buddha, which are displayed in a glass case in a hall on the right side in front of a stunning Buddha image. This image was donated by King Mindon in the middle of the 19th Century and taken by the British at the end of that century. It was returned in 1951. The Botataung is a hollow pagoda with a zigzagging corridor with walls completely — and at times quite unnervingly — covered in mosaic mirror glass. You can actually go inside the stupa, a veritable hall of mirrors.

The **Chauk Htat Gyi Pagoda**, north of the Royal Lake on Shwegondine Road, houses the second largest Buddha (recumbent or reclining) in Burma. It is 216 feet long and 58 feet high. The original was built in 1907 by an exceptionally rich Burmese gentleman, but was destroyed in 1957. Rebuilt in 1966, it was completed in 1974 at a cost of no less than K5 million (allegedly from public donations). Of particular interest are the feet of the Buddha which are inscribed with 108 sacred symbols proving the Buddha's Enlightenment.

The **Eindawya Pagoda** was built in 1846 by Yewun U Win, on the site of the residence of Pagan Min, when he accompanied his father Shwebo Min to Rangoon in 1841. The **Kaba-Aye** (World Peace) **Pagoda** and nearby the **Mahapasana Guha Cave** are also worth a visit. The cave is artificial and is used as an assembly/ordination hall for abbots and monks.

Near the airport at Mingaladon, which is very much a military area, is the **Kyaik-kalo Pagoda** (also spelt Kyaik Ka Lawt), which has a *zaungdan* newly constructed by the SLORC. 'Kyaik' is the Mon (Talaing) word for pagoda and 'kalaw' means 'to do obeisance or revere'. According to tradition, an ogre did obeisance to Buddha Kakusandha on this spot. Close-by (about a minute's drive away) is the **Kyaikkale Pagoda**, which also has a recently-constructed SLORC *zaungdan*. In Mon 'kale' means to disappear. Legend has it that the Buddha Kakusandha disappeared on this spot between the eyebrows of the ogre while playing hide and seek. In the pagoda precinct stands a statue of the ogre called Kaya Heindaka Bulu ('Bulu' means 'ogre'). The pagoda, which was repaired in 1897 and crowned with a *hti* in 1904, is surrounded by monasteries. In the precinct is a tall, standing statue of the Buddha giving prophecy.

This is a wish-fulfilling statue.

About 10 minutes drive away stands the **Ahleinngasint Pagoda**, built by a famous abbot Seiwunkaba Sayadaw. It is unique in style and quite peculiar. Inside is a green Buddha image called Mahasandawshinmyapaya ('The owner of the hair relics emerald statue'). The foundation stone of this pagoda was laid on April 22 1958 jointly by the abbot and the President of Burma, U Win Maung. In the four corners are staircases each with five tiers: the name of the pagoda means 'Five-tiered Pagoda'.

At North Okkalapa, five minutes from Mingaladon Airport, is the **Meilamu Pagoda**, which boasts numerous vast Buddha images. Amongst the myriad of images are: the Buddha on the way to Enlightenment, the Buddha preaching to his five disciples, the Buddha resting, four large images in different postures, a large image of all eight conquests of the Buddha, a reclining Buddha, three laymen offering *sun* (food) to the Buddha, images of Shinthiwali (the most fortunate disciple of the Buddha) and Shinoobagoat (the most powerful of all the disciples), Lord Buddha's son Yahula asking for a legacy from his father, a hermit called Thumayda prostrating himself as a bridge over a stream for the Buddha to walk over (the Lord Buddha predicted that later Thumayda will become Areinmadeya, the future Buddha), Lord Buddha surrounded by two rivals called Dewadut and his follower and two images of the Lord Buddha meditating. All in all, it is an extraordinary and fascinating pagoda.

In the Thamaing area of Rangoon is the **Kyauk-waing Pagoda**, called Kyaik-waing-ut in Mon (Talaing). 'Waing' means 'to play' and 'ut' 'hide and seek'. According to tradition, Buddha Kakusandha played hide and seek with the ogre, the wager laid being that if the ogre was found by the Buddha, he should listen to his preaching, and if not found, the Buddha should be eaten by the ogre.

In the Thingungyun Township of Rangoon and under renovation stands the **Kyaik-kasan Pagoda**, which was built in the 4th Century BC by Sihadipa, king of Thaton, assisted by Yasa and seven other monks, over 16 hairs and 32 bone-relics of the Buddha. In Mon it is called Kyaik-Ha-san, signifying the 'Pagoda of eight monks'. Golden statuettes of these monks were enshrined in the building.

Finally, if you have time, try and pay a visit to the **Htaukkyant War Cemetery**. Situated about 21 miles (or 45 minutes) northeast of Rangoon, it is said to be the resting-place of 33,421 soldiers who perished in World War II.

# BEYOND RANGOON

## Syriam

Syriam or Tanyin was Lower Burma's main trading port in the 18th Century and an old Portuguese Settlement. Today it is a dirty, ugly place which is reached by ferry in about 40 to 50 minutes from Rangoon, but is home to two splendid pagodas: the **Kyaikkauk** and **Kyaikmawwin** (also known as the **Kyauktan Yele-paya**).

Guarded by two massive *chinthes* with black beards (the left *chinthe*'s head is tilted to the right) and under renovation, the Kyaikkauk is located at Payagon. According to tradition, it enshrines one of the two hairs of the Buddha which were given by the sage to 24 Rishis (hermits) on his visit to Syriam at the invitation of Gavampati, the second being enshrined in Rangoon's Kyaik-kasan Pagoda. The pagoda, which is similar in size and design to the Shwedagon, was enlarged by Bhogasena, king of Pada, in 439 BC. It has four pavilions with four seated Buddhas. In front of the pagoda lie the tombs of two celebrated Burmese writers Natshinnaung and Padethayaza.

About two to three minutes drive away is **Natsingone** ('hillocks where there are nat shrines') and a dilapidated stupa called Manawmayazedidaw. Alas, all of the *nats* have disappeared, but their names are written inside the shrines. There is a tomb of the abbot named Sayadaw U Dewataymiza who apparently lived until he was 109 and a marble footprint of the Buddha encircled by two dragons. There is also a monastery called Manawmaya.

Under renovation and reached by boat (K1 there and back) stands the Kyauktan Yele-paya, meaning 'Mid-stream pagoda' which is guarded by two colourful ogres. The water level never reaches the pagoda precinct even if the surrounding area becomes flooded.

To reach Syriam, you have to get to the Thidar jetty. It costs K2 for the taxi to enter the jetty compound, though the ferry trip to Syriam itself costs a mere kyat. The ferry actually crosses the tributary of the Rangoon River known as the Pazuntaungchaung. Be prepared for an unpleasant ride: you have to wait until the ferry is jam-packed before it moves off and if you want a wooden seat you will have to pay 50 pyas (you don't get change for a K1 note, only a hard-boiled sweet from Thailand). The ferry stinks of urine and is full of hawkers selling everything imaginable: quail's eggs, pomelos, bananas, lemons, guavas, coconuts, sugar cane, buns, ice cream, peanuts, newspapers, cigarettes, toys and results of the Burmese lottery.

They even rent out Burmese comics for the trip. Otherwise it's a dull crossing with little of interest, though when you reach Syriam you can take a horse-cart and explore a part of Burma which has probably only seen a handful of tourists in the past decade.

# Twante

The pottery town of Twante lies on the Irrawaddy Delta, en route to Bassein and about a two-hour boat trip down the canal from Rangoon (the Twante Canal, linking Rangoon to the Toe River, used to be the busiest in the country). Twante is 24km from Rangoon. You can watch the potters at work and, if you feel so inclined, purchase some of their handiwork. There are also cotton-weaving industries in the area.

Twante's two most celebrated pagodas are the Kyaikpyaungbye and Shwesandaw. Both are reputed to enshrine two hairs of the Buddha. Those in the Kyaikpyaungbye Pagoda, which is located in *Paya kwin* ('pagoda grounds') neighbourhood, were presented by Mahathera Sumana to Naga-Kumara, king of Ukkalaba. In the construction of this pagoda, the king was assisted by Rishi (hermit) Isi-byaung.

# Pegu

Pegu is located some 80km to the northeast of Rangoon and takes about two hours to reach. If it's included in your MTT tour (as it most probably will be), you'll be taken by bus. If you are on an independent tour, you will be driven there in a private car. It is possible to go on your own accord, by public bus (hot, crowded, uncomfortable but cheap), train (the Rangoon to Mandalay 'express' stops off at Pegu) or by hiring a private taxi. It depends on your budget — and your patience. At present Pegu boasts one hotel for tourists, the Shwe Wa Tun (Tel 21263), which has decent air-conditioned rooms and hot water. Rates (which include breakfast) are US$44.40 for a single room (locals pay K198) and US$64.80 for a double (K246). However, as with the majority of government-run hotels, the service is lousy.

There are two decent restaurants in Pegu: the Burmese Cho Phyone and the Ooktha Biriani Shop, whilst the best coffee shop is the Bandoola Coffee Shop, located within sight of the mighty Shwemawdaw Pagoda.

Pegu was established as the capital of Lower Burma during the reign of Binnya U (1353-85), and was conquered by Tabinshwehti (who founded the Toungoo Dynasty) in 1539. Seven years later, Tabinshwehti pronounced himself king of Burma with Pegu as his capital. In 1599, however, towards the end of the Toungoo Dynasty, an Arakanese fleet laid siege to the city and captured it. During the reign of King Thalun (1629-48), the capital was moved back from Pegu to Ava. During Pegu's golden years, around the time of 1519, it acquired the reputation as a 'rich city and international port'.

Legend, in fact, relates that Pegu's first historical period extended from AD 573 to 1057. According to historical tradition, a king of Thaton had two sons named Thamala and Wimala. They were about to establish a town in the year 573 when they observed a sacred goose (*han-tha*) building its nest on an island nearby. This was an auspicious sign, and therefore they called their town Han-tha-wadi. But people generally referred to it as Pegu (as indeed they do now) because it was located on the Pegu River. Pegu's symbol today are these two mythical *hintha* birds (the spelling and precise meaning of the word vary according to which legend you believe), the smaller female perched on the male's back. The name *hintha* derives from the Pali word *hansa* which means a water bird. A long, busy, bustling town with many beggars, Pegu is wholly dominated by the Shwemawdaw Pagoda.

(Pegu Division, incidentally, includes primarily the area north of Rangoon Division between the Irrawaddy and Sittang Rivers. Its most famous centres are Pegu itself, Prome and Toungoo, all three cities capitals in earlier times).

## SHWEMAWDAW PAGODA

It is impossible to avoid comparisons with the mighty Shwedagon when you first set eyes on the Shwemawdaw Pagoda, 'Great Golden God', for the huge gilded handbell-shaped tower evokes memories of Rangoon's masterpiece. Inside, two hairs of the Buddha lie on a diamond-studded slab of cream-coloured marble, covered with a lid embedded with emeralds, placed inside a gold pagoda, surrounded by Buddha images and buried beneath a mountain of brick. Two earthquakes (in 1912 and 1917) shook the pagoda, before another, even more devastating, brought it tumbling down in May 1930. A brick portion of the toppled spire rests at the base with a small spire balanced on top. Reconstructed in 1952, the Shwemawdaw (whose name derives from the Khmer phrase meaning 'at the tip of the peninsula', a reference to Pegu's former position as a thriving seaport) outgrew even the Shwedagon. And when the diamond-laden golden *hti* was placed on top in 1954, it reached a height of 374 feet. If you climb the *zaungdan* (staircase), you'll encounter what appear to be Buddha images constructed in the mouths of two amazing, vast, salmon-coloured *chinthes*, set out as sentinels at the west (main) side approach. In fact, they are not images of the Buddha but statues of two of his disciples: in the mouth of the left *chinthe* is Shin Oo Pagota (Shinoobagoat), in the right Shin Thi Wali (Shinthiwali). The Shwemawdaw Festival is held annually each April.

## SHWETHALYAUNG

Hidden in the jungle for over a century following the sacking of Pegu in 1757, the Shwethalyaung ('Giant Reclining Buddha') was discovered by chance in 1881 by engineers working on the extension of the railway line to Pegu. An Indian contractor for the supply of bricks and earth began digging the area for stocks when he came across a vast pile of brickwork, of which he decided to avail himself. However, storms of protests arose from fellow-workers conversant with the history of the image and the contractor was obliged to stop his work. The reconstruction of the holy image was started immediately and the once neglected decaying image was restored to its former glory.

Built originally in 994 AD (on the death of King Anuraja) by King Migadhippa (the younger) to commemorate his conversion to Buddhism after years of spirit-worship, this 180 foot long reclining image — the largest in the land — is one of the most beautiful and sacred in Burma. Its dimensions are vast: it is 52½ feet high, its face measures 22½ feet, the palm of the hand 22 feet, the sole of the foot 25½ feet, the little finger 10 feet and the great toe six feet. It is protected by a huge steel *tazaung* (pavilion) erected in 1906.

Foreigners are charged US$2 to visit the Shwemawdaw Pagoda, the Shwethalyaung and the Mahazedi Pagoda. The Mahazedi ('The Great Stupa') was completed in 1560 AD by Hanthawadi Sibyuyin, known as King Bayinnaung to the Burmese and Branginoco to the Portuguese. Its construction was based on that of the Mahacheti stupa of Ceylon. Over the years, the Mahazedi has suffered badly from both earthquakes and vandalism. The placing of the *hti* iron framework crest on top was celebrated in 1982 with festivals of music and dances.

Pegu's two other pagodas of note are the Shwegugyi ('The Great Golden Cave') and **Shwegugale**. The former was built in 1476 AD by

Dhammacheti, king of Pegu after the model of the Bodha Gaya Temple in India; the latter in 1494 AD by Hatthiraja or Byinnya Ran, also king of Pegu. The basement of the Shwegugale's shrine consists of ambulatory corridors containing 64 images of the Buddha, and its superstructure is a cylindrical pagoda.

The Kalyani Thein (Sima, or ordination hall) was first consecrated and built by King Dhammacheti in 1476 AD. The original Sima was a prototype of the famous ordination hall of Ceylon but suffered from various earthquakes and fires subsequently. The present-day Sima was built in 1954 and stands on ground marked by white marble pillars, symbols of a consecrated place. Nearby are 10 stone inscriptions in Pali and Talaing relating the history of the monument as well as an account of the vicissitudes of the Buddhist Church in Burma and of the efforts made by Dhammacheti to reform and purify it.

A few hundred feet off the Rangoon-Pegu Road, almost two miles out of town, stand the **Kyaikpun Pagoda** or Images. Built in 1476 AD by Dhammacheti, king of Pegu, there are four sitting images of the Buddha placed back to back and facing the four cardinal points, recalling the four-faced Brahma of India. Each image measures almost 100 feet in height, though one of the images facing west was destroyed in the 1930 earthquake.

*Novice monk at the doorway of Mandalay's Shwenandaw Monastery.*

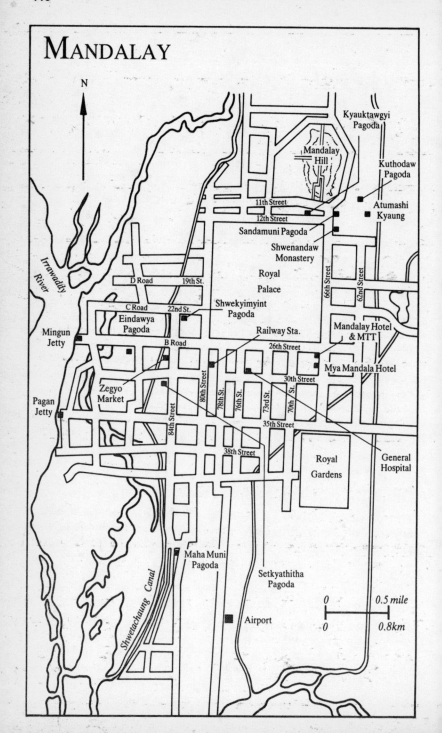

# MANDALAY

N

Kyauktawgyi Pagoda

Mandalay Hill

Kuthodaw Pagoda

11th Street

12th Street

Atumashi Kyaung

Sandamuni Pagoda

Shwenandaw Monastery

Royal Palace

66th Street

62nd Street

Irrawaddy River

D Road          19th St.

C Road     22nd St.

Shwekyimyint Pagoda

Eindawya Pagoda

Mingun Jetty

B Road

Railway Sta.

Mandalay Hotel & MTT

26th Street

Mya Mandala Hotel

Zegyo Market

30th Street

Pagan Jetty

84th Street

80th Street

78th St.

76th St.

73rd St.

70th St.

35th Street

38th Street

Royal Gardens

General Hospital

Maha Muni Pagoda

Setkyathitha Pagoda

Shwetachaung Canal

Airport

| 0 | | 0.5 mile |
| 0 | | 0.8 km |

Chapter Six

# Mandalay and vicinity

'Of all the old capitals of Burma, whose remains, scattered over a
thousand miles from Tagaung to Tenasserim, bear testimony to its
history, Mandalay is the newest. And yet its atmosphere is altogether of
the past. It stands to-day for a dynasty that is no more, for a Court
whose splendour and whose etiquette are already fading into oblivion, for
a sentiment that has all but ceased to exist ... one only wonders how
much longer its crenellated walls and crumbling battlements will survive;
how much longer its gilded pillars and tapering spires will speak to the
eye of things that can never live again.'

V. C. Scott O'Connor, 1907.

## GETTING THERE AND AROUND

If you're not travelling by Myanma Airways, the standard way to
reach Mandalay is by train; but be warned, it's an arduous journey.
The ordeal starts at Rangoon railway station, a disorganised,
overcrowded mess, where you have to fight your way onto the train.
Once on board, you have to locate your seat, which hopefully has
been reserved for you in upper class. The alternative, the so-called
ordinary class, is the ultimate travelling nightmare (a mere K40 or
K63, depending on whom you consult). Thankfully, however, very
few tourists end up being crammed into one of these wooden rabbit
hutches. Most travel first or upper class ('sitting' as opposed to
'sleeping') which costs K171 one way (Burmese pay K155: this

'double-pricing' is prevalent throughout the country, as it is indeed all over Southeast Asia). If you book via MTT, you will have to pay between US$30-38! The trains do actually have sleepers (costing K195 one way, K390 return), but they're seldom allocated to tourists, being primarily reserved for members of the SLORC, various (often non-existent) government officials, diplomats and VIPs. Fares, fortunately, are included in the price of all package tours: trying to purchase a ticket as an independent traveller can be an extraordinarily laborious and bureaucratic procedure.

Upper class is reasonably comfortable, with reclining seats, arm-rests and fans. The train, alas, totters along so lethargically, stopping repeatedly ('Sorry, signal not come'), that the journey can hardly be described as enjoyable. And to add insult to injury, sleep is well nigh impossible as hawkers and vendors of every ethnic race and age, bearing all manner of provisions, march up and down the carriage from the very moment you board the train at Rangoon, until you disembark, shattered, at Mandalay railway station some 14 (hopefully) hours later. Up and down they stomp proffering chickens, eggs, durians, mangosteens, rambutans, bananas, fish, ready-made meals (which they niftily prepare at the end of the corridor), drinks, cigarettes: indeed everything you could possibly need (and much you couldn't) for such an ordeal. As Bernard Fergusson observed so sharp-wittedly in his wonderful book *Return to Burma*: 'As a murderer of sleep Macbeth had nothing on the Burma Railways'. If you are really out of luck, members of the *Tatmadaw* will keep you up all night, growing ever more intoxicated and turning the toilet, by the time morning eventually staggers around, into a flooding stream of urine.

HRH Prince Damrong Rajanubhab, clearly in full agreement with Brigadier Fergusson, remarked back in 1936:

'The railways in Burma have one really bad feature. The railway bed is not smooth, and therefore the carriages jerk badly when in motion. At bedtime, we were shaken so much that it was difficult to drop off to sleep, even though we had a saloon car of the bogie type with paired wheels. The princesses found it so uncomfortable that they begged not to go by Burmese train at night again, unless it was really necessary. I heard complaints from some residents that the Burmese railways are worse than those in any other country.'

In fact, HRH Prince Ramrong's journey back in the 30s took 16½ hours; today it takes 14 hours. Thus in 57 years, 'Burma Rail' have managed to improve their service by 2½ hours.

At least Burmese trains tend to be more punctual than Myanma Airways' Fokkers, though timetables differ depending on whom you consult. At the last count, the following trains were scheduled to run from Rangoon to Mandalay:

Rangoon dep. 6am Mandalay arr. 9.30pm (11 up; that's the name of the train)
Rangoon dep. 5pm Mandalay arr. 7am (5 up)
Rangoon dep. 7.30pm Mandalay arr. 10.30 am (3 up)
Rangoon dep. 9pm Mandalay arr. 11.30 am (7 up)
However, it is also possible that there is a train which leaves Rangoon at 7.30 am and arrives in Mandalay 14 hours later and one which departs at 6.30pm, arriving at 8.30am. Return trains 'might' depart at the following times:

Mandalay dep. 9.30pm Rangoon arr. 6am (12 down)
Mandalay dep. 5.20am Rangoon arr. 3.15pm (6 down)
Mandalay dep. 10am Rangoon arr. 6.30pm (4 down)
Mandalay dep. 12.50pm Rangoon arr. 8.30pm (8 down)
It is just conceivable that a train leaves Mandalay at 3pm and arrives in Rangoon at 5am, that another leaves at 5.30pm, arriving at 7.30am, yet another at 8.30pm, getting into Rangoon at 10.30pm and, finally, one that departs from Mandalay at 5am and chugs wearily into Rangoon railway station at 7pm. As you will have gathered, times *are* rather flexible, or to be precise, 'Burmese'.

Having left Rangoon at 5pm the previous afternoon, you *should* arrive in Mandalay some time around 7am the following morning. Exhausted, you reel off the train to be whisked away by your guide to the hotel. 'Come you back, you British soldier; come you back to Mandalay!'.

Individual travellers have the choice of going by private car, normally spending the night at Meiktila en route. This journey, alas, is no less tiresome than that by train. The roads are bad and it can take anything up to 15 hours to reach Meiktila. Leaving Rangoon, you pass through Pyu, where roughly half of the population is Indian. Here you can lunch at the strangely named Academy Restaurant (Chinese), which has a wholly unacademic menu and an even less academic loo. Then it's on to Toungoo (see Chapter Ten), where it would be sensible (and is now possible) to stop overnight, and Pyinmana. Pyinmana is quite a quaint town, famous for its three Universities: the Institutes of Agriculture, Forestry and Veterinary Science, and for having Asia's only seed bank. It is also noted for its teak production and the celebrated Yezin Dam. Finally, some 14 or 15 hours later, you reach Meiktila (also see Chapter Ten). From Meiktila, it is another three hours to Mandalay.

According to the most recent World Official Airline Timetable (not that this publication has any bearing on events at Mingaladon Airport), there are nine weekly flights from Rangoon to Mandalay. On Mondays, flight UB 775 departs at 0730, arriving at 1055 and UB 783 departs at 1400, arriving at 1500. On Tuesdays, UB 761 leaves Rangoon at 0600, arriving at Mandalay at 0740. On Wednesdays, UB 783 departs at 1400 and arrives at 1500; on Thursdays UB 623 departs at 0700, arriving at 0840; on Fridays UB 789 departs at 0700, arriving at 0915 and UB 775 departs at 0730, arriving at 1055. On Saturdays, UB 625 leaves Rangoon at 0700, getting into Mandalay at 0840 and on Sundays UB 761 departs at 0600, arriving at 0740. For this privilege, MTT will charge you US$82 if you fly from Rangoon, and US$33 if you fly from either Pagan or Heho. The sooner either Thai Airways International or Bangkok Airways introduces flights from Bangkok or Mae Hong Son to Mandalay, the better.

NB: You will gather from the above schedules, that timings differ from those mentioned in Chapter Four. This, I'm afraid, is inevitable in Burma.

Transportation in Mandalay is as diverse as in Rangoon: your best bet, however, is to befriend a trishaw driver and secure his services for the duration of your stay (most wait outside the hotels, in any case, since the SLORC doesn't permit them to enter the hotel grounds). They all speak English (some can even manage French, German and Italian) and are absolutely charming. But don't forget to haggle over the fare: again, any currency or gift will do.

Alternatives to the trishaw include horse-carts (always fun, except for the poor horse), buses (not recommended as they're always packed), jeeps, pick-ups or, if you're really energetic and don't mind the occasional crash or flat tyre, bicycles. Finally — and most importantly — *don't* walk: Mandalay is a vast, sprawling, hot and dusty city. It makes Bangkok seem like a pleasure park.

# HISTORY AND GENERAL DESCRIPTION

'Come you back to Mandalay, where the old Flotilla lay ... Elephants a-pilin' teak ... On the road to Mandalay'.

*Mandalay*, Rudyard Kipling.

'I wrote a song called 'Mandalay' which, tacked, to a tune with a swing, made one of the waltzes of that distant age. A private soldier reviews his love and, in the chorus, his experiences in the Burma campaign. One of his ladies lives at Moulmein, which is not on the road to anywhere, and he describes the amour with some minuteness, but always in his chorus deals with 'the road to Mandalay', his golden path to romance. The inhabitants of the United States, to whom I owed most of the bother, 'Panamaed' that song (this was before copyright), set it to their own tunes, and sang it in their own national voices. Not content with this, they took to pleasure cruising, and discovered that Moulmein did not command any view of any sun rising across the Bay of Bengal. They must have interfered, too, with the navigation of the Irrawaddy Flotilla steamers, for one of the Captains SOS-ed me to give him 'something to tell these somethinged tourists about it'. I forget what word I sent, but I hoped it might help.'

*Something of Myself*, Rudyard Kipling.

So, alas, Kipling never made it to Mandalay; as his biographer Charles Carrington relates: 'Of Burma Kipling knew nothing at first-hand, until he called in a sea-going liner at Rangoon and Moulmein for a few days in 1889. Accordingly, we find his Burmese pieces somewhat remote and romantic.'

The German playwright Bertolt Brecht also never ventured as far as Mandalay, but that never prevented *him* too from passing judgement on this romantic of all cities. Mandalay, it seems, has exerted a mysterious influence on a number of authors.

Alas, there was no enduring romance in Mandalay for Brecht nor, for that matter, for George Orwell in his novel *Burmese Days*. Both writers were a good deal less enthusiastic than Kipling. In his musical *Happy End*, Brecht wrote: 'Mandalay the moon doesn't always stand over you', posing the question 'Is there only one girl in Mandalay?', and finally concluding 'There's nobody left in Mandalay'. Orwell was even more scathing: 'Mandalay is rather a disagreeable town — it is dusty and intolerably hot, and it is said to have five main products all beginning with P, namely, pagodas, pariahs, pigs, priests and prostitutes ...'.

In some ways, all three authors were right, for Mandalay is a city

of many characters. Its evocative, romantic past conjures up all
manner of images: it is the most beautiful city, the cultural heartland
of Burma. But it is also a repressed, forlorn city, whose spirit has
been stifled by a succession of battles, kings and governments. It is
a city that understandably clings on to its past, indeed, to a large
extent, still lives in the past and accepts most grudgingly that it is
today no longer the first city of Burma. Legend has it that when King
Thibaw was forced to surrender to General Prendergast and put on
a ship to be exiled to India, old Mandalay wept and died. Trite as
that may sound, it's actually not far from the truth. Mandalay, like
most of this extraordinary land, is stuck somewhere between the
19th and 20th Centuries; a wonderful timelessness, almost
decrepitude, pervades the city.

However, as Kipling might have said, 'times they are a changin' on
the road to Mandalay'. For Mandalay, it seems, has become
'Southeast Asia's unlikeliest boom town'.

According to a report in the *Bangkok Post*:

'Most of the money is in the hands of local Chinese, residents say. They
add that a lot of it is said to be generated by the heroin trade of the
Golden Triangle in the border area to the east.

People here say there are three lines of business here — the green
line, the red line and the white line. That's jade, rubies and heroin.

This is a trade centre. Some people are getting very rich.'

The report attributes the so-called 'boom' to: 'blossoming relations
with China', adding that 'many Burmese made money by driving
second-hand Japanese cars to the border and selling' — without
any duty or taxes, of course and concludes that 'heroin warlords are
putting their money into Mandalay real estate' and that 'Wa
insurgents ... signed an accord with the government in 1990. This
allows them to still carry weapons and grants them special privileges
in their business dealings ...'

There is no doubt that land prices have rocketed in Mandalay and
that some individuals (almost exclusively the Chinese) are making a
fortune in the process — as the striking advertisement in the
*Working People's Daily* bears witness:

WELCOME TO MANDALAY
TAIN PYU HOTEL
(Silver Cloud Hotel)

AND
RESTAURANT
Mastercard, Visa card and
American express card
are accepted at our hotel.

This new hotel, easily the best in town, was constructed in 1991 by
U Kyaw Than, a local Chinese businessman.

An article in the *Financial Times* of January 28 1993 entitled 'Trade
with China puts Mandalay on the road to riches' and sub-headed
'The free-wheeling economic policy of Burma's junta has spawned
a generation of black marketeers' confirms this recent Chinese
takeover. Indeed, it would appear that the SLORC has gone so far
as issuing Chinese citizens with fake Burmese ID cards.

'BURMA is supposed to be poor and oppressed, but you would have
trouble believing it at the Dynasty. Recently opened on the roof of a
concrete office block, Rangoon's most fashionable restaurant and night-
club is seething with noisy revellers and new money ...

Mandalay, 350 miles to the north, looks even richer. Imported
Japanese cars cruise the streets; shops are full of colour televisions, hi-fi
systems, fake Ray-Ban sunglasses from Thailand, fancy watches and
torch-clock-radios; the market stalls are groaning with toys and textiles
from India and China.

Neighbouring China is the key to Burma's new veneer of affluence.

For the past four years the generals in the Burmese military junta
known as the State Law and Order Restoration Council (Slorc) have
gradually freed the economy from government control, tolerating the
black market, liberalising trade with China and giving free rein to the
ethnic Chinese entrepreneurs who dominate business in Burma as in the
rest of south-east Asia. The Slorc has also struck deals with the warlike
tribes on the frontier.

The chief architect of Mandalay's free-wheeling economic policy is
General Tun Kyi, who until recently was the region's all-powerful military
commander ... 'Tun Kyi is the godfather of Mandalay,' says one Burmese
businessman. 'If the city needs an electric generator he has it imported
from China and then calls in the merchants and tells them to pay their
share.' In return, of course, the government turns a blind eye to the more
dubious business practices of the merchants ...

The free trade boom has spawned a generation of flashy black
marketeers; they smoke imported 555 cigarettes and drink Changlee beer
brewed in the Chinese border province of Yunnan or Heineken shipped
from Singapore; they boast of their ability to buy police chiefs and
immigration officers.

One such free trader explained how he exported gems and jade to China in exchange for Chinese cassette players masquerading as Japanese brand-name products. Mandalay, he declared with not a little hyperbole, 'will be like Hong Kong in three years'.

At first glance it looks as though everyone is profiting from the boom ... But prosperity and the fragile peace on the border have come at a price. Guerillas of the Wa and Kokang hill tribes, who are closely related to the Yunnanese over the Chinese border, have stopped fighting the Rangoon government, but only on the understanding that they are allowed to carry weapons and trade in opium from their strongholds in the Golden Triangle.

China is worried about the spread of heroin addiction on its territory, while the inhabitants of central Burma are appalled by the boorish way in which some of the Wa and the Kokang flaunt their money in restaurants and nightclubs, and resentful of the increasing influence of China and the prosperous ethnic Chinese business community.

Since a great fire in Mandalay a decade ago, the ethnic Chinese are said to have bought up the entire town centre with the exception of one small hotel and one shop, and traders say Chinese nationals are buying Burmese identity cards at the border.

The Slorc, mindful of the Burmese nationalism to which it constantly pays lip service, has recently sought to moderate the spread of Chinese influence and to exert more control over the border trade. Gen Tun Kyi has been recalled to Rangoon, ostensibly to become trade minister, but actually, diplomats believe, because his military colleagues feared he was becoming too powerful in his Mandalay fiefdom.

Gen Tun Kyi and his Chinese friends, however, seem to be holding their own. Although he has been theoretically replaced as military commander of the central region, he is still occasionally referred to as the commander by the official press. And in the karaoke bars of Rangoon, they are singing songs in Chinese.'

Mandalay's economic prosperity (or, if you prefer, 'black market' or 'informal trade') somewhat contradicts the words of Myo Nyunt, current Chairman of the Steering Committee to form the National Convention: 'Capitalists are once again rearing their heads. If they cannot be controlled, the capitalists must be wiped out first.' September 17 1991.

The 'real world' of Mandalay and all that surrounds it dates from the middle of the 19th Century, yet it is the most Burmese of all cities and home of the most traditional Burmese music and dance. They say, too, that Mandalay is where they speak the most eloquent Burmese. It is also the religious core of Burma, with its monasteries, *phongyis* (Buddhist monks) and pagodas.

*Ananda Temple/Pagoda, Pagan.*

*The countless pagodas in Pagan cover an area of 100 square miles. In the 13th Century this must have been one of the most astonishing capital cities in the world.*

*Bassein, the heart of the Irrawaddy Delta. Transportation on the Ngawun River.*

Bassein. (Left) celebrations for the founding of the Shwekyimyint Pagoda;
(right) the author has the great honour of laying the foundation stone.

Burmese-style 'tuk-tuk' in Pegu.

*The Burmese people ...*

*... and a recommendation from the military*

မြေပေါ်မြေအောက်အဖျက်သမားသတိထား:

BEWARE OF ABOVEGROUND AND UNDERGROUND DESTRUCTIVE ELEMENTS

Mandalay is the city of King Mindon. There may be little left of the palace: some broken walls, some tombs, the moat, but round the 954-feet high Mandalay Hill his spirit lingers on, for it was he who sponsored the myriad of monasteries and pagodas that are the hallmark of Mandalay.

The city covers an area of 25 square miles, practically one-third of which was razed during World War II due to the principal offensive against the Japanese being centred in and around Mandalay Hill. With the loss of its palace and its magnificent woodcarvings, a large part of Mandalay died. Worse was to follow: in 1981 a devastating fire destroyed much of the northwest of the town and left 35,000 people homeless.

The city itself forms a near-perfect geometrical pattern, the roads cutting at right angles. The long, broad streets running east-west are alphabetically named (A, B, C, D, etc) and the cross-streets running north-south numerically, in the American style. Traffic can be chaotic (there never seems to be any order) and at times quite terrifying. Break-downs are frequent, horns toot continuously, but everyone keeps smiling. Enjoy it.

Mandalay Division covers an area of 14,294 square miles and is made up of 29 townships with a total population of 4½ million.


# PLACES TO STAY AND EAT

At present there are two principal choices for most tourists: either the large, colonial-style Mandalay Hotel (Tel 22499) or the Mya Mandala (Tel 21283). The Mandalay has improved in the last couple of years: it has decent air-conditioned rooms (rates vary from US$20-55) and the bathrooms have been considerably upgraded. However, because it is government-run and used to dealing with large groups of grumbling travellers, the service is surly and the restaurant dire. Just round the corner lies the smaller and friendlier Mya Mandala (which even boasts a swimming pool). Room rates are US$36 for a single room, US$48 for a double, which may be 'negotiable' for the independent traveller.

Mandalay does have other more recent hotels, such as the brand new Chinese-built Silver Cloud Hotel (as mentioned above) on 73rd Street. Room rates are K200-600 for locals, but US$30-75 for tourists. The telephone numbers are 27059 and 25228. The smartest hotel in town, it is popular with the military, businessmen and visiting VIPs. There is also the Innwa Hotel (Tel 27028/27029) on Eastern Moat

Road (two blocks to the north of the Mandalay Hotel) which some guide books and Burmese travel agents recommend: steer clear of this place, it has a dodgy reputation and a bad security record. Rates, incidentally, vary from US$25-45. Mandalay also has the Manmyo Hotel by the Central Railway Station (Tel 26889, US$15-20), the Kaung Myint Lodging House (Tel 22790/24615/22447) on 80th Street, between 30th and 31st Streets (US$25-40), the Hotel Venus (Tel 25612) on 28th Street, between 80th and 81st Streets (US$30-40), the Golden Express Hotel on 9th Street (US$30-60), the Tiger Hotel (Tel 23134, US$30-50) on 82nd Street, between 36th and 37th Streets and the Sabai Byu (Tel 25377/22122, US$15-35) on 81st Street, between 25th and 26th Streets. As in Rangoon, new hotels and guest houses are springing up all over town, but only time will tell which ones survive and which can be recommended.

  Mandalay has a fair collection of restaurants: the top two Chinese eateries are the Honey Garden Restaurant at the corner of 70th and 29th Streets (Tel 24098), which has no prices on the menu and is consequently very expensive, and the Shwenandaw. The latter is located at No 110, between 28/29-73 Streets (Tel 24588) or so it says on the visiting card (it's actually on 73rd Street, at the corner of 29th Street) but then, on the visiting card, it also calls itself 'Shwe Nung Daw'. Mistranslations like this are commonplace not only in Burma, but all over Southeast Asia. Take a look at the Shwenandaw's menu, for example:

Stean Pork with Kyunchys
Fried Hat Mince-Pork
Special Pig Feet
Guyland with meat
Fried chicken gablet
Mid vegetable
With and Red Soup

I never sampled the 'Hat' nor the 'gablet', but the sweet and sour pork wasn't bad.

  There is also the Pyigyimon Restaurant (Chinese) on the moat opposite the Mandalay Hotel, but, owing to its splendid location, is extremely expensive. The Pyigyimon is in fact the Royal Barge which was constructed during the reign of King Bodawpaya, the founder of Amarapura and it was used to transport the celebrated Mahamuni image, which had been brought over from Dhanyawady in Arakan State, from Amarapura to its present site along the Nadi stream. The

Royal Barge has been reconstructed at a cost of over K7,300,000 and, apart from serving as a restaurant, affords a superb view of Mandalay Hill.

A cheaper Chinese restaurant is Min Min, No 194, 83rd Street, between 26th and 27th Streets, though I would be loath to recommend either the 'Pecking Roast Duck' or the 'Chicken State'.

The best Burmese restaurant is Too Too on the south side of 27th Street between 74th and 75th Streets; not far from there is the Naganee Tea and Coffee Shop which serves, not surprisingly, tea and coffee and Burmese-style pancakes. Another excellent Burmese restaurant is the Shwe Ayin Nan, No 90, 30th Street, between 73rd and 74th Streets. For the cheapest and coldest Pepsi in town, try the Pinya Cold Drink on 74th Street (between 27th and 28th Streets), but don't bother paying a visit to the inappropriately-named Lucky Cold Drinks on 35th Street: it only serves lukewarm beverages. For breakfast, there's Savoury Burger, No 121, 37th Street, between 77th and 78th Streets.

# ENTERTAINMENT/SHOPPING

Like Rangoon, Mandalay now has a night-life. On the moat by the Palace is the Manmyo Thayar Recreation Centre where locals belt out songs in Burmese, Thai and even English. It's open from 7.30pm to 10.30pm and entrance costs a mere K2, though if you want a table in the restaurant section, you'll have to pay an extra K20. Practically everyone in Mandalay seems to hang out here, particularly now that the curfew has been lifted. There is also the State School of Music and Drama on East Moat Road but no one seems to have much information about it: ask your guide if you're interested. Otherwise for entertainment simply trundle around town in a trishaw, take a stroll by the banks of the Irrawaddy (where you can watch exhausted water buffaloes hauling huge teak logs up the riverbanks) or sip a few Mandalay Beers (if stocks haven't run out) by the swimming pool at the Mya Mandala Hotel, where, if you're lucky, 'There's a Burma girl a-settin.'

Zegyo Market dominates the shopping in Mandalay. Situated in the town centre and overlooked by the Diamond Jubilee Clock (dating from Queen Victoria's reign), this vast bazaar was designed in 1903 by an Italian called Count Caldrari, first secretary of the Mandalay municipality. The original market has been pulled down and a new one is presently being built at a cost estimated to be no less than

K124,000,000.

Zegyo Market offers an extraordinary range of goods, many smuggled in from Thailand, China and India. Local delicacies include what appear to be stir-fried cicadas and a host of weird-looking and even fouler-smelling fish. Definitely not for the faint-hearted. A word of warning: don't run out of shaving-foam in Mandalay, you'll be hard pressed to find any in the market. It's lucky most Burmese men don't need to shave.

Mandalay's night market, situated on 84th Street, between 26th and 28th Streets, offers little of especial interest: the ubiquitous *longyi*, toiletries, cosmetics and various bits and bobs. However, it's a great place to meet locals and is open from 6pm to 10pm.

Ivory, gems, woodcarvings, tapestries, silk and lacquerware are readily available in town. Try to avoid the touts (and, on this occasion, your trishaw driver who'll be after his commission) and search out the shops by yourself. Mandalay also boasts an interesting array of stone (marble and alabaster) and wooden Buddha image and ivory carvers, gold leaf makers and beaters and silk weavers. Visits to these establishments will probably be included on MTT's agenda: if you're in Mandalay independently, ask any trishaw driver.

# MANDALAY HILL AND ENVIRONS

Mandalay Hill, with its 1,729 steps and under whose shadow the city lies sprawling, gives Mandalay added distinction. When you eventually reach its 954-feet peak, past the drinks, cheroot and betel vendors and U S Sayatin the fortune teller (whose predictions are remarkably accurate), you have a superb panoramic view all round: the crenellated walls of the old palace with its wooden spire on one side, and the long line of the distant Shan Hills on the other. It is truly a magnificent sight. And all the while, the huge, golden **Shweyattaw Buddha** stands guard, his right hand pointing to the city way below. At the foot of one of its two southern staircases, there are *chinthes* with permanent curls in their manes. Tin roofs cover the steps all the way up the hill, but it's still an arduous climb. You can always jump on to a pick-up truck if you don't fancy the walk.

Mandalay Hill has three covered approaches; on the southeastern slope are the **Peshawar Relics** (sacred relics of the Buddha), while near the southern approach stands the **Kyauktawgyi Pagoda** built by King Mindon in 1878, having taken 25 years to complete. The Buddha image here was carved out of a huge single slab of marble brought from the nearby mines of Sagyin. Legend has it that the marble block was so big that 10,000 men had to be employed for 13 days to transport it from a canal to the site of the pagoda. Round the shrine are figures of 80 disciples of the Buddha, 20 on each side. To the east is the **Sandamuni Pagoda**, constructed on the grounds on which the temporary palace of King Mindon stood while the new palace was being built. This pagoda is also known to have been raised over the graves of the crown prince and some members of the royal family, who lost their lives in the palace rebellion of 1866 when there was an attempt to assassinate King Mindon. It enshrines an iron image of the Buddha cast in 1802 by King Bodawpaya and brought from Amarapura 72 years later and marble slabs inscribed with commentaries on the *Tripitaka* (the 'three baskets' of notes from Buddha's teaching).

Northeast of the Sandamuni Pagoda lies the **Kuthodaw** ('Royal Bounty') **Pagoda**, also known as the Maha Lawka Marazein Pagoda. Modelled on the Shwezigon at Nyaung-U (Pagan), it was built by King Mindon in 1857. In the eyes of Burmese Buddhists, the Kuthodaw holds pride of place in Mandalay, for there are over 729 monoliths of white marble on which the *Tripitaka* have been inscribed. Often referred to as the 'world's largest book', the inscriptions were made during the Fifth Buddhist Synod convened at Mandalay in 1871-2. It is said it took 2,400 monks six months to recite the entire text. Each slab has a small temple erected over it, making the Kuthodaw a vast and venerable pagoda.

South of the Kuthodaw lie the imposing ruins of the **Atumashi Kyaung** ('The Incomparable Monastery') which dates from the same period (1857) and was built by King Mindon Min at a cost of 500,000 (five lakhs) rupees. The building was of wood covered with stucco on the outside, and its peculiar feature was the fact that it was surmounted by five graduated rectangular terraces instead of the customary *pyatthats* (wooden spires). In it was enshrined a huge image of the Buddha having dimensions mentioned in the Buddhist scriptures. It was made of the silken clothes of the king covered with lacquer, and its forehead was adorned with a huge diamond, which was presented to King Bodawpaya by Mahanawrata, governor of Arakan. In the building four sets of the *Tripitaka* were deposited in large teak boxes. During the troubles following the British annexation of Upper Burma, the valuable diamond disappeared, and the whole building, together with its contents, burnt down in 1890. The monastery was also renowned for the many ecclesiastical conventions which took place within its walls. All that remains of this great monument, which drew rapturous accounts from travellers who saw it in its former glory, are the brick-work platforms and the carved compound gates. As one anonymous English traveller wrote in 1885:

'In Mandalay, King Mindon erected a monastery — the like of which there is not, the great Incomparable — which possesses a beautiful hall, unquestionably the finest in all Mandalay. It would be no great stretch of truth to say that it is the finest in the world. The building is composed of a series of bold terraces, seven in number, rising one above another, the central one being the highest. The golden hall is carried on thirty-six pillars, some of which are seventy feet high, the ceiling reaching its greatest elevation in the high central terrace. And there a colossal figure of Gautama sits, meditating beside a golden throne intended for the King. The boldness of the general design, the noble proportions of the immense hall, and the great height of the golden roof soaring over the throne and the statue, fill the mind with surprise and pleasure. Pillars, walls, and roof are richly gilt, glass inlaying heightening the brilliancy. When the Viceroy comes to Mandalay to promulgate the decree which announces the future organisation of Burma, the ceremonial will probably be held in this noblest of throne rooms.'

By the side of the 'Incomparable Monastery' stands the only vestige of the magnificently carved and gilded timber buildings that were around before the palace was destroyed. This is the superb **Shwenandaw Monastery** (known to the Burmese as the 'Shwe-kyaung-gyi') which contains a replica of the royal throne. It is said that Thibaw would come here to meditate; indeed the couch he used to sit on can still be seen. Inside were once some masterly examples of glass-mosaic craftsmanship, though most have been lost through the passing of time. The Shwenandaw Kyaung was originally an apartment of the Royal Palace; it was also the place where King Mindon passed away. His successor King Thibaw, believing the building to be haunted by Mindon's ghost, ordered it to be disassembled and moved to its present location in 1880. The Shwenandaw Monastery, which was built at a cost of about one lakh and 20,000 rupees, is a wonderful archetype of mid-19th Century Burmese woodcarving with an array of stunning *nagas* (serpentine dragons); it is also a supremely relaxing place to wander around and to watch the novice monks peering curiously and timidly through the exquisitely-carved wooden portals. Tourists are sometimes charged an entrance fee of US$3.

## OTHER ATTRACTIONS

Mandalay's original **Royal Palace** (known in its heyday as 'The Golden City' or 'The Centre of the Universe') is no more, but parts of it have been reconstructed. Built in 1857 by King Mindon, it formed a perfect square: 2 km square to be precise. The walls were 27 feet high and 10 feet thick with gates and wooden spires (*pyatthats*) and with a 225 feet wide and 11 feet deep moat all around. Each side had three gates and the Palace itself was divided into 144 square plots: 16 square plots for the Palace, the rest for the royal staff. In these 16 square plots there were over 131 buildings: the eastern ones for the kings, the western ones for the queens. On the left side stood the clock tower and on the right side the tooth relics tower. In 1885, under the reign of King Thibaw, Mandalay was occupied by the British and the Royal Palace, having become a British military area, was renamed Fort Dufferin. The Palace remained under British rule until 1945 when the Japanese invaded and seized control. The British, however, bombed the Palace and a series of fires razed it to the ground. Only the city walls, the moat, the towers and the mausoleum survived. The most vivid description of the Palace appears in V. C. Scott O'Connor's marvellous book *Mandalay and other cities of the past in Burma*.

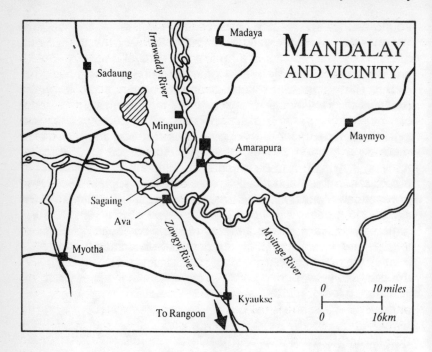

In recent years the SLORC have embarked on the huge task of recreating this once-wonderful Palace. About seven buildings have been reconstructed including the great audience hall and the watch tower. The latter, known as the Nan-Myint Watch Tower, measures 108 feet from the base to the top, and was finished in July 1990 at a cost of just over K2 million. Reconstruction work on the Lay Thein Gate (the entrance to the northern wall of the Palace) took almost eight months to complete and cost K800,000, while the U Htake Gate of the eastern wall has also been renovated. The SLORC are determined to carry out the reconstruction work despite the vast expense. As they explain:

'Lack of maintenance after the annexation of Myanmar Naing-Ngan (*Burma*) by the English colonialists and their bombing during the Second World War destroyed not only the Palace and its walls and 'pyatthads' but also the handicraft of the Myanmar civilization fine arts that had been inherited. Thus, the Golden Palace, the walls and 'pyatthads' have been renovated and rebuilt so as to boost nationalism and patriotism in the Myanmar people who see these with their own eyes.'

Foreigners are charged an entrance fee of US$8.

Within the enclosure of the Royal Palace lies the mausoleum erected over the remains of King Mindon, who died in 1878. Before he died, he left instructions that his body should be buried and not cremated, thus violating the time-honoured custom of burning the dead bodies of members of the royal family. Close-by lies the tomb of Sinbyumayin, the only daughter of the notorious Nanmadaw Me Nu, chief queen of King Bagyidaw, who was Mindon's second queen and mother-in-law of Thibaw. She died in Rangoon in 1900 and her body was permitted to be buried near Mindon's tomb. The chief queen of Mindon, Nanmadawgyi, who died in 1876, was also buried in the Palace stockade, the third tomb to be erected within the sacred precincts of the Royal Palace.

Right in the heart of Mandalay stands the **Shwekyimyint** ('Golden Bird Sighted') **Pagoda**, built by King Minshinzaw, exiled son of King Alaungsithu (1114-1167) of Pagan, who had come to the shores of the Aungbinle Lake to cultivate rice, and to make a heap of his produce as high as the Mandalay Hill. This shrine has two especial attractions: the image is the original one consecrated by the builder himself and has now become the repository of many images of the Buddha salvaged from the Palace at the time of the British occupation in 1885: images made of gold and silver, adorned with invaluable precious stones, representing the collections of successive monarchs. There is also a small golden palanquin (a covered litter for one person, usually carried by four or six men) and outside, on a verandah, a wooden palanquin used by a lesser queen. There are numerous Buddha images in the quadrangle of the pagoda. (For a more detailed description of the history of this pagoda, see Khin Myo Chit's atmospheric book, entitled *A Wonderland of Burmese Legends*).

On 85th Street, just south of Zegyo Market, stands the **Setkyathiha Pagoda**, where the Buddha image was cast at the command of King Bagyidaw at Ava in 1823 (just before the outbreak of the Anglo-Burmese War in 1824) and subsequently shifted to Amarapura in 1849. 35 years later it was brought to Mandalay when the third war broke out and the Burmese monarchy became extinct. Measuring 16ft 8ins, this huge bronze image is artistically crafted. The temple, which is on an elevated masonry platform, was badly damaged during the war but has since been renovated. In the courtyard of the pagoda there are numerous images of the reclining Buddha and also the sacred *Bo* tree (Banyan-tree, under which the Buddha reached Enlightenment) planted by former Prime Minister U Nu in an enclosure to the right of the entrance.

A little to the northwest of the Setkyathiha Pagoda lies the **Eindawya Pagoda**, built by Pagan Min in 1847 on the site of the palace in which he resided before he ascended the throne. Heavily gilded, this beautifully proportioned shrine houses a chalcedony (a type of quartz mineral mixed with opal) Buddha image said to have been brought from Bodh Gaya in India in 1839.

To the south of the city is the much-venerated pagoda which is variously called the **Maha Muni** ('Exalted Saint'), the **Payagyi** ('Great Pagoda') and the **Arakan Pagoda**. The 12½ foot high seated image, which is heavily gilded with gold leaf (and consequently badly misshapen), dates back to ancient times and was brought over by the son and heir of King Bodawpaya in 1784 from Myohaung in Arakan State. Legend has it that the Burmese had tried three times previously (but unsuccessfully) to steal it from the Arakanese. Bodawpaya, whose capital at that time was Amarapura, also built a road paved with brick from the capital to the eastern gate of the pagoda. Remains of this paved King's Highway can still be seen. The original temple was destroyed by fire in 1884 and the present pagoda, with its terraced roof of gilded stucco, is of more recent construction. In the courtyard is a small building housing six bronze figures, Khmer statues brought back from Arakan State at the same time as the Maha Muni image (there were originally 30 figures, but the remaining 24 were melted down by King Thibaw and cast into cannons for his struggle against the British). These figures have had a chequered past: they had been appropriated by the Siamese from Angkor Wat to Ayutthaya in 1431, and then by the Burmese to Pegu. From there the Arakanese King Razagyi had them removed to his own state, only for them to end up eventually in Mandalay. The courtyard also contains a five-ton traditional Burmese gong and various inscription stones accumulated by King Bodawpaya. The SLORC have spent a fortune renovating the pagoda, the museum of Buddha's holy autobiography, the garden, turtle pond, fish pond, clock tower, shops and roads. Individual tourists are required to pay an entrance fee of US$4. (The full history of this pagoda also appears in *A Wonderland of Burmese Legends*).

# AMARAPURA

## Getting There

Lying 11km south of Mandalay, the ancient capital of Amarapura is almost certain to be included in your schedule. In the unlikely event of it not, you can always go by bus. Bus 8 passes through Amarapura on its way to Ava; it departs from the corner of 84th and 27th Streets. Another alternative is the bus which goes to Sagaing from between 84th and 85th Streets; you could also go by 'tuk-tuk' or even horse-cart.

## History, What To See

Amarapura ('The City of Immortals') was described in its heyday as 'a microcosm of Burmese civilisation with a concentration, not only of the wealth, fashion and beauty, but also learning and scholarship'. As a capital it was founded by King Bodawpaya in 1783, the year after he came to the throne, and it superseded Ava. However, Bodawpaya died in 1819 and his grandson Bagyidaw shifted the capital back again to Ava in 1823. That was not the end of Amarapura though, for in 1841, during the reign of Tharrawaddy (the brother of Bagyidaw), it became the capital once more. 16 years later, with King Mindon in power, Amarapura was finally displaced by Mandalay.

Unlike its successor, Amarapura has little to show for its past glories. All that remains of Bodawpaya's palace are just two buildings, the Royal Palace Tower (Pangon) and the Royal Treasury Building (Shwedaik). The city walls have been demolished. There are also the tombs of King Bodawpaya and his grandson King Bagyidaw. Bodawpaya's body was burnt on the site of the so-called tomb, and the ashes were placed in a velvet bag and thrown into the Irrawaddy. Likewise, Bagyidaw's body was cremated on the site of his 'tomb' and his ashes also thrown into the river. The body of Bagyidaw's brother, Shwebo Min, suffered an identical fate.

In the Amarapura city area lies the **Bagaya Monastery**, built in 1785. It is noted for its collection of Pali manuscripts made from palm leaves (downstairs), its myriad Buddha images (upstairs) and a vast collection of various antiques.

The **U Bein Bridge** (named after the former town mayor) was constructed out of materials salvaged from the forsaken Ava Palace. The bridge, the longest made from teak in the world, is about three-quarters of a mile in length (3,967 feet) as it crosses the

**Taungthaman Lake**; it takes about 15 to 20 minutes to walk it. Repair work on the bridge started in February 1989 and was completed just over a year later at a cost of K400,000. At the head of the bridge stands the Taungmingyi Statue.

If you do decide to wander over, you'll end up at the **Kyauktawgyi Pagoda**, which was built by King Pagan in 1847 in the style of the Ananda Temple. Unlike the Ananda (which was constructed by Indians), the Kyauktawgyi is wholly the work of Burmese craftsmen and is the best preserved of the numerous religious buildings in the deserted capital of Amarapura. The temple itself is raised a few feet from ground level and has broad steps and huge doorways; unlike the Ananda, it has wooden beams or rafters. The stone image is seated on a high platform and there are also 88 stone figures of the disciples of the Buddha at the back and 12 of *manussiha*, half-man and half-beast (twin-bodied mythical creatures), all around. The Kyauktawgyi is noted for its frescoes in the four porches. These represent religious buildings in various styles of architecture, built or repaired by Pagan Min at Sagaing, Amarapura, Ava, Pakangyi, Prome and Rangoon, and the planets and the constellations according to Burmese ideas of astronomy. The human figures depict the dresses and customs of the period.

Re-crossing the bridge you'll eventually come to the **Patodawgyi Pagoda**, which was built by King Bagyidaw in 1820 (some sources quote 1816) and is one of the largest of its kind. It goes up in a series of five terraces finishing up with a small *sikhara* (beehive-like dome, a spire of North Indian type) and a finial. On white marble panels on the three lower terraces are illustrations and scenes from the Jataka Tales (stories of the life of the Buddha), while there is also an inscription-stone relating the history of the pagoda and a large brass bell.

Besides the twin pagodas, the Shwe Kyetyet ('Golden Fowl's Run', named, because, according to the legend, the place was once the habitat of the Buddha-to-be, who in one of his former lives was born a Golden Fowl) and Shwe Kyetka, which were originally built by King Asoka but subsequently repaired and enlarged by a king of Pagan in the 12th Century AD, located on the banks of the Irrawaddy opposite Sagaing, there is one small but interesting pagoda called the **Nagayon** with a distinctive architectural feature embodying the motif of a hooded snake. Amarapura also boasts a Chinese joss-house, which has stood since the time of King Bodawpaya. Legend has it that when King Mindon switched the capital to Mandalay, the Chinese stuck fast and refused to move with the king.

The nearby village of **Kyithunkhat** is renowned for its craftsmen who cast Buddha images in bronze; gongs and cymbals are also manufactured here. Amarapura is home to a number of silk and cotton weavers and it is here where many a silk *longyi* (Burmese sarong) is turned out.

# AVA

## Getting There

If you want to go on your own, take bus 8 which passes through Amarapura on its way to Ava. You could always jump on a pick-up which is heading for Sagaing, get off before it crosses the Ava Bridge and follow the dusty road to the Myitnge River where a 'ferry' will take you to the other side. From there, hire a horse-cart to the ruins.

## History, What To See

'Ratanapura, the City of Gems, Inwa or Ava, the Fish-pond; such are the varying titles by which this city that was a capital for four and a half centuries is known to Burmese history, and of these the Fish-pond long preceded the City of Gems.'

After the disintegration of the Kingdom of Pagan, Ava emerged as the capital of the Burmese kings, having been founded by Thado Minbya in 1364 AD. It remained the capital for more than 300 years until King Bodawpaya moved over to nearby Amarapura. Ava enjoyed another brief spell as the King's City during the reign of Bodawpaya's grandson Bagyidaw, as it did subsequently on two further occasions. Ava was on an artificially-created island which was formed by linking the Irrawaddy and Myitnge Rivers by a canal. The name 'Ava' actually means 'lake's entrance'.

Unlike Amarapura, Ava's city walls can still be seen, and near the northern gate, opening out on the Irrawaddy, they remain practically intact. From here you have a marvellous view of the Ava Bridge and the river itself flowing by the pagoda-studded hills of Sagaing.

Little remains of the palace area save for a 90-feet high masonry watch tower, the **Nanmyin** built by King Bagyidaw, which was shaken by the earthquake of 1838 and is now regarded humorously as the Burmese 'Leaning Tower of Pisa'. Nearby there is an impressive example of Burmese architecture, the **Maha Aung Mye Bonzan Monastery** which was specifically built in 1818 by Bagyidaw's chief queen for her favourite *Sayadaw* (chief abbot). Unfortunately, the 1838 tremor damaged this structure as well and what is left today is the result of renovations undertaken in 1873 by Sinbyumashin, queen of Mindon. It is a dome-like construction, with a seven-tiered spherical top. Inside there is the room where the *Sayadaw* resided and a Buddha image on the original glass mosaic pedestal. Curiously enough, it has a teak floor. Approach steps, two on each side, three in front and one at the back, lead up to the monastery. Outside there is an inscription giving the name of the monastery and carved figures of a peacock, a hare, the sun and moon and some leogryphs. The Maha Aung Mye Bonzan Monastery still stands today because, unlike most of the monasteries, it was constructed out of masonry and not wood.

Nearby lies a huge unhewn block of white stone on a brick and mortar platform, in an enclosure, marking the site of Let Ma Yoon Prison in which the first American Baptist Missionary, Dr Adoniram Judson, was incarcerated during the reign of King Bodawpaya from June 1824 until May the following year. According to the inscription, the Rev Judson 'endured unrecordable sufferings'; perhaps he, too, was forced to travel on Myanma Airways.

*Water-buffalo: an integral part of Burmese agricultural life.*

# SAGAING

## Getting There

Sagaing (pronounced 'Sa-guy') is not always included in the tourist's trip to Mandalay, but it certainly should be: it is one of the most beautiful spots in Burma. If it's not in your programme, go by yourself by hiring a 'tuk-tuk' in town and ideally taking a Burmese friend with you (any of the trishaw drivers who hang about outside both the Mandalay and Mya Mandala Hotels will be delighted to accompany you and offer helpful advice).

It is a marvellously scenic route from Mandalay to Sagaing as you cross the Ava Bridge, strangely enough, the only bridge spanning the Irrawaddy. Built by the British in 1934 and destroyed by them eight years later, it was eventually repaired in 1954. For so-called 'security reasons' you are not allowed to take photos in the vicinity of the bridge. On your way, you will also be stopped frequently by officials (as indeed you will whenever you travel on the roads in Burma), allegedly to pay 'customs charges' (the Burmese humorously refer to them as 'official beggars'). An alternative means of transport is to take a pick-up from Mandalay; but it's better to go either by 'tuk-tuk' or private car.

If you travel at the week-end, you will notice many people from the various townships sweeping and cleaning the roads. These citizens are forced by the SLORC to tidy the streets every Saturday and Sunday without any remuneration.

## History, What To See

Like other capital cities, Sagaing, preceding Ava, experienced a brief, chequered history. Athin Kaya, a Shan chieftain, made Sagaing his capital in 1322 AD, when he set himself up independently, having freed himself from the overlordship of the Shan Kingdom of *Pinya*. It was his grandson Thado Minbya who transferred the capital to Ava and became its first king. Alaungpaya's son Naungdawgyi installed his capital again at Sagaing for four years (1760-64) and when he died, Ava once again became the seat of royalty. The name 'Sagaing' has two possible meanings: either the 'start of the rounding of the river', or 'the branch of the *sit* tree (Albizzia procefera) leaning over the river'.

Historically, that would have been the end of Sagaing were it not for the bloody scenes that took place between August 9 and 11 1988. Hundreds of students and monks demanding democracy were ruthlessly gunned down and subsequently dumped into the Irrawaddy River (those who didn't die immediately were, according to horrified by-standers, swiftly finished off with rifle butts). A few days later on Naukchinkyun Island at least twenty bodies were washed up — though the actual total massacred was many more than that. The one-time capital Sagaing had, some 224 years after its fall, witnessed an even darker hour.

The best views of Mandalay and the Irrawaddy River are from the **Ponnyashin Pagoda**, which is reached by a long staircase (not dissimilar to that of Mandalay Hill, only fortunately somewhat shorter and, for some inexplicable reason, with only one *chinthe* for protection). Another mystery is why the area is known locally as 'Thayetpinseik', which literally means 'Mango Tree Port', as there is not a single mango tree to be seen.

The Ponnyashin was built by U Ponnya (from whom its name comes), who was the minister of the founder of Sagaing, Athin Khaya and is dominated by two vast Buddha images. Legend has it that the spirit of the minister Ponnya still does his daily dawn offering of alms food at the shrine earlier than anyone else — a unique honour conferred on him by the king — and if you go there before dawn with your offering, you will find that someone has already been there before you. Thus the pagoda is known as the 'Soon-oo Ponnyashin': 'Shrine of the earliest dawn offering'.

NB: There is a charge of US$3 to visit the pagodas on Sagaing Hill and the surrounding areas.

Standing beside the Sagaing Kaunghmudaw Road is the **Hsinmyashin Pagoda** ('The Lord of Elephants' or 'Pagoda of Many Elephants') which was constructed by King Mohnyin of Ava in 1429. Originally called Ratna Ceti, it was destroyed by an earthquake in 1485 and renovated by King Mingaung II of Ava. However, another tremor razed it in 1955 and it was subsequently rebuilt. As the name implies, it is surrounded by innumerable statues of elephants and enshrines relics from Sri Lanka.

Located about six miles northwest of Sagaing is the **Kaunghmudaw** (Rajamanicula) **Pagoda**. Built by King Thalun in 1636 to commemorate the re-establishment of Ava as the royal capital, this hemispherical pagoda (the only one of its type in Burma), with three circular terraces and a base circumference of 400 ft, was modelled on the Mahaceti Pagoda in Sri Lanka. It has a vast dome, reaching 151½ ft, with a *hti* on top which has a diameter of about 17 ft 7 ins. Along the base are hollowed-out recesses housing 120 figures of *nats* or *devas*. The most remarkable feature of this pagoda, which enshrines a left lower tooth relic of Buddha brought from Sri Lanka and King Dhammapala's emerald begging bowl, is the original arrangement for flood-lighting made through 812 stone posts, 4½ ft high with niches for oil lamps to be found on all the four sides. There is also an 8½ft high marble stone inscription, in Burmese script, in one corner of the innermost yard, relating details of the construction of the pagoda. Recently renovated, this vast, white, bell-shaped stupa is an awesome, dazzling, imposing sight. Inside, its Buddha image with glittering lights adds to the splendour and aura of this wonderful pagoda.

The **Ngadatkyi Pagoda**, to the west of town, was built in 1657 by Minyenandameik, son and successor of King Thalun of Ava, and houses the largest sitting image of Buddha in Upper Burma. One of the most celebrated pagodas in Sagaing is the unfinished Tupayon, sponsored by the Ava King Narapati in 1444, which stands 90 ft high and is unusual in that it is circular in plan with three storeys, marked by vertical or dormer window-like hollows with niches, enshrining a number of small Buddha images. It was destroyed in the 1838 earthquake and partially restored (though never completed) 11 years later. In a shed next door is a rich collection of inscription stones dating from the 14th and 15th Centuries. The Tupayon has been described as a 'pagoda of very rare type in Burma and of peculiar architectural interest as marking a certain phase in the development of these structures'.

The **Aungmyelawka Pagoda** (also known as the Eindawya Paya), built in 1783 by King Bodawpaya on the ground on which his residence stood before he ascended the throne, stands on the river front, not far from the Tupayon. Its distinguishing feature is that it is wholly built of sandstone and designed to emulate the Shwezigon Pagoda at Nyaung-U (Pagan). It has a slender, tapering spire and is cylindrical in form with five pairs of leogryphs.

The **Datpaungzu Pagoda**, whilst not as old as most of the others, houses relics collected from all the pagodas which were dismantled to make room for the construction of the railway through Sagaing. The **Umin Thonze** (30 images and 30 caves) Pagoda was built by Padugyi Thingayaza (chief of the *Sanghas*). 30 images of the Buddha are housed in a crescent-shaped building on the side of Sagaing Hill. Padugyi Thingayaza also constructed the **Padamyazedi** (in 1300) — and repaired by the late Sinbyumayin, queen of Mindon — which resembles pagodas of the Mandalay period. It is cylindrical in form, and its bell-shaped dome is covered with glass mosaic. Its original type may well have been changed to its present day appearance by numerous repairs and reconstruction.

In and around Sagaing there are hundreds of pagodas and monasteries. One of the most celebrated monasteries, nestling on the slope of a hill, is the **Pa Ba Gyaung** with a sign in Burmese which reads 'Of the original nine, this is the first'. It is over 900 years old and enjoys a wonderfully peaceful location. Approaching it, you may well hear the chanting of hymns from all sides and novices, in the traditional semi-recumbent posture, with their legs tucked in and poised on their elbows, taking their lessons in Buddha *Dhamma* (Buddhist doctrine) from the *Sayadaw* or some other learned monk.

On the right bank of the river lies a rather dilapidated old fort, where the Burmese put up a last-ditch effort against the British forces during the operations culminating in the annexation of Upper Burma. If you climb the old wall, you can see the Irrawaddy, Ava Bridge and the hills of Sagaing and Mandalay. In the nearby village of **Ywataung**, a couple of miles out of town, live numerous silver-workers who, for generations, have produced silverware from their forges. You can watch them inscribing and engraving, untouched by events elsewhere in the world.


# MINGUN

## Getting There

A trip to Mingun, unfortunately, is not always included these days in MTT's (and some other private companies') programme: if it isn't, go by yourself. It's a must. Ask your trishaw driver to take you to the banks of the Irrawaddy (actually at the bottom of 26th Street or B Road) and hop onto one of the innumerable boats that ply the muddy waters: it's a day's journey really so it's best to start early in the morning and before the heat becomes intolerable. You can either take the communal boat with all the locals (though you'll have to wait till it's completely full) at a cost of K10 one way, or hire your own boat for around K300. The outward trip, which offers a marvellous insight into life on the Irrawaddy, can take up to 90 minutes, though the return leg can be done in half the time. Mingun itself is a village located on the west bank of the Irrawaddy, roughly 7 miles (10.5 km) north of Mandalay.

Disembarking at Mingun, you first pass through the Methodist Infirmary (**Daw Oo Zoon**) which is home to 70 old ladies and 31 gentlemen. The friendly staff here take pleasure in showing tourists around, and in return you can make a donation and receive a certificate.

## History, What To See

Mingun has two remarkable objects both the brain-child of King Bodawpaya: the Mingun **Bell** and the Pagoda, and both are candidates for the *Guinness Book of Records*. You will have already gathered by now that Bodawpaya was something of a lunatic (he considered himself to be the Buddha reincarnated); he was also a brutal megalomaniac with a penchant for madcap projects. The first was the construction of the **Mingun** (Pahtodawgyi) **Pagoda**, which began in 1790 and was to have been the largest in the world (at 150 metres high — as intended by the king — it would have been no less than 20 metres taller than the vast chedi at Nakhon Pathom in Thailand). It took years to build (nobody is quite sure how long), by which time most of the workers had expired and, even worse for the king, money had run out. So in 1813 he abandoned his scheme, leaving little more than a vast pile of bricks. The entire plan was a total fiasco and had a devastating effect on the community, as villagers fled to escape being called upon to continue the construction.

In 1838 an earthquake struck and part of the building collapsed; today you can still see a huge fissure in the giant slab. Guarded by a pair of dilapidated brick *chinthes*, the Mingun Pagoda is truly a bizarre and incongruous sight. Square in plan, it rests on five receding terraces with porches projecting slightly on all four sides. The bottom terrace is a square of 450 feet and the top terrace 230 feet. Above the main square block are three receding terraces which have small square panels decorated with colourful glazed plaques. In a building close-by are plaques glazed in green, brown and yellow which depict scenes from the five Buddhist Councils.

'A pathway has been worn along the rent by the feet of many climbers, and up this one may now climb to its summit. In clear weather it offers a great view of the river and its ceaseless life; of the spires and turrets of Mandalay and the blue walls of the Shan highlands beyond. Immediately behind it there rise in tiers the barren hills of Sagaing. The ruins of two colossal leogryphs, one ninety-five feet in height, stand between it and the river. These also the earthquake destroyed. They are in keeping with this place of gigantic but abortive conceptions'.

V. C. Scott O'Connor.

Today it is still possible to climb to the very top, 162 feet high and local kids will follow you all the way. Unfortunately, you have to leave your shoes at the bottom, which makes the ascent rather uncomfortable. Within the pagoda, according to the *Royal Chronicle of Burma*, 1,500 figures and images of gold, 2,534 of silver and 36,947 of 'other materials' lie buried. All you can actually see inside the pagoda is an uninspiring Buddha image accompanied by a foul and musty smell of bats' droppings.

Mingun may not have the largest pagoda in the world, but it does have the biggest uncracked bell, 14 times the size of that of St. Paul's. There is a larger one in Moscow (one-third bigger), but that one is flawed. Naturally, this was also the idea of Bodawpaya, who made sure it could never be copied by having the designer executed promptly afterwards. Cast in 1790 (some say 1808) to be dedicated to the Mingun Pagoda, it is 12 ft high, weighs 90 tons and has a diameter at its outer lip of 16 ft 3 ins. It's possible to crawl inside, and pray that none of the entourage of giggling kids rings it while you're underneath! Not surprisingly the bell fell off during the earthquake of 1838 and it lay on the ground until 1896 when it was re-mounted. It is now covered by a shelter open on all sides.

'King Bodawpaya who reigned in Amarapura City in 1782-1819 had an idea to hang a bell near Mingun Pagoda which was his merit at Mingun region. The bell was cast with pomp and ceremony in Alai-kyun on the east bank of the Ayeyarwady River on 5th waxing of Kason, 1170 M.E. (1808 A.D.). Administrator to cast the bell was Pan-di-wun (Minister of Blacksmiths) Nanda Kyaw Thu. It is said that the bell is made of bronze and some bits of gold and silver inside. The weight of it is 55.555 viss (90.52 tons).

The bell was completed in Nayon, 1173 M.E. (1811 A.D.). To move such massive bell to Mingun Pagoda was a big burden. But the Myanmar people's intelligence is very great and smart. The management to shift the bell was easy like this.

People dug the soil beneath the bell and took it out. Then they made a canal in which two barges could pass well to the river. Similarly, they also canalized from the opposite bank to the fixed point. After digging the canals, they built the barges which were 120 feet (36 metres) long below the bell and guilded them. In Waso-Wagaung (July-August), the canals were flooded by the river and so the bell was successfully carried to the permanent place in the barges.

The bell was hung on three parallel bars of wood covered with metal plate. Those bars were on two upright posts which were of teakwood covered with stucco on the outside. The bell cannot swing to and fro. The British gazettes expressed that two carts could drive and turn well under such voluminous Mingun Bell. Moreover, the diameter of the outer lip is 16 feet 3 inches, the diameter above 4 feet 8 inches of the inner lip 10 feet, the height on outside 12 feet and the diameter of the inner top 8 feet 6 inches. The thickness of the bell is from 6 inches to 12 inches and the weight of it is roughly about 80 tons the English estimated.

However, according to the measurements of the bell shown in *Kon-baung-set Maha Raja-wun* (Great History of the Konbaung dynasty), the diameter of the outer lip is 5 metres, the girth 15 metres, the height 6 metres and the weight 90.52 tons (91972.56 kilograms).

The brick-posts sustaining the bell were crashed by earthquake on 23rd March, 1839 (*sic*). So the bell also fell nearly onto the ground and a few bits of it cracked. It was lifted by logs on the surface of the earth. In 1896 A.D., a Scottish officer of the Ayeyarwady Steamer Company shifted the bell from its original hanger onto the double iron-bars supporting with the steel-posts. The bell has been covered over by a *pyatthat* or pavilion of wood with 16 pillars open on all sides. Now it is maintained by the Archaeology Department.

It is claimed to be the world's third biggest bell in Myanmar Encyclopedia Vol. 2 although Mingun Bell is said to be the world's largest one in Amended List of Ancient Monuments in Myanmar, Sagaing Division, Serial-5: published by the Archaeology Department. But *Guinness Book of World Records*, March 1982 expresses, 'At present, the heaviest bell in use is Mingun Bell which is 101.4 tons weigh and in Mandalay District in Myanmar'.'

*MYANMAR REVIEW.*

Just as you leave the boat and reach the bank there is a small white pagoda, **Pondawpaya**, only 15ft high which was designed as the working model for the giant pagoda. Downstream from the Pondawpaya lies the **Settawya Pagoda**, a hollow vaulted shrine built in 1811. There is a footprint here of the Buddha in brick and stucco.

A few hundred yards from the bell is the **Hsinbyume** (Myatheindan) Pagoda, built by Bagyidaw in 1816 in memory of his wife Princess Hsinbyume when he was still crown prince. Modelled on Pagan's Sulamani Temple, it is of a circular construction with seven concentric terraces designed to represent the seven mountain ranges surrounding Mount Meru, the legendary home of the gods. There are four flights of steps on the four sides and the white marble figures in the niches of the balustrades are supposed to be the mythical monsters who stand guard on Mount Meru. This too was damaged during the earthquake but was restored by King Mindon in 1874. From the top terrace you have a panoramic view of Mingun.

# MAYMYO

## Getting There

Some 42 miles (67km) northeast of Mandalay lies the hill station of Maymyo, and whilst it is possible to get there and back in one day (by pick-up truck or even train), it's far more sensible to stay overnight. If you manage to go on your own, it can take up to 2½ hours to reach (always assuming the pick-up doesn't break down on the way) and maybe 1½ to 2 hours to get back. The train, which can take anything up to five hours, isn't recommended. Around town you can hire a bicycle, a horse-drawn carriage (a sort of mini stage-coach) or even travel in a wooden bus.

## History, What To See

Situated at around 3,500 feet (roughly 1,100 metres) above sea level, Maymyo took its name from Colonel May ('Maymyo' literally means 'May Town') of the 5th Bengal Infantry Regiment which was stationed in the town in 1886. Because of its pleasant cool climate (and strawberries) it served as a summer resort for the British Government in Burma. Maymyo's 17 square miles are practically hedged in by low hills, the highest being 'One Tree Hill' at 4,021 feet. Eucalyptus, silver oak, pine, innumerable flowers including chrysanthemums, coffee, pineapples and strawberries are plentiful, along with 'colonial' vegetables such as cabbages and cauliflowers.

Of principal interest are Maymyo's vast **Botanical Gardens**, laid out by Sir Harcourt Butler, governor of Burma, established in 1914 and located just south of town, a Chinese temple (*Tayokebaye*), and a waterfall (*Pwekouk*), five miles from town on the Lashio Road. Further out of town lie the **Anisakan** and **Wetwun Waterfalls** (seven and 15 miles out respectively), while 35 miles on the Maymyo-Lashio Road (see Chapter Ten) is the **Goteik Viaduct**, built between two forest-studded plateaus of the Shan Hills and across a deep gorge. This railway bridge crosses the valley at a height of 870 feet. Maymyo also has a market, where many ethnic groups from Shan State can be seen. There is an excellent view of the surrounding area from the Naung Kan Gyi Pagoda on the hill top.

## Places to Stay and Eat

As with the Strand Hotel in Rangoon, Maymyo's very own colonial masterpiece, the Candacraig (Tel 2118), is alas no longer what it was. Originally constructed in 1906 in the style of an old Scottish manor as a holiday retreat for British employees of the Bombay Burmah Trading Company, it has subsequently suffered an ignominious decline, not to mention numerous name changes in the intervening years. It appears to have been called the Maymyo Government Rest House, the Maymyo Inn and — now that the SLORC have renamed the town Pyin U Lwin — the poor old Candacraig has become the Pyin U Lwin Government Rest House or 'Thiri Myaing' (meaning 'Magnificent Copse'). At least the roast beef, Yorkshire pudding, strawberries and raspberries are still on the menu.

The top hotel in Maymyo is now the Cherry Myaing which was originally the British governor's residence and subsequently the state guest house for high-ranking officials and foreign dignitaries. Rooms here cost up to US$100, so it's unlikely you'll be dining alongside members of the SLORC. Standard (ie basic) accommodation is provided by the Nann Myaing (Tel 2047), Gandamar Myaing, Yuzana Myaing and Thazin Myaing Hotels. These generally charge between US$15-25 a night. Maymyo has no outstanding restaurants.

# MONYWA

Open once again to tourists, Monywa, the commercial centre of the Chindwin Valley, lies 84 miles (136km) northwest of Mandalay and takes some three hours to reach by car. Located by the banks of the Chindwin River, it is an unprepossessing town whose economy is wholly dependent on illegal trade with India but with a fascinating background.

It was actually founded during the Pagan period, and was only given the name 'Monywa' in 1888. Prior to that, it was just a sleepy little village (though according to research, the surrounding areas were the dwelling places of mankind as long ago as a million years). Monywa is indeed recorded in Pagan inscriptions and King Thalun's Royal Register. Subsequently it was a village in Alon District during the Konbaung Dynasty. When King Alaungpaya led his troops to Manipur, the Burmese Armed Forces passed through Monywa. The town of Alon was formerly called Badon, and became a sizeable village with a big market during the late Konbaung period. The municipality of Monywa was constituted on April 25 1888 and the town was made the headquarters of the Lower Chindwin District. At that time the population was just 2,000 with 345 houses and two wards.

Today Monywa is a thriving black market city with a population of more than 100,000, 18 wards and six markets.

The town itself is rather a dreary place with just one hotel for foreigners, the Monywa on Ah-lone Road (Tel 21549), though very few tourists stay here. Rates vary from US$30-35. Fortunately there is plenty to see in the surrounding area. Foremost is the **Thanboddhay Temple** (also known as the Moe-hnyin-thanbuddhe Temple), which lies seven miles southeast of the town. A recent construction, built by Moe-hnyin Sayadaw in 1939, it houses literally thousands of Buddha images. All in all, there are reckoned to be 582,357 images, though I don't know how anybody managed to count them all. The Thanboddhay Temple is one of the most beautiful in Burma and attracts worshippers from all over the land.

In **Kyaukka** village (which is famous throughout the country for its lacquerware), about 10 miles to the east of Monywa, stands the **Shwe-Gu-Ni Pagoda**. Founded in the 14th Century, it was given its present name in 1638 during the reign of King Thalun. It is 108 feet tall and is one of Burma's many 'wish-fulfilling' pagodas (see Chapter Nine).

West of the Chindwin River in Min-Zu village tract among the Townships of Yin-Mar-bin, Sa-lin-gyi and Pa-lei lies **Pho-Win Hill**. It derived its name from *Zawgyi* Pho Win who, as legend has it, haunts the hill. A *Zawgyi* is a complex character (an alchemist or magician), who, according to Khin Myo Chit:

'began as a human male who practised austerities and contemplation. He collected magic herbs and concocted things like magic stones, wands and medicines. When he attained the state of a *Zawgyi*, he took a new form, a glamorous figure in flaming red robes with a magic wand in hand. The human shell he left behind was the size of a seven month old baby. It emitted a smell of ripe bananas. If anyone found it and ate it such a person would be endowed with super-strength and invulnerability. A *Zawgyi* is endowed with supernatural powers, like flying in the air, walking on water, going underground. He can also create things like flying chariots. Above all, he is blessed with longevity of life that runs into centuries and what is more important, eternal youth and vitality. He is a permanent character on the marionette stage'.

Wood and stone sculptures and frescoes of the Nyaung-Yan Period are to be found here.

Situated in Budalin Township, about two miles east of the river, is **Twinn Hill**. According to geologists, this was the crater of an extinct volcano about five to seven million years ago.

In the northeastern part of Monywa is the **Lei-di Monastery** which was constructed in 1886 by Lei-di Sayadaw, a scholar of Burmese literature and scripture. Today the monastery serves as a large monastic university. The Lei-di Inscription Hall built in 1925 features 806 upright stone slabs on which are inscribed scriptures in Burmese and Pali.

The most interesting excursion from Monywa is to the **Powlntaung Caves**, which is a sandstone mountain sheltering numerous carvings of pagodas, images, pavilions and various other ancient woodcarvings. To reach the caves, you have to cross the Chindwin River to a place called Nyaungbingyi and then drive for about 20 minutes.

The best restaurant in town is the Pann Cherry Chinese Restaurant on Bogyoke Street, though I'd steer clear of the Pig's Stomach Quail Egg Soup and the Quail Egg Pig's Brain Sweet.

*Mingun Bell: the largest uncracked bell in the world.*

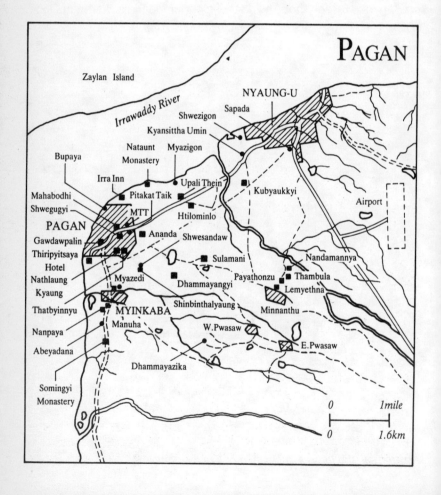

# PAGAN

Zaylan Island

*Irrawaddy River*

NYAUNG-U

Shwezigon   Sapada

Kyansittha Umin

Nataunt   Myazigon
Monastery

Bupaya

Irra Inn   Upali Thein

Pitakat Taik   Kubyaukkyi

Mahabodhi

Shwegugyi   MTT

PAGAN   Htilominlo

Ananda   Shwesandaw

Gawdawpalin

Thiripyitsaya   Sulamani   Nandamannya
Hotel

Nathlaung   Payathonzu   Thambula

Kyaung   Myazedi   Lemyethna

Dhammayangyi

Thatbyinnyu   MYINKABA   Minnanthu

Shinbinthalyaung

Nanpaya   Manuha

Abeyadana   W.Pwasaw

E.Pwasaw

Dhammayazika

Somingyi
Monastery

Airport

0   1mile

0   1.6km

Chapter Seven

# Pagan

## GETTING THERE AND AROUND

Pagan's Nyaung-U Airport is served sporadically and unpredictably by the occasional Myanma Airways Fokker Friendship, which totters in from both Rangoon (about 1¾ hours away and costing US$71 from MTT's office) and Mandalay (a mere half-hour's flight; MTT charges US$33). Other alternatives are rail (since there's no line all the way to Pagan, this isn't a very sensible choice). You have to travel from Rangoon to the railway junction at Thazi, for which MTT charge between US$27-33, and then catch a bus from Thazi to Pagan, or boat (scenic but very time-consuming; indeed it can take 20-24 hours from Mandalay on an ancient paddle wheel steamer. It is hard to believe that these boats carry some 14 million passengers each year and belong to the world's largest 'fleet' of river steamers). Private car for individual travellers is the wisest option or lastly the Myanmar Travels & Tours bus for government-organised groups. Most tourists will be coming from Mandalay, which is about six hours away. En route, however, you can stop off at Meiktila (either overnight or just for breakfast), which is roughly equidistant between Mandalay and Pagan (see Chapter Ten).

Once safely ensconced in Pagan, you can either stay with your group, go your own way by horse-cart (bargain madly for the fare) or rent a bicycle for about K15 an hour. If you decide to go by bike, check thoroughly that the contraption (most likely of Russian or Burmese origin) is roadworthy and that — most importantly — the brakes function. It can be quite hard work (but hugely rewarding) under Pagan's scorching sun and on the slippery sand, so be careful. For good measure, take with you a Burmese friend, a good map, a torch and a water-bottle.


# GENERAL DESCRIPTION

If Kipling did indeed remark 'This is Burma, and it will be quite unlike any land you know about' (*Letters From the East*, 1889), then he ought to have been referring to Pagan, arguably the most awe-inspiring sight in all of Southeast Asia. Pagan's Dynasty and past history have been well documented in Chapter One: suffice to say that in its palmiest days, there were thousands of temples and pagodas. Even now, the remains of about 5,000 can still be traced.

The ruins of Pagan cover a tract of land measuring about 16 square miles along the east bank of the Irrawaddy. The monuments, which are now in various stages of decay and disrepair, were erected mostly from the 11th to 13th Centuries when Pagan was the seat of the Burmese Dynasty. Tradition has it that a long line of 55 kings ruled over Pagan during the 12 centuries beginning from 108 AD and this is corroborated by local chronicles. The present walled city of Pagan is ascribed to King Pyinbya, the 34th king of the Dynasty, who in 874 AD transferred the capital from Tampawadi (now known as Pwasaw). The latter was built by Thaiktaing, the 12th king, and there were two other capitals, namely Thiripyitsaya built by Thiligyaung, the 7th king, and Paukkan (Yonhlutkyun) built by Thamudrit, the founder of the Dynasty in 108 AD. The authentic history of the Dynasty (as supported by epigraphic evidence) begins only with the reign of Anawrahta (1044-77) in 1057 AD.

Besides being both royal and holy, Pagan was also a solemn seat of serious study, particularly of the Pali language, with its celebrated university. Here for several centuries learning continued, not only during the long line of kings but also after the Dynasty had died out and been replaced by Ava, as evidenced by structural remains of the 15th-16th Centuries. Yet it was the end of the 13th Century that bore witness to the fall of the Pagan Dynasty. Thousands of pagodas were plundered by the Chinese, and the king, fleeing from the invaders, dismantled a considerable number of the monuments in order to assemble forts to defend himself against the pillagers. Since those days, the great mass of religious edifices have been left to decay and ruin (including a terrible earthquake in 1975) and today there are no more than 100 wondrous monuments to admire, which still remain a place of worship.

Until May 1990, Pagan was a marvellously atmospheric town with guest houses, shops, stalls, and people all milling about. The temples were abuzz, alive, vibrant: then, ruthlessly and without warning — and in a fashion not dissimilar to Pol Pot's treatment of the Cambodians — the *Tatmadaw* moved in and forced out the entire population at gunpoint, allegedly to disperse government dissenters. As an old man bemoaned despairingly:

'We were given just 10 hours to move', an old man told me. 'The *Tatmadaw* suddenly appeared and ordered us to destroy our houses and take all our belongings with us. Those who refused were taken away and shot. Now all 6,000 of us have been relocated in a terrible place seven kilometres out of town. We've got nothing left, we lost all our possessions in the rush to get out. There's no work for anyone; some people have even resorted to stealing Buddha images from the temples and selling them on to the Thais. All that remains of old Pagan are two government hotels and Tourist Burma.'

Pagan is a ghost town, lifeless, deserted. The only occasions when there is any spark at all are on the Buddha's birthday and the full moon days. Old Pagan still weeps today, mourning its passing in 1287 when sacked by Kublai Khan and again, 703 years later, when the *Tatmadaw* stepped in so savagely.

# PLACES TO STAY AND EAT/SHOPPING

Tourists invariably stay at one of two hotels: the Thiripyitsaya (which has the dubious distinction of being Burma's finest) and the Irra Inn, now renamed the Ayeyar Hotel by the SLORC. The only good thing that can be said about either is that they occupy wonderfully scenic locations by the banks of the Irrawaddy. The Thiripyitsaya has the better reputation since it is laid out in beautifully landscaped grounds and offers accommodation in fairly large bungalows (it even takes American Express, though at the official exchange rate, that's a positive disadvantage). However, the air-conditioning has a mind of its own, the showers are grim, the murky waters of the 'swimming pool' haven't been touched for years, the restaurant is dismal and the bar regularly runs out of Mandalay Beer. As with all government-run hotels in Burma, the service is slow and the receptionists surly. Rooms (which they have recently attempted to upgrade, though the ceilings still leak) cost US$45 a single and US$55 a double.

The Irra Inn (Ayeyar Hotel) has sizeable rooms with a balcony, but no air-conditioning (only noisy ineffective fans) and dreadful bathrooms (with the inevitable cockroaches). Room prices here vary from US$20-50. Breakfast, which consists of a piece of pineapple, two pieces of cold stale toast, rancid butter, bizarre looking jam, fruit juice (not fresh, but the ubiquitous lemon pop), dire eggs, coffee or tea (indistinguishable from one another and quite possibly straight from the Irrawaddy), costs US$5, while lunch costs US$7 and supper US$10. Supper, incidentally, must be ordered before 4pm or you won't get anything, whilst lunch must be ordered at breakfast (very Burmese). As the sign at the reception says 'All plus 10% service charge and 10% sale tax. Bill payable in foreign currency converted at the current rates', though this may be open to 'negotiation'. There is also the Thande Hotel, which is ridiculously overpriced, whilst on the main road to Nyaung-U stands a brand new hotel called the Golden Express, which charges between US$30 and US$90. Located near the Irra Inn is the Co-Operative Inn, the cheapest in the area. Rates here start at US$8, going up to US$35. It also has an excellent, cheap Chinese restaurant. As with the Silver Cloud Hotel in Mandalay, tourists have only recently been permitted to stay at places like the Golden Express so desperate are the SLORC for foreign currency.

Pagan's most exclusive restaurant is the River View, a modern yet raj-like construction owned by Skyline Travel of Bangkok (ie governmental) and inevitably empty when there aren't any tourists about. It seems quite out of place. The set menu costs K120 and consists of lentil soup, the unavoidable curry (beef, chicken, pork or fish), vegetables, dessert and Chinese tea: at the black market rate, a snip at US$1.20. *A la carte* costs more, and there is also 20% extra in various taxes to be added on. Tea or coffee cost K10, bottled water (a distinct rarity in Pagan: be warned) K35, Coke and 7 Up K65 and beer K88. The River View is some way out of town and you need to hire a horse-cart: there and back plus waiting-time should cost you between K150-200 — bargain hard. You need to reserve a table in advance (not because the restaurant will be fully booked, but to make sure the chef remembers to go to market that day).

Other restaurants include the Nation on the main road and the Myayadana which serves Burmese fare, whilst there is a pleasant little noodle shop near Nyaung-U market called the Sein Yatana Restaurant (rather a misnomer, but friendly all the same).

Pagan is the home of lacquerware and you won't be able to

escape from it anywhere. If you feel inclined to buy, go to U Kan Htun, Daw Hla Myaing & daughter Ma Moe Moe, Ywar Thit Quarter. This is one of the rare non-government shops, so you can bargain hard. You can also 'pay' in cigarettes and whisky, swop items or change money. Nyaung-U Market has the usual collection of comestibles, cosmetics, *longyi* and smuggled goods.

# PAGODAS AND TEMPLES

It is obviously impossible to visit all the pagodas and temples during your stay in Pagan. Most guidebooks tend to classify the structures according to their location: there are five main areas — Pagan village (near the two hotels), Nyaung-U (near the market and northwest of the airport), Minnanthu (southwest of the airport), Myinkaba (south of Pagan) and Pwasaw (situated between Myinkaba and Minnanthu). However, since Pagan is essentially a place for those with a keen interest in history and architecture, it may be more useful to categorise the buildings according to their architectural style. Incidentally, independent tourists must pay an entrance fee of US$10 and register at Pagan's National Museum (don't forget to have your FED form stamped) before they are permitted access to any of the sites. An additional charge of US$3 is levied for every extra night exceeding two nights.

In Chapter One I discussed the nine architectural types in Pagan, and I shall now give specific examples of each style:

### Stupa whose dome is modelled on a reliquary (a receptacle for relics)

A fine example of this is the Bupaya Pagoda, which stands on the brink of the Irrawaddy in Pagan, above rows of crenellated terraces, not far from the Irra Inn (Ayeyar Hotel). The dome resembles that of the Ngakywenadaung assuming the form of a cylindrical relic casket. Above it stands a bold convex band upon which rises a tapering stupa finial. Tradition attributes the Bupaya to King Pyusawhti of Pagan who reigned from 168 to 243 AD, though stylistically it may be ascribed to about the 11th Century. According to tradition, it was constructed on the spot where a gigantic *Bu* or gourd creeper grew. Within its precincts is a shrine dedicated to the God of Storms (*Mondaing Nat*). It was completely destroyed during the 1975 earthquake but has subsequently been restored. It is a marvellous place from which to watch the sunset.

**Stupa whose dome is modelled on a tumulus (ancient sepulchral mound)**

Located by the banks of the Irrawaddy at Nyaung-U and accessible both by land and water, the Shwezigon is one of the holiest pagodas in Burma since it is believed to contain the frontal bone and a tooth of the Buddha. It is a solid, cylindrical structure resting on three square terraces, a prototype of Burmese stupas. It has a bold waist-band round the bell-shaped dome, above which rises a series of concentric mouldings ending in a finial and crowned by an umbrella (*hti*). It was constructed by King Anawrahta who left it in an unfinished state and completed by Kyansittha (1084-1113 AD). Around the terraces of the pagoda, set in panels, are enamelled plaques illustrating scenes of the previous lives of the Buddha. On each of the four sides of the pagoda is a small temple enshrining a standing Buddha, 13 ft high. On either side of the east approach is a square stone pillar with Mon inscriptions on all four sides dedicated by King Kyansittha. Figures of the 37 *nats* can be seen in a rather dreary shed at the northeast corner of the pagoda precinct.

Since the Shwezigon is one of the most popular pagodas in the area, there are touts and child beggars everywhere. Even monks occasionally demand money to have their photo taken (the Thai influence no doubt). If you do want to take any photographs, you will have to pay K5 to a surly Burmese official.

**Stupa of a Sinhalese type**

Southeast of the Shwezigon is the Sapada Pagoda, which was built in the 12th Century AD by Sapada, a native of Bassein, who had been ordained a monk in Ceylon and who founded a sect at Pagan on his return to Burma. The pagoda was constructed after the model of a Sinhalese shrine, and is the prototype of similar structures in the province. The Sapada's distinctive feature is the cubical relic-chamber above the bell. It is a landmark in the history of Buddhism, and commemorates the religious relationship between Burma and Ceylon (Sri Lanka).

**Temple based on North Indian model**

The most celebrated temple both in Pagan and Burma itself is the Ananda, which was built by Kyansittha in 1091 AD (some sources say 1090), and constructed according to a plan furnished by Indian Buddhist monks. It symbolises the endless wisdom (*Ananta Pañña*) of the Buddha. The name 'Ananta', which was later changed to 'Ananda', was the name of Buddha's cousin.

In plan the Ananda forms a square of nearly 200 feet, broken on each side by the projection of large gabled vestibules which convert the plan into a perfect Greek cross. These vestibules are rather lower than the main mass of the building, which elevates itself to a height of 35 feet in two tiers of windows. Above rise successively diminishing terraces, the last of which just affords sufficient breadth for the spire which crowns and completes the edifice. The lower half of this spire is in the form of a mitre-like pyramid adapted from the temples of India; the upper half is the same moulded taper pinnacle that completes the common bell-shaped pagodas of Pagan. The gilded *hti* caps the temple at a height of 168 feet (51 metres) above the ground.

The interior consists of two vaulted and high but narrow corridors running parallel to each other along the four sides of the temple. They are connected by low and narrow passages and further intersected by four large corridors into which access is obtained through the porticoes. In the centre is an enormous cube, on the four sides of which are deep and high niches enshrining four colossal standing Buddhas. Each Buddha rises 31 feet high above his throne, which itself measures almost 8 feet in height. Of these images (which represent the four Buddhas who have attained nirvana), only those on the north and south are the original ones; those on the east and west are copies made 100 years ago to replace the originals which were destroyed by fire.

Other interesting features of the Ananda are the numerous glazed terracotta tiles ornamenting the base and the receding terraces which represent the Jataka stories. Each of these plaques is inscribed with a Mon legend. The inner walls are a honey-comb of niches in which are set small stone Buddhas in various postures. The western sanctum of the temple enshrines the life-size statue of its founder Kyansittha. In the porch on the west face are two footprints of the Buddha placed on a pedestal.

There are numerous stalls leading to the temple, offering lacquerware, books, drinks and various souvenirs.

### Temple of Central Indian type
Southeast of the Bupaya Pagoda stands the Mahabodhi Pagoda, built by Nantaungmya in 1215 AD based on the temple at Bodh Gaya in Bihar which commemorates the spot where the Buddha attained Enlightenment. It is the only one of its type in Burma. The basement is a quadrangular block of no great height, supporting a tall pyramidal spire. The finial is a small slim stupa. The entire

structure is covered with niches bearing seated Buddhas and interspersed with ornamental panels and mouldings.

## Temple based on South Indian model

At Minnanthu, about three to four miles southwest of Nyaung-U, stands the Sulamani Temple which was built around 1183 AD by Narapatisithu. It consists of two storeys, set back one behind the other, each crowned by terraces ornamented with battlemented parapets; small stupas at each corner surmount a deeply moulded cornice set with glazed plaques of different sizes and patterns. In plan each storey is a square and four porches facing the cardinal points project from each, the porch on the east face being larger than the rest. This temple, which in plan resembles the Thatbyinnyu, affords superb views of Pagan.

## Cave temples based on Indian model

Situated close to the Shwezigon Pagoda is the Kyansittha Umin, a low brick building half under ground and half above. Despite its name, it has been attributed to Anawrahta. The interior consists of long and dark corridors, some walls of which are ornamented with frescoes dating from the 11th to 13th Centuries. Those dating from the 13th Century were most probably painted during the Mongol occupation of 1287 and represent Mongolian people, nobles, captains and warriors.

## Ordination hall

Northeast of the Ananda Temple is the Upali Thein, named after a celebrated monk Upali and dating back to the second quarter of the 13th Century (though repaired in the 17th Century). It is a structure of fine proportions enclosed within brick walls and is rectangular in plan, containing a hall with a Buddha image placed on a pedestal near the western end. The roof is ornamented with a double row of battlements in simulation of wooden architecture, and its centre is surmounted by a small, slim pagoda. The arches on which the superstructure rests are well-built and the brilliant frescoes covering its walls and ceilings are in a fair state of preservation. These date from the late 17th or early 18th Century.

## Library

West of the Ananda, within the city walls, is the Pitakat Taik which was built in 1058 by Anawrahta to house the 30 elephant-loads of

Buddhist scriptures in Pali which he had brought from Thaton. The structure was repaired in 1783 by King Bodawpaya. It measures 51 feet square and 60 feet high with the entrance on the east and perforated stone windows on other sides. The inner cell has a corridor round it. The Pitakat Taik's chief peculiarity is its approximate simulation of architectural forms in wood: that's to say it is covered by five multiple roofs in a style similar to that of the Mandalay Palace, and ornamented with peacock-like finials in plaster carving.

There are scores of other pagodas and temples, the most interesting of which are located at Pagan. These include:

**Htilominlo Temple**: constructed around 1211 AD (some sources quote 1218) by King Nantaungmya to commemorate the spot where he was chosen to be crown prince out of five brothers, it is one of Pagan's finest, marvellous to climb and and an ideal spot from which to take photographs. There are four Buddhas facing the cardinal points on the ground floor as well as on the upper storey, which is reached by two staircases built in the thickness of the walls.

**Thatbyinnyu Temple**: approached through the crumbling city walls, this temple stands 201 feet high (the highest in Pagan) and is a superb place for watching the sunset, offering stunning views of the Ananda Temple. Meaning 'omniscience', the Thatbyinnyu was built in 1144 by King Alaungsithu after the model of the temples in Northern India. It has five storeys: the first and second were used as the residence of monks; images were kept on the third; the fourth was used as a library; and on the fifth a pagoda was constructed containing holy relics. The building is thus a combination of a stupa and vihara and its history is recorded on its walls. Like all the structures of Pagan, the Thatbyinnyu has suffered badly from tremors and the ravages of time, having been restored on numerous occasions.

**Shwegugyi Temple**: located northwest of the Thatbyinnyu, it was built in 1131 (some say 1141) by Alaungsithu after the model of the Buddha's sleeping chamber. Standing on a high brick platform, this temple faces north and access to it is by a flight of steps at the northwest corner. The Shwegugyi's history is recorded on two stone slabs set in the inner walls; it apparently took just seven months to complete.

**Nathlaung Kyaung**: this is the sole remaining Hindu temple in Pagan and was built by King Taungthugyi in 931 AD (over a century before the introduction of the Southern School of Buddhism from Thaton). Partly in ruins, it is dedicated to the god Vishnu and is decorated on the outside with stone figures of the 'Ten Avatars' (past and future incarnations), Gautama Buddha being the ninth. Occupying the centre is a huge square brick pillar, around which there is the usual circumambulatory passage, vaulted over; this pillar supports the dome and *sikhara* above.

**Gawdawpalin Temple**: almost equidistant between Pagan's two best known hotels, the Gawdawpalin was constructed by Narapatisithu (1173-1210 AD) in order to commemorate the ceremony of paying homage to the manes (deified souls) of his ancestors, and its general arrangement resembles the Thatbyinnyu. It has a vestibule on the east, but unlike the Thatbyinnyu, the upper storey is reached by narrow stairs built in the thickness of the walls, and Buddha images are placed against the central cube on all sides on the ground floor. Both the *sikhara* and stupa are elongated but the temple is only 180 feet high. The Gawdawpalin was severely damaged during the 1975 earthquake and its restoration, one of the most major ever undertaken, was completed in the 1980s. It offers splendid views of the Irrawaddy and the plains of Pagan.

**Shwesandaw Pagoda**: this is a cylindrical stupa with five terraces, the first to be built by King Anawrahta after his conquest of Thaton in 1057. Enshrined inside are some sacred hairs of the Buddha. The chedi, rebuilt over 60 years ago, fell down in 1975 and was restored in 1977, painted yellow (it was originally white). From here, you have a marvellous view of the sunrise. This pagoda is also known as the Mahapeinne or Ganesha Pagoda, from the fact that each of the four corners of its lowest terrace is guarded by three Hindu gods, Brahma, Vishnu and Siva, the third being often identified with Ganesha.

**Shinbinthalyaung**: in a brick shed, within the confines of the Shwesandaw Pagoda, lies a 60 ft long reclining Buddha (in the sleeping position) which dates from the 11th Century. Unlike the recumbent image of the Buddha in the Manuha Temple, its head points to the south, whereas that of the Manuha Temple points to the north, a position assumed by Gautama Buddha when he was lying on his death-bed between two *Sal* trees at Kusinagara. It is a good idea to bring a torch if you decide to enter.

**Mingalazedi Pagoda**: built in 1284 by Narathihapati and located just south of the Thiripyitsaya Hotel, this pagoda is noted for its beautiful terracotta tiles with Burmese legends around the terraces. It stands on a low square basement with a broad staircase on each side. It has fine proportions and indicates the high watermark of Burmese religious architecture, because it was constructed a few years before the subversion of the Pagan Empire by the Mongols.

**Dhammayangyi Temple**: built in 1170 AD by Narathu, this temple is similar in plan to the Ananda, but only the outer corridor is accessible as all the entrances to the inner ones are for some unknown reason blocked by brickwork, which is reputed to be the finest in Pagan. It is the biggest building of its kind in Burma, and attached to it are two inscriptions dated respectively 1205 and 1253 AD. King Narathu, incidentally, was also known as the 'Kalagyamin' or the 'King killed by the Kalas', and while the construction of this temple was in progress, Narathu was assassinated by some Kalas, who were probably natives of Chittagong, and the temple itself was never completed.

**Kubyaukkyi Temple**: located at Myinkaba and built in 1113 by Rajakumar, son of Kyansittha, this temple consists of a square basement surmounted by a *sikhara* with curvilinear roofs resting on terraces. The interior has a sanctum around which runs a vaulted corridor adorned with niches enshrining stone Buddha images. The architecture of this temple is typically Mon, and some of the paintings in the sanctum are among the earliest still in existence in Pagan.

**Manuha Temple**: built by Manuha, the captive king of Thaton, in 1059, this square structure contains three seated Buddha images and a vast reclining image representing the Buddha in the act of entering nirvana. The central roof collapsed during the earthquake, in the process badly damaging the largest, seated Buddha, though it has subsequently been repaired.

**Nanpaya Temple**: close to the Manuha, this temple served as the residence of the captive Mon king, Manuha. It is built of brick and mud mortar, surfaced with stone, and is square in plan with a porch projecting on the east face. Flanking the sanctuary in the main building are four stone pillars on the sides of each of which are carved triangular floral designs and the figures of the Brahma holding lotus flowers in each hand. Like other earlier temples at Pagan, the Nanpaya has perforated stone windows to admit light into the building. The arch pediments over the windows and the carvings of the frieze are fine examples of architectural motifs in stone.

**Abeyadana Temple**: this temple faces north and consists of a square basement surmounted by a stupa with a pronounced relic-chamber and a tall spire; the porch on the north has three entrances. The basement is ornamented with perforated stone windows, and there is a vaulted corridor running round the central block. In the latter there is a deep recess forming a sanctum on the north, and in it is enshrined a large brick image of a seated Buddha. The most interesting aspect of the Abeyadana are the paintings with which the inner faces of its walls are decorated. They represent the Brahmanical gods and divinities of the Mahayana pantheon. Scenes from the Jataka with Mon legends cover the walls of the front hall. The temple was built by King Kyansittha on the spot where his wife Abeyadana waited as he sought refuge during one of his flights from the wrath of Sawlu.

**Somingyi Monastery**: this is one of the typical monasteries of the Pagan period built in 1218 AD and is situated south of the Thiripyitsaya Hotel. It consists of a brick-enclosed platform surrounded by a lobby on the east, a chapel on the west and small cells on the north and south, all of which are connected by narrow passages. The chapel is a small square two-storeyed building with a single door opening on the east, connecting it with the central platform by a passage. In the lower chamber of the chapel, on a brick pedestal, the remains of an image were found placed against the west wall.

**Nandamannya Temple**: located at Minnanthu, east of the Sulamani, this temple has a small vaulted chamber with only one entrance on the east. The interior walls are decorated with fine frescoes. Inside there is a seated image of the Buddha in a state of disrepair. The temple dates from the mid 13th Century.

**Thambula Temple**: just south of the Nandamannya, this temple was built in 1255 by Thambula (Sumlula), wife of King Uzana. It is a square building with a circumambulatory corridor running round the central square pile sustaining the *sikhara* above. It is adorned with frescoes and mural writings. Thambula is a misreading of Sumlula, 'The Moon of The Three Worlds', which is the briefest Burmese rendering of the Pali 'Tilokacandadevi'.

**Lemyethna Temple**: southwest of the Thambula and built in 1222 by minister Anantathura, this badly neglected temple rests on a high platform and faces east. The interior walls are decorated with frescoes and the exterior is all painted white. It is topped by an Indian-style spire, similar to the Ananda.

**Payathonzu Temple**: in between the Thambula and Lemyethna Temples lies the Payathonzu, consisting of three distinct small square temples with vaulted corridors and porticoes, joined together by two vaulted narrow passages leading from the one into the other. There is a pedestal in each sanctum, but the images have disappeared and their exact nature is not known. The walls of the corridors and the vaults are covered with beautifully painted and well preserved frescoes. The half-decorated middle sanctum and the plain walls of the western temple indicate that the work was abandoned before completion. The date of the foundation of the temple is not known, but it can safely be attributed to the late 13th Century.

**Dhammayazika Pagoda**: located at Pwasaw and built by Narapatisithu in 1196, this is a solid circular pagoda similar in style to the Shwezigon but its design is elaborate and unusual. The three lower terraces, which are adorned with terracotta tablets illustrating the Jatakas, are pentagonal, and at the base of each side there is a small temple with a square basement enshrining a Buddha image. They are all built on a raised platform enclosed within a wall, and there is an outer circuit wall which is pierced with five gateways. There are some ink inscriptions on the interior walls of the projecting porches.

If you have had enough of temples, stroll down from the Irra Inn (Ayeyar Hotel) to the riverbank and ask for Winswe who owns a boat on the Irrawaddy and whose family runs a restaurant ('Toe Toe': where a Burmese meal costs just K70 per person) and the ubiquitous lacquerware store. Take a trip on the river; barter for the price in kyat or dollars: it should cost around K450 or US$5 (or

perhaps a couple of T-shirts). The boat passes children frolicking in
the Irrawaddy as their mothers do the daily washing. First you'll
come across the Nataunt Monastery, which has nine novice monks,
two *phongyis* and some interesting woodcarvings and frescoes
dating from the 11th Century AD, some of the earliest mural
paintings in existence in Pagan. Then there's the Myazigon, a small
white stupa and monastery. Eventually the Shwezigon appears: this
time, of course, from a different angle. You can moor the boat here
and wander up to the pagoda, but don't forget to leave your shoes
at the bottom. Finally ask Winswe to cross over to Zaylan Island,
where the fishermen work at night for four months each year,
retreating to the centre of the island when the river rises. Selling their
catch at Nyaung-U Market, the 11 fishermen earn K400 a day in total
between them. They'll greet you with typical Burmese hospitality, so
bring along some cigarettes as a gift. This river journey, just like the
one to Mingun, offers a rare glimpse into a world that few tourists
are privileged to experience.

*The pagoda-studded plains of Pagan.*

# ARCHAEOLOGICAL MUSEUM

Opened in October 1979 at a cost of K1.4 million, this rather dull museum features a rectangular open hall housing inscriptions and stone sculptures, and an octagonal structure with a spire-like skylight exhibiting smaller antiquities. Of no great interest, it serves as a fair introduction to the history of Pagan. Independent travellers must come here to pay their US$10 Pagan entrance fee, plus an additional US$4 to visit the museum alone. Open daily (except Mondays and public holidays) from 9.30am to 3pm, though, as with all things Burmese, these times are flexible.

# MOUNT POPA

'Even from afar, Mount Popa casts its spell on travellers ... Like all marvels of nature, Popa fulfils the need of the people, spiritual as well as intellectual. If the great mountain's overwhelming majesty awakens the lyrical in the heart, its baffling mystery challenges the mind to explore it.'

Khin Myo Chit.

Between 50 and 60km southeast of Pagan rises the sugar-loaf Mount Popa ('Popa' is Sanskrit for flower) 4,981 ft high, like a massive, misplaced pillar. It was created from a violent volcanic eruption way back in 442 BC to become the dwelling place of the gods. For 700 years from the 4th to 11th Centuries, every king had to make a pilgrimage here to consult the spirits before his reign could begin. Even today, Mount Popa is considered the earthly font of power for the mystical world of the *nats*. A shrine to the Mahagiri *nats* (the blacksmith Nga Tin De and his sister Shwemyethana, 'Handsome and Golden Face', guards of Pagan's Sarabha Gateway) stands half way up the steep path to the summit, which itself is covered with pagodas and other religious structures. According to legend, they perished in flames as a result of evil designs of the local king. Henceforth the 4th Century king of Pagan Thinlikyaung made Mount Popa the official home of the brother and sister spirits with the intention of providing a national centre for *nat* worship.

As Maung Htin Aung describes so evocatively in his book *Folk Elements in Burmese Buddhism*:

'It was near the time of the full moon, and according to the English calendar it was December. The fields had been reaped, the harvest had been successfully gathered, and the people were in festive mood. The images of the two *Nats* were put on golden palanquins and attended by the king himself, they were carried along the road to Mount Popa. Red was the colour associated with *Nat* spirits and red flags and red streamers were carried by the people taking part in the procession and by the people who lived along the route. Everyone danced and sang, and when the procession halted at villages on the way, food and toddy-wine flowed free. The procession reached the summit of Mount Popa on the full moon day and a golden *Nat* shrine, newly constructed, awaited the two images. The images were set up in the shrine with great pomp and ceremony, and the king proclaimed that the village on the slope of the hill, Popa Ywa, was given as a perpetual fief to the two *Nat* spirits. As spirit mediums danced in abandoned joy, hundreds of white oxen, white horses, and white goats were sacrificed to the *Nat* spirits.

It was the ninth month of the Burmese year, and it seemed so propitious that the month associated with the magic number nine should now be associated with the two *Nats*. Both were now given by the king the title of 'Lords of the Great Mountain'. The brother was given the title in a Burmese-Pali form, 'Min Maha-Giri'. (*Min* in Burmese means 'Lord', and *Maha-Giri* in Pali means 'Great Mountain'.) The sister was given a title in its pure Burmese form, 'Taunggyi-Shin', *Taunggyi* meaning 'Great Mountain' and *Shin* meaning 'Lord'. However, the sister continued to be affectionately called 'Shwe-Myetnha', 'Golden Face'. The king further ordered that the month be renamed 'Nat-Taw', or 'the month of the Royal *Nats*', and fixed the full moon day in this month as the date of the annual festival in honour of the Popa *Nats*. The name of the eighth month of the Burmese year, Tazaung-mon, means 'the month of the Festival of Lights', and before the advent of the Lords of the Great Mountain the full moon day of this month was the occasion for the offering of lights to the gods of the planets in particular and to all gods in general. But the king now ordained that the festival of lights was to be held one month later, in the month of Nat-Taw.'

During the month of *Nayon* (May to June), Mount Popa is busy with pilgrims celebrating the annual 'Festival of Spirits'.

It is an quite an arduous climb, particularly as all the way up you are pestered by hordes of rabid-looking monkeys. When you eventually reach the top, it is rather disappointing: there are no interesting pagodas and the view does not match up to that from any of the temples of Pagan.

Chapter Eight

# Prome and Shwedaung

## HISTORY, WHAT TO SEE

Located by the steep banks of the Irrawaddy, some 5½ hours (161 miles) northwest of Rangoon, lies the city of Prome, known to the Burmese as Pyay. Prome is actually two towns, both situated on the east bank of the river, where the Nawin stream flows into the Irrawaddy: the other one being the historic city of Sri Ksetra, about 6km away ('Sri Ksetra' is its classical Sanskrit name; the Burmese pronounce it 'Thaye-khit-taya'). In reality the whole area is known as either Prome (to the British) or Pyay (to the locals). The actual name Sri Ksetra is found only in ancient texts and used purely by students of history and archaeology.

Legend has it (and even by Burmese standards it is quite a far-fetched tale) that the Buddha came to the area for the benefit of all creatures and stayed on a mountain to the northeast of Prome. He saw a lump of cow-dung floating in the sea. At that moment a snake came out of a clump of bamboo and moved up close to the Buddha's feet, behaving in a very reverent way. When the Buddha smiled, his disciple Ananda asked why. Buddha then prophesied that in later times five miracles would occur in that place: the earth would tremble; the sea would recede, leaving dry land; the mountain on which the Buddha sat would collapse, leaving a swamp; a river would appear; and a new range of mountains would arise. After these five miracles occurred, this snake would be reincarnated, named Duttabaung. One hundred and one years after Buddha had entered nirvana, this king would establish Sri Ksetra as his royal capital at the spot where the cow-dung was floating. He would be a patron of Buddhism, causing it to spread and flourish in this land. According to popular history, all five miracles did occur, just as the Lord Buddha had foretold. However, they all occurred as a result of the eruption of Mount Popa, thousands of years *prior* to the Buddhist era.

There is no record of the founding of Prome on the banks of the Irrawaddy. After Pagan became the capital, a number of people were probably sent back down the river to re-establish the former city of Sri Ksetra. But by that time the river had shifted its course considerably leaving the original site on higher ground far inland. Prome was thus built on the riverbank near the hill of the Shwesandaw Pagoda, positioned right between the rich lands of the Delta in the south and the dry zone (of peanuts, cotton, tobacco, sesame seeds and toddy palms) in the north. Prome came under British rule in 1852 after the second Anglo-Burmese War, but was completely destroyed by a terrible fire ten years later. Completely rebuilt, Prome today is euphemistically referred to as a 'thriving trading post', famous for its custard-apples.

Unlike the road from Rangoon to Meiktila, the stretch from the capital to Prome is generally good and flat. However the town itself has distinctly limited accommodation: to be precise, just one hotel, the Pyay (on Strand Road, Tel 21890), where the rooms, though sizeable and with air-conditioning and fridge, have no washing facilities. There are only communal showers, ant-infested wash-basins and disgusting toilets. Rates vary from US$24-36, though at least you can pay for meals in local currency. The drawbacks of Prome are that nobody speaks English and it gets stifling in the hot season. Just round the corner from the Pyay Hotel is the inappropriately-named San Francisco Chinese Restaurant (No 775 Strand Road), which is filthy but serves adequate fare (and warm Singha Beer).

Around **Hmawsa** (five miles south of Prome, where there is an archaeological museum) stands a trio of unusually-shaped ancient pagodas: the Bawbawgyi, Payagyi and Payama. Tradition ascribes them to the 5th Century BC, but judging by their architecture, their construction could not have been earlier than the 5th or 6th Centuries AD when Chinese, Cambodian, Talaing and South Indian influences were blended at Prome. The **Bawbawgyi** is a solid brick structure over 150 feet high. It rests on five terraces and is cylindrical in shape with a slight indentation in the middle. Both the **Payagyi** and **Payama Pagodas**, which are more conical in shape, were said to have been erected by King Duttabaung in 443 BC.

Two other pagodas of interest are the Lemyethna and Bebegyi. The **Lemyethna**, a low brick construction, allegedly dates from the 9th Century AD and consists of a vaulted corridor running around a central pillar in a style similar to certain pagodas in Pagan. Against the central pillar are embedded four sculptured stones facing the cardinal points. The figures on the eastern and northern faces have been destroyed; but of those on the remaining sides, one is still in a fair state of preservation, while the other has broken away near the top. The strange aspect about the Buddhas on the southern and western faces is that the right hand, instead of resting on the lap or pointing towards the earth, is outstretched.

The **Bebegyi** is a brick construction, surmounted by a *sikhara* with a single entrance facing the east. It is decorated with plaster carvings. The interior is covered with a vaulted roof, and in the wall facing the entrance a sculptured stone representing the Buddha in a sitting position is embedded, with the left foot not upon but below the right. He is flanked by two disciples in a prayer-like attitude wearing robes similar to those of Chinese or Tibetan monks, and having their legs drawn up like those of the Brahma in the Nanpaya in Pagan. At the foot of the stone is an inscription probably in Pyu script but barely legible. Judging by the inscription and its architecture, the Bebegyi can be assigned to the 10th Century AD.

Down a side road, where children will gawp at you in amazement, lies the **Kanbaung Nat Shrine**, which dates back about 60 years. Here stand 12 *nats*, though by far the most important are the brother and sister (ogre and ogress) Saw Bya Thakhingyi and Ma Saw Oo, who originally came from Arakan State. Each day locals offer food to the *nats*; they also must seek permission from the *nats* to take their photographs. If they don't ask, legend has it, then the photos will turn out blank.

Prome Town's crowning glory — and indeed one of the most sacred pagodas in the whole of Burma — is the stunning **Shwesandaw Pagoda**. To many Burmese Buddhists, the Shwesandaw ('The Sacred Hair Relic Shrine') is the third most revered pagoda in the land, after the Shwedagon in Rangoon and the Shwemawdaw in Pegu. Said to have been erected in the 6th Century BC by two brothers, Ajjika and Bhallika, it contains four hairs of the Buddha and one tooth. There are two large lion statues in front of the entrance to the staircase that leads up the hill (though, for a fee of K3, you can take a lift) and the entry gate is a spired pavilion. The staircase itself is an enclosed corridor, roofed over, with spired pavilions interspersed along the way with stalls on both sides. There is an ambulatory terrace on the level just one tier below the terrace of the momument. The Shwesandaw is four feet taller than the Shwedagon and in shape differs both from Rangoon's masterpiece and the Shwemawdaw. In fact the lower part (from the ambulatory terrace up to the bell) resembles the Shwezigon in Pagan, that's to say a typical Burmese stupa. There are assembly halls for paying reverence on the terrace around the monument, and looking out from the compound itself are stunning views of the Irrawaddy and the surrounding areas. There is a charge of K25 to take photographs (for some reason no 'professional photography' is permitted).

From the Shwesandaw one sight stands out above all others, and that is the 219 feet tall Buddha image in pink robes poking through the **Sehtatgyi** (ten-storey) **Pagoda**. It is one of the tallest statues of Buddha in Burma, having been originally constructed in 1919, and is too large to have a roof on it. Legend, in fact, relates that every time a roof is built to house the image, the wind blows it off.

About 15 minutes drive from Prome lies the town of **Shwedaung** (pronounced 'Shway-dao'), home of two outstanding pagodas as well as a major Chinese-built textile mill and an oil exploration base. There is one hotel in town, the Shwedaung, though very few tourists have ever been known to stay overnight.

The most famous (and indeed most fascinating) pagoda is the **Shwemyethman** or 'Golden Spectacle' **Pagoda**, which houses the only image in the world of the Buddha wearing glasses (see the back cover of this book). In years gone by, the local people removed the spectacles but various disasters ensued and so now they do not dare take them off. The spectacles that the Buddha wears now are actually the third pair: the first were stolen, the frames of the second were enshrined in the body of the statue, and the present ones were offered by a British general during the colonial rule. The pagoda was built by King Duttabaung of Sri Ksetra, but in the intervening years was covered by vegetation and subsequently discovered by the commissioner of Shwedaung, Zeyanandameik, on clearing the site.

Some 12 minutes down a side road stands the **Shwenattaung** or 'Golden Spirit Mountain' **Pagoda**. The Buddha himself visited this spot in BE (Buddhist Era) 104 (one year after attaining Enlightenment) and prophesied that there would be a venerated pagoda constructed here. In those days the place was called Pyitsandirit. Legend has it that the pagoda was built portion by portion by humans and *nats* (indeed there is a *nat* shrine in the precincts of the pagoda). Prince Thuratapa, son of King Paukkan, was responsible for part of its construction in the Buddhist year 283 (over 2,000 years ago). The pagoda was originally 16½ feet high, and during the reign of King Thihathu of Pagan it was raised to 33 feet. Later King Kyanyit raised it to 44 feet. Then King Duttabaung raised it to approximately 90 feet. Thanks to donations the height went up to 115½ feet. During the Buddhist year 1220 (1858) a severe earthquake shook the area and the umbrella (*hti*) fell to the ground. After the *hti* had tumbled down, the pagoda was renovated by means of further donations to its present height of 122 feet.

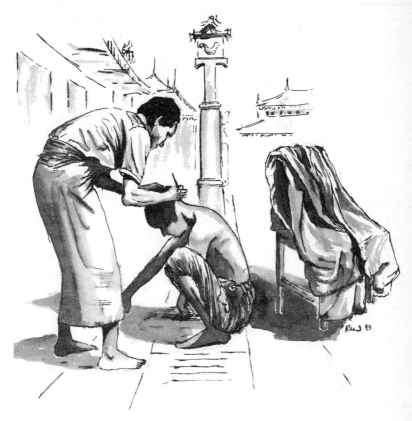

*Head-shaving of a Buddhist monk at Prome's Shwesandaw Pagoda.*

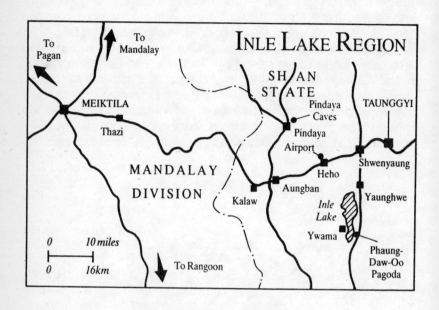

*Leg-rower of Inle Lake with his unique conical net-cage.*

Chapter Nine

# Inle Lake Region

## GETTING THERE, GENERAL DESCRIPTION

The Inle (pronounced 'In-lay') Lake region consists of the lake itself
with its floating market, gardens, villages and celebrated 'leg-rowers',
Taunggyi (the capital of Shan State, pronounced 'Towndjee'), Heho
(the airport), the hill-station of Kalaw and Pindaya (with its famous
caves). En route from Pagan you pass through the towns of Meiktila
and Thazi, the latter serving as the railway junction for trains to
Rangoon and Mandalay.

Whilst it is possible to fly to Heho Airport from Mandalay
(approximately 30 minutes, for which MTT charges US$33) or
Rangoon (roughly 1 hour 25 minutes at US$71), you're better off
relying on ground transportation. The journey from Pagan to Meiktila
takes about three hours. You may well stop off for lunch at a village
called Yinmapin in Shan State which has a Chinese restaurant called
Shan Lay. From Yinmapin it's another two hours to Kalaw, a scenic
route which at the same time is reminiscent of both the Swiss Alps
and West Sumatra. In fact you're in the Shan Hills and as you climb,
passing cotton plantations, the road twists and turns past houses
resembling those of the northern Thai hilltribes. If you're lucky you
may even catch the odd glimpse of an elephant splashing about in
the Shan River.

# KALAW AND THE HILLTRIBES

Nestling in the heart of the pine-studded Shan Hills at 4,319 feet (about 1,300 metres) above sea level is Kalaw, another former British hill-resort littered with colonial-style houses. Meaning 'pan' because of the shape of its location in the mountains, Kalaw has a population of around 25,000 and is surrounded by craggy slopes, numerous hilltribes and a large military base.

Kalaw boasts just one hotel for tourists — but what a hotel! For the Kalaw Hotel, a sprawling colonial-style Tudor mansion, is wholly out of character with a country in Southeast Asia. But here it has stood since about 1915 (originally it was a rest-house solely for the British) with vast chambers, grubby bathrooms with sporadic hot water which flood regularly and the inevitable leaking ceilings. Room rates vary from US$30-57, though locals only pay K230. The receptionist is a remarkable Burmese gentleman who goes under the name of Mr Anthony Andrews, yet hails originally from Madras. A charming and fascinating man with many a tale to tell, he has, as do many elderly Burmese, a highly idiosyncratic command of the English language.

Kalaw is a cool peaceful town with a fascinating market where the various hilltribes come to buy and sell their goods: vegetables, fruits, flowers, and even skewered eels are amongst the many items on offer. In the area there are five main tribes (not including the Intha who are based in and around Inle Lake), these are:

**Pa-O**: the women wear black dresses and turbans, the men a black jacket and trousers. The most fascinating Pa-O village in the vicinity is Kyauksaungmycha, about 10 miles southeast of Kalaw. The Pa-O are Buddhists of Karen stock and speak a Tibeto-Burman language.

**Palaung**: they are noted for their colourful hats which they weave themselves and which vary according to their marital status. Married women wear a hat with white beads, a purple or blue jacket with red facing and a collection of thin lacquer bands around the waist. Single women, though, wear a fenced woollen cap and a thick red-striped *longyi* with an embroidered green jacket. At work however the velvet jacket is replaced by an embroidered cotton one and the hat by a band around the forehead to support the load of the basket carried on the back. About six miles northeast of Kalaw lies the Palaung village of Tawyaw with a population of around 150-200. The Palaung are Buddhist and speak a Mon-Khmer language.

**Danu**: they dress like the Burmese, though they speak a different dialect. One mile from the Kalaw Hotel lie two Danu villages: Pinmagone and Ohnbin. The Danu are Buddhist.

**Taungyo**: the women wear black skirts and brass rings on their legs and the men wear black jacket and trousers similar to the Pa-O. There are Taungyo villages around Kalaw and near Heho. They are mainly farming peoples of Tibeto-Burmese stock.

**Padaung**: this is the famous tribe of the 'giraffe-necked' women who wear up to 28 brass rings on their neck and rings on their arms and legs. The rings were originally worn to stave off would-be kidnappers (others say to protect them from tiger bites) which to Westerners may seem rather bizarre. The men dress in similar fashion to the Pa-O. The most interesting villages are located in the Loikaw area of Kayah State about 96 miles (155km) southeast of Kalaw. The Padaung are also of Mon-Khmer stock.

Visits to all the above tribes can be arranged either via your guide or through the Kalaw Hotel's charming and helpful staff.

For a great view of Kalaw and the surrounding areas go up to the **Theindaung**, a Buddhist monastery located on the hill near the market. The best restaurant in town is the Dragon (Naga) Restaurant, a Chinese eatery on the main road near the petrol station. It is infinitely preferable to the Kalaw Hotel, whose dining room is positively grim and cuisine even grimmer.

# PINDAYA

The journey from Kalaw to Pindaya takes about 1¼ hours (though it's only 28 miles, 45km). If at all possible ask the driver to stop off at the village of Pwehla en route. Around 2,000 hilltribe peoples live here, Pa-O and Danu, and there is also a primary school with 95 children and four teachers. They're sure to give you a warm welcome in their very best broken English.

Pindaya itself is home to around 20,000 inhabitants and is essentially a farming community producing tea, cabbages, ginger, yams, potatoes, avocados, pineapples and oranges. The main hilltribe in the area are the Danu. The locals are absolutely charming, some of the most hospitable you will encounter on your travels throughout Burma. Pindaya lies beside a beautiful lake **Nattamiekan** (meaning 'Angels' Lake') and is surrounded by a range of mountains called the Menetaung. It is very relaxing simply to sit beside the lake and watch the locals fishing, washing and playing in the water: quite idyllic. Transport is by horse-cart.

Tourists are accommodated in the Pindaya Hotel where as ever the notice proclaims 'Foreigners shall have to settle all bills in foreign currency.' Room rates vary from US$25-40 (plus 20% tax), though locals pay between K150-240 (plus tax). It's not a bad place; the showers have hot water, the rooms, alas, only sporadic electricity (so make sure you've got a torch handy).

There is one decent restaurant in town, a Chinese place called Kyintlight.

Tourists essentially visit Pindaya for its celebrated caves (**Shweumin** or 'Golden Cave'), formed 200,000 million years ago, though both the spontaneous charm of the people and the scenic location have enormous appeal. The caves themselves are stocked full of Buddha images (apparently 8,094 in total) many covered in gold leaf and carved by the locals at the end of the 17th Century in a variety of styles. There are also numerous stalactites and stalagmites. The stupa inside the cave was built by King Alaungsithu in the 12th Century (again a torch is necessary). Every March a festival, *Tabaungpwe*, is held and there are shows and parties throughout the area. Two other places of interest in the vicinity are the **Shwe Ohn Hmin Pagoda** and the **Padah Lin Caves**, where archaeologists have been excavating a neolithic site.

NB: There is a charge of US$3 for tourists who visit the Pindaya Caves.

# INLE LAKE

The drive from Pindaya to the jetty at Inle Lake takes remarkably long, bearing in mind the actual distance covered: on the map it doesn't look very far at all. The approximate journey time is 2½ hours as you travel through Aungban, Heho (past the airport), the junction town of Shwenyaung, finally arriving at Yaunghwe. Still, it's a scenic mountainous route past the water buffalo, some working, some grazing and some being ridden by kids, horse-carts, ducks, lotus flowers in waterpools, farmers at work in the rice-fields — and always a multitude of curious, smiling faces. Some tourists have managed to stay at Yaunghwe's Inle Inn and Guest House where room rates are as little as K50 (if they allow you to settle up in local currency), but there's no particular reason to spend the night here.

Inle Lake actually has two meanings: 'little lake' and 'four lake' (because there are four big villages on the lake, though 200 in all on and around the lake). It is 70 miles from one end to the other (which lies in Kayah State) and 30½ miles from Yaunghwe to the famous Phaung-Daw-Oo Pagoda. The lake reaches a depth of five metres though this obviously diminishes during the dry season. The 'people of the lake' are the Intha of which there are approximately 70,000, hailing originally from the Tavoy region of Tenasserim. They began migrating to the lake area as early as the 14th Century completing their resettlement during the 18th Century. To survive, they became fishermen and developed their unique style of leg-rowing and catching fish in conical traps. Their wives planted floating gardens and grew all manner of crops: tomatoes, aubergines, chillies, beans, maize, potatoes, limes, bananas, oranges and flowers, which they sold at the market. And since the land fronting the lake belonged to the Shans, they were forced to build their homes and villages on the water itself. Thus sprung up Ywama village where the floating market is held once every five days and Thala a weaving centre of fine cloth.

If you are on one of MTT's programmes (or that of another agency), your ride on Inle Lake will be included in the price. This is just as well, considering that if you managed to travel by yourself and intended hiring a boat on your own, you would have to pay an exorbitant US$110 for the day (if you were allowed to pay in kyat it would only cost K660 or just under US$7 at the black market rate). An 'entrance fee' of US$5 (payable *only* in dollars) is also demanded.

Departing from the jetty (where there is a shabby restaurant serving fried noodles, fried rice or ghastly fishballs for K42 and where the office of MTT is also located), you pass through a narrow canal before coming out onto the lake proper. Inle Lake elicits mixed responses: some find it stunningly beautiful, others, particularly those who have visited West Sumatra, may feel that it doesn't really compare with Lake Maninjau for example. Still the leg-rowers and floating gardens are unique, though make sure you arrive on the day when the floating market takes place, otherwise the trip isn't half as interesting.

Eventually you reach the **Phaung-Daw-Oo Pagoda** where the famous boat festival is held each October. Built at the beginning of the 18th Century, but renovated and repainted every year to make it look new, the Phaung-Daw-Oo houses five extraordinary Buddha images. These are scarcely recognisable as they have been disfigured by layers of gold leaf which men stick on both for good luck and as an act of piety (women aren't permitted to do so; the Burmese don't consider women sufficiently holy). All in all, the pagoda is quite incongruous, almost perched on the lake, with its television set keenly watched by an intrigued group of Burmese monks and children. The television was a gift from the SLORC to appease the monks and get them to listen to their propaganda.

As you near the villages and the pagoda, be prepared to be pestered by touts and vendors offering Buddha images, opium weights, bananas and lotus flowers. At the hand weaving-centre you can purchase Shan shoulder-bags, cloth and *longyi* but they're all grossly overpriced. There is a hotel by the lake (Inle Hotel, Khaung Daing), but rooms must be booked in advance and since it doesn't have a telephone, it's not easy to make a reservation. There is also the Golden Express Hotel, Tel. 37. The Inle Hotel charges between US$20-30, the Golden Express at No 19 Foungtawpyan Road, US$30-55.

# TAUNGGYI, HEHO, THAZI

Taunggyi (meaning 'Great Mountain') is one of the very few disappointing towns in Burma. As the Shan capital it's a much more affluent (and thus more westernised) place and the people scoot about on brand-new motorbikes and wear jeans not *longyi*. Affluence has come from smuggling, black market trading and opium trafficking and as its centre Taunggyi is markedly wealthier and exhibits more of a Thai influence than either Kalaw or Pindaya. Consequently the locals are far less friendly: in fact they'll barely give foreigners a second glance. They're more concerned with seeing what's on at the cinema and, of course, making money. Taunggyi itself is not dissimilar to many a northern or northeastern Thai town (Chiang Mai excluded): long, drab and characterless. It has no charm, few smiles and even fewer sights.

Another former British hill station, **Taunggyi** is about an hour's drive from Inle Lake and situated at 4,690 feet (1,430 metres) above sea level. The region (consisting mainly of 'traders', a frequently-expressed Burmese euphemism) is home to roughly 150,000 people and is famed as the main cheroot-growing area in the land.

Tourists invariably stay at the Taunggyi Hotel (Tel 21127), which is located a long way from the town centre (but that's not such a disadvantage). It's a large, rambling, smelly place boasting some of the most decrepit bathrooms in Southeast Asia. There is occasional hot water though you may find that the hot water taps don't actually function (sneakily the knobs have been removed). Room rates vary from US$36 up to US$60 (or for locals K210-300). A new hotel called Taung Paw is scheduled to be built by 1993 and is expected to accommodate foreigners: it will be located near Paya Phyu village three miles from Taunggyi in the mountains. In the meantime, other guest houses will most probably surface.

In Taunggyi itself there is little to do, just the Shan State Museum (open 9am-4pm Monday to Friday) which is of no particular interest, General Aung San Park and the inevitable market, with very much a northern Thai flavour to it. You soon notice the difference between Taunggyi and, say, Mandalay for here there is an abundance of quality goods, fruit, vegetables, fish, meat. At times you'd hardly believe you were in one of the most destitute countries in the world. At the daily market there is always a fascinating array of hilltribe costumes, and indeed of most interest in the vicinity are the various hilltribes: for example the Pa-O, who live in Paya Phyu and Pantin, two miles out of Taunggyi.

In the southwestern part of Taunggyi stands the **Yat Taw Mu Pagoda** which features a large standing Buddha. There is also a new pagoda 3km south of town built in 1985 called the **Sutaungpyi**, which means 'Wish Fulfilling' or 'Lucky Hill' Pagoda. As the name implies, Buddhists from all round come here to make a wish (though the wish should remain a secret, many Burmese have confessed to me that their sole desire is to win the state lottery!). There are several Buddha images in this pagoda, including one of the Buddha in the position of entering nirvana: feet on top of each other, left hand on the side and right hand by the head. From the Sutaungpyi, which is also in the southwestern part of Taunggyi, you have a marvellous view of the surrounding area.

A kilometre further out lie the **Montawa Caves**, which were formed by an underground river. The entrance to the Caves contains numerous Buddha images and inscriptions. If you fancy exploring them, bring a torch.

If you are interested in cheroots, there is the **Ma-Oak** cheroot factory northeast of the market where you can watch Burmese girls slaving away. Each girl earns K4 for a roll of 100 cigars (which takes roughly 45 minutes to produce); if they're lucky they'll manage 1,000 cheroots a day — a whopping K40. The girls (45 of them) work from 8am to 4pm; to earn enough money to feed themselves and their families, many of the girls are obliged to take cheroots away to roll at home. Tobacco is shredded with tamarind juice and some nuts and left to dry for two days before wrapping the cheroot. A filter is made from the dried outer skin of the maize cob.

Finally, there are a number of decent restaurants in town (ignoring the phenomenally expensive Coca-Cola Restaurant). There's Maxim's, a Chinese place that's smart and clean and will cost around K230 for two, the Lyan You Restaurant (K90 for two) and the Maw December Chinese Restaurant. Nearby there's supposed to be an excellent Indian restaurant called Parbathie, but it looked very much closed when I last wandered by.

# HEHO

Tourists can't stay at Heho (an hour's drive from Taunggyi), but they can fly there (according to one of Myanma Airways' latest 'schedules' there is a daily flight, except for Friday, departing Rangoon at 0715 and arriving at either 0840, 0910, or 1035, depending on whether it stops off en route. But check with UB in Rangoon first). Heho is the domestic airport for the Inle Lake region, though of much greater interest is the market held every five days. This is a rotating market and each day it moves from town to town: so make sure you see it at either Heho, Taunggyi, Kalaw, Ywama (the floating market on Inle Lake) or Yaunghwe (and sometimes even at Shwenyaung). The market is vast, offering all kinds of fruit and vegetables; they even sell cattle (one buffalo apparently goes for no less than K15,000: what average Burmese citizen on a daily salary of about K40 can *possibly* afford that? This is where the black market or so-called 'informal trade' really come into play). All the hilltribes are here in their myriad of costumes: Pa-O in black and dark blue with orange trim and with what appear to be brightly-coloured tea towels on their heads, Taungyo women with red-stained lips and teeth and clad in short black dresses sequinned with shells, Danu and Shan in khaki and brown, and Intha men (the 'people of the lake') in plaid sarongs and Intha women in bright flower prints. As Mi Mi Khaing observes in her book entitled *The World of Burmese Women*:

'The five-day bazaar system is an ancient institution in these northern parts of Burma. Marco Polo, travelling through these parts bordering on China and Burma in the 13th Century, remarked on a regular bazaar to which hill peoples from the surrounding higher regions walked down. The description holds true of bazaar meets in the Shan States of today ... All capitals held their bazaars on the same day, and other towns within a radius of about 25 miles held bazaars on days in between. Even in a cosmopolitan town like Taunggyi where there is a bazaar every day, Bazaar Day is noticeable. The swell on every 5th day, with country folk, fresh produce and 5-day-orientated town-wives makes its own hum.'

# THAZI

Assuming you're not flying back to Rangoon, you'll have to get to the railway junction at Thazi: 'get to' being the operative words. From Heho it's a helluva journey. It may not look very far on the map — indeed as the proverbial Burmese crow flies it's only about 50 miles (80km) — but alas Burmese buses or cars don't fly (nor very often do Myanma Airways' Fokkers). So it's an exhausting and bumpy 4 hours 20 minutes ride, with perhaps an hour's stop for lunch in Kalaw. And don't think the fun ends in Thazi's grim MTT railway station office, where you're rudely informed that 'THE TATMADAW SHALL NEVER BETRAY NATIONAL INTERESTS', because it doesn't. In fact, it's only just begun. You'll then have to wait for the Mandalay-Rangoon 'express' to stagger through, for by now you're ready to embark on your return to Rangoon: quite possibly 11 hours 9 minutes of sheer hell which only costs K154 (around £1 on the black market). If you have time, there's one interesting pagoda in Thazi: the heavily-gilded Zedihla which was built by King Narapati of Pagan in 1196 AD. Thazi's sole accommodation is the Moon Light Lodging House (US$5-$20), on the Meiktila-Taunggyi Road, No. 5 Quarter (Tel 56).

*Native of Bassein celebrating the Nigyawday Pagoda Festival.*

Chapter Ten

# Other destinations

## SHAN STATE

### Tachilek and Kengtung

For years, much to the frustration of *farangs* (foreigners), Thais (but not tourists) have been able to cross the border from Mae Sai to Tachilek (pronounced 'Tat-jee-lek). Likewise, Burmese, noticeable by their *longyi*, wander over the bridge to the 'Land of the Free' ('Thai' means 'free') to sell goods and to experience a brief taste of Southeast Asian-style democracy. Counterfeit gems (notably rubies) and hilltribe children clad in fake costumes, demanding a minimum ten baht to be photographed, abound in this dusty border town, whilst a sign proclaims 'THE CITY OF GOLDEN TRIANGLE'.

Since October 1 1992 for the cost of K400, or the equivalent in US dollars (Thai baht not acceptable), foreigners — issued with a one-day pass — can now sample life in Tachilek, where MTT has set up its first office. The border opens at 6am and closes at 5pm: and you must return before the post shuts.

A three-day visa to Kengtung ('Chiang Tung' in Burmese), in the depth of the Shan State and very much the heart of the 'Golden Triangle', 167km to the northwest of Tachilek, costs 400 baht at the Burmese Embassy in Bangkok or US$18 at the border. At present only group tours of at least ten (and not more than 50) can make the six/seven hour road journey to Kengtung owing to insufficient accommodation. MTT charges an excessive US$150 per person for a group of 15 and US$200 for a group of 20 or more. Rates at the Kyaing Tong Hotel are US$25-30.

Kengtung's major interest (excluding opium production) lies in the vast numbers of hilltribes: Hkum, Lem, Lur, Ekaws, Miaos, Muhsos or Lahus. The ruling tribe in this area is the Hkum who are similar to the western Shans except that their features are more Chinese. They are also fairer in complexion and slighter in build. They mainly inhabit the Kengtung Plain, while in the hill villages live the Kaws or Ekaws, who with the Lahus, form the majority of the tribes in this area. The Kaws and Lahus have a long history of hostility against the Thais (Siamese). The Kaws are also known for their destructive slash-and-burn (or swidden) form of cultivation. There are also some Was in the Kengtung area though they are principally based in the Wa States on the frontier between the Shan States and Yunnan, an extremely hilly district which is bordered on the west by the Salween River.

# Lashio

'There was a vista of blue wooded hills in the near distance and the first glimpse of Lashio in a wonderful setting of range upon range of hills, reaching away eastward into China.'

Ethel Mannin, 1954.

On October 12 1992 the SLORC officially opened up Lashio, the northern Shan administrative centre, but for some reason they remain extremely reluctant to grant tourists permission to visit it. Lashio is accessible by plane from Rangoon (UB 629 is scheduled to depart every Tuesday at 0715, arriving at 1050), by train from Mandalay or by MTT package tour from Ruili and Wantin in Yunnan Province via Muse (you can stay at the Muse Motel, US$25-40) and Kyukoke. Easily the most spectacular route is the train journey, which takes up to 14/15 hours going, and no less than 17 hours coming back. Trains normally leave Mandalay Station early in the morning, between 0530 and 0545. Tourists have to pay for the trip in dollars: a return costs US$23. The scenery en route is breathtaking, over the stunning Goteik Viaduct, through tropical forest, jungle, waterfalls, steep wooded hills and ravines, tunnels, jungle jasmine, past orange, mandarin and citrus groves and all the time with sharp-peaked mountains thrusting up in the distance. The train zigzags up to Maymyo (there are four famous 'zigzags', called *Ion-toe* in Burmese), then over the Goteik Viaduct, through the town of Kyaukme (famed for *lepet*, green tea and its Shan Festival in the springtime) and finally on to Lashio.

Lashio itself has numerous markets, hot springs (the most celebrated are 24 miles out of town) and caves. The hotel with the best location is the privately-run New Asia Hotel (near the markets); there is also the Parkview Guest House (under Chinese management) and the government-run Mao Shwe Li Guest House, which charges K100 for a single room, K500 for a suite.

# UPPER BURMA

## Meiktila

There's not a great deal to see in Meiktila, whose name, pronounced 'McTealah', makes it sound more like a town situated somewhere north of Inverness. Tourists tend to stop over at the Wun Zin Hotel, en route to Pagan (from Mandalay; or vice-versa). Complete with tennis court, the Wun Zin Hotel (Tel 21559) has air-conditioned rooms with a fridge but foul bathrooms and room rates which vary from US$20-30. You can, however, relax on your balcony overlooking the splendid man-made Meiktila Lake, the highlight of a trip to this town. Tourists are now permitted to stay at the higher-grade Meiktila Hotel on the Rangoon to Mandalay Road (Tel 21892), where prices range from US$30-40. The town itself boasts one truly outstanding Chinese restaurant called Seng Hein Restaurant. Transportation is by horse-cart. Bring a torch with you: there are nightly power failures (as indeed there are in all areas outside Rangoon).

Meiktila Lake was built in pre-Pagan times, most likely during Sri Ksetra's prominence in the 7th Century AD. It was fed by the Chaungma ('main stream'), which received its waters from numerous auxiliary streams originating in the range of hills southeast of Mount Popa. Two of these streams that run north and south at Meiktila were dammed to form the lake. An inscription of the 19th Century describes the lake:

'Four-sided ... its perimeter is 10,000 *tas* (15,800 feet); 300 streams and 250 streamlets flow into it. The area drained by these feeders is 3 *yuzanas* (40.5 square miles). The surface of the lake measures 10,000 *tas* on the Northern, Eastern, and Southern sides. The area irrigated by the lake is capable of being sown with 10,000 baskets of seed paddy. One thousand pairs of buffaloes were originally set apart to be used in connection with the lake. In the rainy season, the depth of the water is 18 cubits and 3 *maiks* (about 20 feet); and the surface of the lake measures 1,500 *tas* from east to west, and 1,300 from north to south.'

*Meiktila Settlement.*

Apart from the lake, Meiktila houses the Burmese Flight Training School which, judging by the safety record of Myanma Airways, isn't living up to its name. In the vicinity of the Wun Zin Hotel, there's also Meiktila Jail; tourists have more chance of getting in there than into the Burmese Flight Training School (the lesser of two evils, I suppose).

Meiktila is not especially renowned for its pagodas but there are four in the area worth a visit: the **Shwegu** and **Shwezigon** (both built in the 11th Century by Anawrahta), the **Shweyinhmyaw** and the **Yazamani**, which was constructed by King Thibaw in 1882. The last-named is probably of greatest interest since it is one of the last examples of a royal pagoda. Situated on the northern extremity of the south causeway of the lake is an inscription shed which shelters an inscription set up in 1856 by King Mindon to commemorate the repairing of the lake. The inscription states that the only repairs to the lake were carried out by King Aniruddha (Anawrahta) of Pagan.

# Toungoo

Roughly equidistant between Rangoon and Meiktila (and consequently a sensible place to overnight), Toungoo is being slowly touted by the SLORC as a tourist destination. In truth, Toungoo's past is far more interesting than its present: it's an ugly, dull town, bereft of restaurants (save for the Happy Chinese Restaurant with a distinctly unhappy loo) and with just one hotel, the Toungoo (Tel 21764, US$10-30). The town wallows in a glorious past (for a particularly fascinating account of Toungoo's history, I strongly recommend HRH Prince Damrong Rajanubhab of Thailand's narrative in *Journey through Burma in 1936*), and you can still see the city walls surrounded by the moat dating from the Toungoo Kingdom and the toddy palm grove where King Tabinshwehti (whose name, extraordinarily, translates as 'Premier Golden State Umbrella') is said to have enjoyed his relaxation.

Tabinshwehti became king at the tender age of 13 and is supposed to have keenly partaken in toddy-drinking and cockfighting. Unfortunately, the incompetent ruler met a painful and particularly humiliating end — he was assassinated whilst sitting on the toilet during a bout of dysentery.

Toungoo's most famous pagoda is the **Myazigon** which houses a portrait of the ancient monarchs, while just outside the town lies a Japanese World War II cemetery. Other pagodas of interest in the locality include the **Shwesandaw** (founded in 1597), **Shwedaung-U** (said to have been built almost 250 years ago by Maung Tha Zan, clerk to the Burmese governor) and the **Pawdawmu**, constructed many years ago by three Karens: Ka-la-be, Bu-naw-le and Na-mi-e.

# LOWER BURMA

## Moulmein and vicinity

'By the old Moulmein Pagoda, lookin' lazy at the sea, There's a Burma girl a-settin', and I know she thinks o'me ...'

*Mandalay*, Rudyard Kipling.

As your boat crosses the Salween River past the silver pagoda, Gaungsekyunpaya, on Gaungsekyun ('Shampoo Island'), you espy a golden stupa. It is Kyaik-than-lan, Kipling's Pagoda, the locals say, in Moulmein. You are not 'On the road to Mandalay', there are no 'flyin'-fishes' in sight, and if you're out of luck, barely even 'a Burma girl a-settin', just Moulmein, one of the most beautiful locations in all Burma.

Special permission is required to visit Moulmein (pronounced 'Moolmain'), capital of Mon State and the British administrative centre in the first half of the 19th Century, for it does not figure on MTT's list of approved places (owing to so-called 'security reasons'). But Moulmein, at the mouth of the Salween River, is a must: tranquility, charm, hospitality and pagodas. It can be reached by plane (UB 379 departs every Monday and Saturday at 0630 and arrives at 0905; UB 369 departs on a Wednesday at 0730 and arrives at 1005), but you're much better off going by car: it's a reasonable road and you'll reach the river crossing at Mottama in about six hours (punctures permitting). En route you can stop off for lunch at Kyaikto, which has a decent Chinese restaurant called Panyoma.

Once at Mottama, you are confronted with a typically Burmese problem: is there a ferry (known to the Burmese as a 'zed ferry') to transport you and your car over to Moulmein? Well, that all depends on what time you arrive in Mottama and on the depth of the river. If you're in luck, the car ferry will be ready and waiting, and the journey will take 40 minutes. If you decide to leave the car at Mottama and go by normal ferry, it'll take 30 minutes. If you wish to hire your own boat, the crossing will take just 20 minutes and cost you K120, but then your car, of course, will still be in Mottama.

Moulmein boasts the finest pomelos in Burma, and, more surprisingly, the finest hotel, the Mawlamyine on Strand Road (Tel 22560/21976). Recently renovated and enjoying a wonderful location by the water's edge with views of 'Shampoo Island', the Mawlamyine has air-conditioned rooms, TV, fridge and hot water. But these luxuries don't come cheap, even in a provincial hotel. A single room costs US$48, a double US$66 (locals pay K288 and K396, inclusive of taxes, respectively). But it's worth it just to watch the myriad boats plying the waters, to glimpse the stunning sunset, the curiously-named Gaungsekyun — or simply to chat with the ever-smiling children of Moulmein. There is also the Thanlwin Hotel on Lower Main Road, Bo Kone (Tel 21518, US$15-25).

Pomelos, pagodas, 'Shampoo Island' — and the best coffee shop in Burma: Ngwe Lwin Oo Coffee Shop on Roman Road, run by a delightful old Burmese gentleman called U Naing Hok Shein, where there's 'many a Burma girl a-settin'', but I don't think they were looking at me. The best (and only?) restaurants in town are the Peking and Padamya (both Chinese and directly opposite each other) and the Burmese Daw Pu. Transportation in Moulmein is by horse-cart, trishaw or Burmese 'tuk-tuk'. Once again, don't forget your torch: on average there is a power failure 20 days (or rather evenings) a month.

> 'In his visit to Burma in March 1889, Kipling put in briefly at Rangoon and Moulmein. He clearly drew on his memories of this visit when writing 'Mandalay'. In From Sea to Sea, Kipling's third letter describes Moulmein and tells how he fell 'deeply and irrevocably in love with a Burmese girl' on the steps of the pagoda.'
> Robert Hampson, editor of Kipling's autobiography Something of Myself.

Though no one can say for certain, Kipling's pagoda was in all probability the **Kyaik-than-lan**, and it is one of the most beautiful in the land. Originally constructed in 875 AD, it is similar in structure to the Shwedagon and offers stunning views of the river and the

*Chaungtha's beach pagoda, the Kyaukpahto.*

*'By the old Moulmein Pagoda ...' The Kyaik-than-lan, Kipling's pagoda in Moulmein.*

Kyaiktiyo, the Golden Rock Pagoda. The rock is balanced over a cliff, and to the Buddhists is not only a marvel of nature but also a manifestation of their ancestors' faith in the teaching of the Buddha.

*The Laykyunyanaung Pagoda in Bassein, formerly the wish-fulfilling Phaung Daw Oo. Renovated in the style of Pagan's Ananda Temple.*

The Htaukkyant War Cemetery, where 33,421 allied soldiers who gave their lives in the Second World War lie buried.

surrounding areas. There is a lift to take you up, and you can then climb to the very top. The name 'Kyaik-than-lan' is said to be a corruption of 'Kyaik-shan-lan', the shrine commemorating the defeat of the Shans or Siamese. The pagoda has twice been enlarged — once by Pon-nu-rat, king of Moulmein, and again in 1538 AD by Wareru, king of Martaban. When Tenessarim was ceded to the British after the first Anglo-Burmese War of 1824, the Kyaik-than-lan was in ruins and was repaired by U Taw Le, an Extra Assistant Commissioner, with funds collected by public substription. It measures 152 feet in height and 377 feet in circumference at the base.

Moulmein's other celebrated pagoda is the **Uzina**, a wish-fulfilling pagoda with a reclining Buddha, which was built in the 3rd Century BC over a hair of the Buddha. It was repaired about 100 years ago by Uzina of Moulmein. Located between these two pagodas is the **Aungthiekdi Stupa**, one-third gold, one-third silver and one-third white. From this stupa you have superb panoramic views.

About one hour 40 minutes south of Moulmein on the coast lies **Kyaikkami** (formerly Amherst and pronounced 'Jye-ke-mee'), where, for K45, you can enjoy a fine Burmese meal on the beach at Anawa Restaurant. Kyaikkami is best known for the **Yele-Paya** (the 'In-Water-Stupa'), where 11 hair relics along with 21 small Buddha images are enshrined. The pagoda, which juts out into the sea, was renovated at a cost of over 140 lakhs (one lakh equals 100,000 rupees) and is due to be renovated again later in the year. Legend has it that the pagoda came floating from the sea and was stranded on the present ridge of rocks. It derives its sanctity from the fact that, owing to cross undercurrents, the basement of the shrine is never touched by sea-water even at high flood. Women are not allowed inside the pagoda precinct.

Not far from Kyaikkami is the beach resort of **Setse**, which is completely unspoilt and only frequented by locals. You can stop off here for a while, enjoy the sun and sea and a vast coconut for a mere K15. Also located in the vicinity is the World War II cemetery of **Thanbyuzayat**, where countless Allied prisoners-of-war, who perished whilst constructing the railway to Thailand under the command of the Japanese, lie buried. The cemetery is located about one and a quarter hours south of Moulmein.

Two towns you shouldn't miss in this area are Mudon and Thaton. **Mudon** is on the way from Moulmein to Kyaikkami — it is 18 miles from Moulmein — and must be one of the most tranquil spots in all of Southeast Asia. Before reaching Mudon, you will notice the

Kyauktalone Mountain, with numerous pagodas perched on top, while the town of Mudon itself enjoys the most idyllic position beside two lakes: Kangyi and Kanlay. Sit by the lake, watch the children frolic in the crystal-clear waters and sample *buthigywa* (fried gourd dipped in chili sauce) and *pebinbauk* (fried beansprouts). The two celebrated pagodas in Mudon are the **Kangyi Paya** and the **Kangale Paya**, which were said to have been constructed in the lifetime of the Buddha.

Roughly halfway between Mottama and Kyaikto is **Thaton**, which like Toungoo is a town whose past is of far greater interest than its present (save for the stunning Shwezayan Pagoda). A former capital of the Mon Kingdom of Suvannabhumi under the rule of King Manuha, Thaton was captured in 1057 after a long siege by King Anawrahta, founder of the Pagan Dynasty, thereby enabling him to gain control of Lower Burma. Anawrahta brought the Mon king of Thaton, Manuha and some 30,000 captives back to Pagan and the city was completely destroyed:

'Since the downfall of Manuha, the ancient city — most ancient, it would seem, of all the cities of Burma — has never again held up its head ... Its life is in the past, and its glory has departed.'

Thaton's crowning glory today is the beautiful golden pagoda, the **Shwezayan** which is guarded by two colourful *chinthes*. Built in the 5th Century BC by King Thuriya-Candar Duttabaung, it enshrines four teeth of the Buddha. Situated nearby is the **Thagya-paya** or **Myatheindan**, which has a square base, resembling the Northern Indian style. Around the central and uppermost terraces are panels which were filled with plaques illustrating scenes from the Jataka Tales (stories of the Buddha's previous existences).

# Kyaiktiyo and vicinity

'Kyaiktiyo — the name spells magic, fantasy and spiritual exultation to the Burmese Buddhists, among whom the conversation often leads to the question: 'Have you been to Kyaiktiyo yet?'. It means: 'You haven't really lived until you've been there.' ... It is an overwhelming sight ... '

Khin Myo Chit.

Some may say that the most awe-inspiring sight in all Burma is the Shwedagon in Rangoon or the pagoda-studded plains of Pagan, but for me it is Kyaiktiyo (pronounced 'Jy-tea-owe'), the 'Golden Rock

Pagoda'. Suddenly, after trekking for three to four hours, as if from nowhere, appears a huge golden boulder, perched precariously on the hillside. At first, in case it rolled off, I was afraid to approach, but the closer I came, the more secure it seemed.

Like Moulmein, Kyaiktiyo does not figure on MTT's approved list, so special permission is required to make the ascent (which is certainly not possible during the rainy season and not recommended during the hot season). On arrival at the base camp of Kinpun, tourists must first register with the immigration authorities. You will then be assigned your own personal armed guard (they say for 'security reasons'). The guard is under strict instructions never to leave your side, unless, of course, you need to go to the toilet or to bed. No doubt, if you *are* sufficiently worried about your own security, he will be happy to accompany you to both the bidet and the boudoir.

It is an invigorating 7½ mile trek up to the top (I suggest you purchase a bamboo pole at the bottom to assist you) and, if you feel so inclined, there are porters to carry your bags (highly recommended!). The porters charge K8 per viss (one viss is 3.65lb) and, my word, do they earn every kyat!

> 'Porters carry the pilgrims' luggage, and the carriers the pilgrims who are unwilling or unable to make the long climb on foot.
> Children are carried in cane baskets hanging from poles flung over the carriers' shoulders. Adults go up in hammocks, a strong cotton blanket tied lengthwise to a bamboo pole and carried by two men.'
>
> Khin Myo Chit.

*Zayats* (rest-houses) and stalls line the entire route, selling an amazing array of souvenirs and Burmese medicines, including monkey's blood (*myaut-thwe*), python's gall (*sabagyi-thechay*) and seal's penis (*phantho*). When you reach **Ye Myaung Gyi Camp** ('Big Stream' Camp), you are a third of the way up and certainly entitled to a rest (and an excellent Burmese meal) at the Mi Tha Su Restaurant. From here to the top, you will be cheered on by friendly Burmese fellow climbers and stared at by curious kids. As Khin Myo Chit explains:

> 'Some of the climbs are quite steep and challenging, especially to the residents of the flat-lands. They have expressive names like 'Shew-yin-so' ('Heaving Chest') and 'Pho-pyan-taung ('Old-Man-Turns-Back-Hill'). There is a flow of pilgrims going up or down the path. Those coming down hail the up comers with words of encouragement; 'Come on, the pagoda is

just ahead,' or 'You are doing fine — keep it up'. At one of the stops, called 'Myin-daw-mu' ('The View') pilgrims have a real glimpse of the Kyaiktiyo pagoda — something really exhilarating. The pilgrims then are convinced the trip was worth everything they had gone through.'

The Chinese, in fact, believe that if you climb Kyaiktiyo three times, you will become rich.

Derived from the Mon-Sanskrit, 'Kyaiktiyo' means a 'pagoda shouldered on the head of a hermit' and the celebrated shrine is on the crest of the Paunglaung ridge (one of the ridges of Eastern Yoma). The diminutive Kyaiktiyo Pagoda, just 18 feet high, is built on a huge boulder which balances precariously on a projecting tabular rock. The rock itself is separated from the mountain by a deep chasm which is spanned by an iron bridge, thus enabling the pilgrims (but not women) to pay close homage at its feet and to make merit by gilding the boulder with gold leaf. Legend has it that in the time of the Lord Buddha, hermits resided in the mountains and after obtaining sacred hairs from the Buddha enshrined them in the pagoda on their respective mountains. But the hermit from Kyaiktiyo, reluctant to part with his share of the sacred relic, treasured it in his hair-knot. And only after finding a boulder resembling his head, did he enshrine his cherished share in a pagoda built on it (as is the case throughout Burma, there are other tales as to how the pagoda came to be). For centuries the pagoda lay buried in the jungle; the wonderfully balanced boulder withstanding the rigours of wind, rain and earthquakes before being discovered in 1823 by Minhlathinkha-thu, the mayor of Sittang. As Khin Myo Chit concludes in her marvellous book *A Wonderland of Burmese Legends*:

'It is impossible to be in the vicinity of the Kyaiktiyo Pagoda ... and not be emotionally involved ... There's fantasy, magic and adventure and very little, if any, history, — but who minds?'

There is just one hotel at the top, the Kyaikto, which has the effrontery to charge tourists US\$24 (locals pay K210). The hotel has wafer-thin walls, sporadic electricity and only provides cold running water between the hours of 6.00-6.30 am and 6.00-6.30pm. At other times, guests have a daily ration of two buckets of ice-cold water. There is no need to eat in the hotel: restaurants and food-stalls abound in the vicinity of the pagoda. I particularly recommend the Kyu Kyu Win Restaurant. There are four essential items to bring with you: a torch, a sweater (as the evenings and mornings can be very cold), a raincoat and an umbrella.

Further up the mountain is **U Ahbaw Cave**, which contains an image of a Chinese monk who came from the Irrawaddy Delta and who practised at Kyaiktiyo for 26 years before attaining Enlightenment. Daily he would go out begging for food for up to 16 miles. Also on the mountain is a shrine to the guardian *nat* Mo Po Shin Gyi. An hour's stiff trek from Kyaiktiyo is the Hermit Mountain ('**Yathetaung**'), which was named after a hermit called Eithsathara who practised on the mountain and also attained Enlightenment. In his memory a pagoda, Aungmingalapaya, was built during World War II by U Khanti, a hermit from Mandalay. During your ascent of 'Yathetaung', you will pass groups of Burmese constructing roads and paths and clearing the way: this is forced labour (they receive no remuneration from the SLORC). They will ask for money to buy drinks, so do give as much as you can. (There are other mountains in the region which you can climb, but they are technically 'off-limits').

## Bassein and Chaungtha

A newly-constructed road, they say, leads from Rangoon to Bassein (pronounced 'Bassane'), but maybe 'newly-constructed' has a different meaning in Burmese, for the 118 mile (190km) journey takes over five hours. The route is often unpaved, dusty and very bumpy; occasionally it disintegrates into mere sand.

First stop (after 25 minutes) is Insein jetty for a five-minute crossing over the Hlaing River to Hlaingthaya. Then it's another one hour ten minutes to Nyaungdoon to traverse the Irrawaddy. After a frenetic scramble to board the ferry, Setkaw, some 40 minutes away, emerges as the next port of call. From Setkaw to Bassein, count on three hours (including a drive over a stretch of railway line) — and a thick coating of dust.

Those with time on their hands can make the journey from Rangoon to Bassein by water: boats depart daily at 3pm and 5pm and take about 16 hours. The trip offers a wonderful insight into life around the Irrawaddy Delta. Tickets are bookable at the Inland Water Transport Office in Rangoon, and if you're lucky, you'll be assigned a private cabin and dining room facilities. Bassein, incidentally, does have an airport but no domestic flights these days.

The highlight of the land route is a brief stopover at the town of **Nyaungdoon**, which has three marvellous pagodas. The **Nangaingayepayagyi** has a giant Buddha image, the **Mahazedi**

**Stupa** is noted for its two large *chinthes* painted in red, green and white with black beards, and the **Mohokepayagyi**, in front of which two smaller *chinthes* stand guard.

At present, accommodation in Bassein is limited to the Pathein Hotel which looks like a prison from the outside and isn't much better inside. It has pokey fan rooms with hard beds, foul bathrooms, frequent power failures and cannot be recommended. Tourists pay US$10 for a single room and US$20 for a double (plus 20% tax); locals K120 and K168 respectively. Fortunately a new 'luxury' hotel, the Kanthaya, has just been completed and tourists will soon be able to stay there.

Good Burmese food is available at the Shwezinyaw and Shan-Myanmar Restaurants, while two restaurants offering Chinese fare are the Golden Swallow and the Zee Baeinn. The best coffee shop in town is the Nayi Soe, though I would also recommend the Shwelatha Coffee Shop and the Oasis Cold Drinks Shop.

A quaint town, situated by the Ngawun River and thronging with bicycles, Bassein is famous, amongst other activities, for its umbrella production — and, of course, pagodas. Umbrellas can be purchased direct from the manufacturers at Yon Taseit Pathein Htisaing (pronounced 'tee-sine' and meaning 'umbrella shop') on Twenty Eight Pagoda Road. Prices start at K20 and go up to K1,800: there are all sizes available from the minute to the gigantic and, if you've changed your money on the black market, are an excellent buy.

The town of Bassein is dominated by the celebrated **Shwe-mok-htaw Pagoda**, which started life as a small stupa about seven and a half feet high with a circumference of about four and a half feet and dates back to around the time of 305 BC. It was named Shwe-arna or 'Grand Power' and inside the Emperor Asoka enshrined sacred relics of Buddha along with a solid-gold bar, six inches in length. In the year 1115 AD Alaungsithu, king of Pagan, constructed a larger pagoda right over the smaller one, increasing the size to 36 feet and renaming it Htu-par-yone. In 1263 AD King Smodagossa and his Queen Ommadanti enlarged the pagoda to 130 feet in height and changed the name to Shwe-mok-htaw, meaning 'a bar of solid gold half a foot in length'. Following subsequent renovations, the pagoda reached its present height of 153 feet. In memory of the three kings, a three-tiered sacred crown called a *shwe-hti* was placed on the top of the pagoda. The top tier is made of solid gold and weighs about 14 pounds, the second is of pure silver and the third (and largest) is of bronze. Both the silver and bronze tiers (as well as the entire structure) are thickly coated with gold leaf. The *shwe-hti* supports about 40 pounds of gold, 829 pieces of diamond, 843 pieces of ruby and 1,588 pieces of various other precious gems.

In the south shrine of the Shwe-mok-htaw reposes the famous **Thihoshin Phondawpyi** statue of Buddha, one of four images which floated down originally from Ceylon (the others are at Kyaikto, Kyaikkami and Tavoy). Around the year 1418 AD Sri Prakkama-barhu VI, king of Ceylon, had four statues of the Buddha engraved in order to help spread the word of Buddhism abroad. The four images were constructed from branches taken from the sacred banyan tree which were grounded and mixed with cement composite. They were then placed on four wooden rafts and set adrift, with a vow that the statues would land where Buddhism took firm root. The one which landed in Tavoy is called the Shin-mokhtee, the one at Kyaikkami is in the Yele-Paya (the so-called 'In-Water-Stupa') and the third is at Kyaikto, where it was named the Kyaik-pawlaw or 'the statue of the moving sacred mole'. The statue in the Shwe-mok-htaw Pagoda originally ran aground at Phondawpyi, a sea-side fishing village about 60 miles south of Bassein. During the reign of Shin-Sawpu, the sovereign-queen of the former Mon Empire, the statue was brought to Kuthima-nagara, the present day Bassein, and was placed in the Shwe-mok-htaw campus somewhere round about 1455 AD. Stalls line the entrance to this magnificent pagoda, where there is also a reclining Buddha at the stage of entering nirvana.

Hexagonal in shape with five terraces, surrounded by a number of small stupas and noted for its vast Buddha image is the **Tagaung Mingala Zeditaw**, which in former times was called the Tagaung Pagoda. It has eight pavilions (*tazaungs*) and four entrances. According to the *Amended List of Ancient Monuments in Burma* it was built in 984 AD by Samuddaghosa, king of the Talaings, and his Queen Ummadandi, though the pagoda-keeper relates a different history. Similar in style but smaller, is the **Tha-Yaunggyaung Pagoda** (whose correct name in fact is the **Thayaung Mahazedidawgyi**). This pagoda is unusual in that it has three *htis* (umbrellas). It is located in a wonderfully peaceful, countryside setting.

The **Mahabodhi Mingalazedi** is at present under renovation: eventually the entire stupa will be covered by glass mosaic. Instead, you can visit the **Laykyunyanaung Pagoda**, which is quite extraordinary in that it has been renovated in the style of the Ananda Temple at Pagan. Formerly called the Wish-Fulfilling Phaung Daw Oo, the SLORC enlarged and reconstructed the pagoda around the old one.

In the precincts of the **Settawya Pagoda** stands a giant statue of the Buddha; close-by the local people are constructing a new pagoda called the **Shwekyimyint**. I had the great honour of helping lay the foundation stone, a ceremony known as *paned* in Burmese. The pagoda will take three months to complete.

One other pagoda well worth a visit is the **Twenty Eight Pagoda** on Twenty Eight Pagoda Road (very near the umbrella shop): it is so called because it houses 28 statues of the Buddha.

Burma is renowned for its festivals, and one particularly enjoyable *pwe* takes place each year in Bassein on December 27: the **Nigyawday Pagoda Festival**. It relates one of the Jataka Tales, when the Lord Buddha came to preach to 550 Shan traders. On the way they were robbed, yet they still came to listen to the Buddha's preachings. The festival involves much dancing, singing, and cheering with everyone dressing up in ethnic and formal costumes. A procession follows involving various modes of transport: an image of the Lord Buddha heads the parade followed in strict order by his 28 disciples, the Shan traders on bullock carts, numerous beautiful maidens (also on bullock carts, to accompany the traders) and, at the rear, the robbers or dacoits, as they are known in Burmese. As they proceed through the town, the dacoits re-enact the robbery. The whole performance is hugely entertaining.

# Chaungtha

If you glance at a map of Burma, the beach resort of Chaungtha looks tantalisingly close to Bassein: perhaps some 20 to 30 miles to the northwest (it's impossible to say exactly how far). But don't for one moment be fooled: it's a terrible journey. For once, I think, if they constructed an airport at Chaungtha, I'd be tempted to fly. But that's an unlikely scenario, as indeed is the completion of the so-called 'road' from Bassein to Chaungtha.

It's hard to describe the route from Bassein to Chaungtha: dusty, exceptionally bumpy with the certainty of at least one puncture on the way. It takes about 2½ hours in total, but it is extremely uncomfortable and not really recommended for cars (jeeps, maybe).

After 35 minutes, you cross the Ngawun River at Shwemyintin and arrive at Thanlyetsun (which takes 15 minutes) and then proceed to Chaungtha, continuously bounced up and down and caked in dust and sand.

Tour companies in Rangoon describe Chaungtha in clichéd terms: 'Unspoilt beaches with swaying palms', they say, but for once they've got it dead right. Chaungtha is stunning: a deserted, undiscovered seaside paradise, where Burmese kids frolic in the sea without a care in the world, the Kyaukpahto Pagoda stands serenely and immovably on the beach and the fishermen haul in gigantic prawns. Every now and then a bullock cart meanders by over the sands, as the sun sets behind a distant island.

Chaungtha's location and way of life are truly idyllic, and at first glance the Chaungtha Beach Hotel (which you can book direct from Rangoon, Tel 042 22587) appears likewise. But you soon discover the truth: it's a government-run hotel and consequently the service is appalling. Admittedly the well-appointed bungalows have TV, fridge and air-conditioning, but often the rooms aren't made up, the toilets don't flush and you can't even tune in to TV Myanmar. Room rates are US$35 a day, and in true Burmese bureaucratic fashion, tourists are obliged to take breakfast (US$7), lunch and supper (both US$10) in the hotel, whereas locals can pay K350 for just a bungalow. As the surly manager gruffly remarks: 'Breakfast, lunch and dinner compulsory in hotel for tourist.' (Fortunately, there is a new private hotel under construction). Although you will lose money, I suggest you ignore the manager's commands and head to Ywa-win-lan, Chaungtha's one street, which is littered with fine restaurants, tea and coffee-shops, souvenir stalls, a pagoda and a hospital. The hotel manager will tell you: 'Very dangerous to eat outside. Unhygienic and security risk'. Nonsense: the *mohinga* is excellent and cheap, as are the *lepet* and the many sea-food dishes, and the local Burmese could not be more hospitable.

On a rock on the beach is the **Kyaukpahto Pagoda** with a Buddha image inside. Local children tend to congregate round here, paying homage, foraging for shells and crabs and diving off the rocks into the sea. The sight of a foreigner will send them into raptures of delight and they will show you around and take care of you. The town itself is unremarkable, though it may be of interest to have a look at the hospital which, like most in Burma, is dirty, very run down and suffers from a dire shortage of Western medicine. Pinned on the wall is a notice listing the cases of malaria in the area: the hospital staff are grateful for any donations. Nearby stands the Pyilonechantha Pagoda and a field where you can watch the locals skilfully playing volleyball.

From the beach at Chaungtha, take a boat for K5 to Foh-ka-lah Island, which has a population of around 200 who rely solely on fishing for their living. They sell their catch in the market at Bassein, making around K125 a day. However, there are fears that increased poaching by Thai fishing boats in the area will damage their livelihood — and indeed a Thai boat, captured for illegal fishing, has been held off Chaungtha for some time. On **Foh-ka-lah Island**, on Palitaung (Pali Mountain), is the four-year-old Suutaungpyay Pagoda, which offers stunning views of the beaches. What bliss.

# ARAKAN STATE

'Slowly out of the mist, like a coloured slide coming into focus, there appeared the coast of Arakan, forty thousand feet below us. I could see the whole sweep of it, from Cox's Bazaar to Akyab: the white ribbon of surf along the beach, the three broad rivers with their muddy banks, and the ranges in between, like the backs of prehistoric saurians.'

*Return to Burma*, Bernard Fergusson.

# Sandoway and Ngapali

The beaches around Sandoway, of which Ngapali is the best known, were opened to foreign visitors in 1983, and have oscillated subsequently between being 'on' and 'off-limits'. At the time of writing, they once again figure on MTT's list of approved destinations, although you can safely forget this area during the rainy season (May to October).

For foreign travellers, Sandoway can only conveniently be reached by plane, a fact which deters most overseas tourists: UB 403 is scheduled to depart every Wednesday, Friday and Sunday at 0630, arriving at Mazin Airport at 0740 and costs US$47 (one way). During the peak tourist season, Myanma Airways attempts to lay on extra flights (which are always overbooked), but this is a hopeless task. They simply do not have enough planes and their timetables and scheduling are depressingly chaotic. Some tourists (and most locals) make the journey by road: an arduous trek via Prome and down to Rangoon.

Sandoway's most popular beach resort is Ngapali (a regular haunt of the SLORC, diplomats and VIPs), which was supposedly given its name by a homesick Italian, who thought the beach reminded him of Naples. In fact in Burmese, Ngapali actually means 'A fish who is pulling a face', so nobody can really say if the story is true.

Ngapali (pronounced 'Na-pah-lee') attracts many more visitors than either Chaungtha or Setse, particularly the more affluent members of Burmese society, but, despite being Burma's main seaside destination, is hardly in the Phuket or Pattaya league. It enjoys an idyllic, peaceful, scenic location but is less intimate than Chaungtha. And since Ngapali itself has no real village to speak of, there is little atmosphere. To cap it all, the rich Burmese visitors (often the Chinese) are less friendly and a good deal more arrogant than those at Chaungtha.

Ngapali has three hotels: the old favourite is the **Ngapali Beach Hotel**, which charges between US$25-45 (locals pay K180-350) for beach-side bungalows. Typically, this hotel is beginning to fray at the edges: the rooms are grubby and the bathrooms grotty. A notice on each door reads: 'There is a battery operated emergency light. The switch of which is located behind your bedside table. Please use it when the electric lights fail or when the town electricity supply is cut off at 10 pm everynight. Please switch off to conserve the battery.' Electricity is only available between 6pm-10pm, so a torch is a must.

Breakfast is compulsory in the hotel for foreigners and, as with all government-run establishments, the receptionist is surly and inefficient. It is quite remarkable in Burma that every time a tourist checks into a hotel, it is as though it has never happened before (this is also the case when buying train, boat and aeroplane tickets).

Directly to the right of the Ngapali Beach Hotel (looking from the main road) is the **Shwewar Gyaing Hotel** (US$10-40, K100-280) which has a pleasant enough location but is much more down-market than its neighbour. To the left is the 'star' of the trio, the **New Ngapali Beach Hotel**, which charges an exorbitant US$60-100 (K750-1500). All the rates are plus 10% service charge and 10% government tax.

Next to the New Ngapali Beach Hotel is an ice factory, which, in true Burmese style, produces no ice. This is because it used to receive its water supply from the Ngapali Beach Hotel, but for some reason refused to provide the hotel with ice. So in revenge the hotel cut off the water supply — and thus 'very little' (ie no) ice is available in Ngapali.

There is little point in taking lunch or supper in the hotel: simply wander over to **Zaw Restaurant**, which is virtually opposite the Ngapali Beach Hotel (meals must be ordered in advance). The charming owner can also arrange visits to the three famous pagodas in Sandoway (the Andaw, Nandaw and Shwesandaw) and boat trips to the neighbouring islands. An alternative to Zaw Restaurant is the **Kyi Nu Yeik Restaurant** next door run by a delightful couple U Tin Phe and Daw Tin May. Seafood (large prawns and crab) are particularly appetising and a speciality of the area. *Gananhin*,

Arakanese crab curry, is especially recommended.

Past the two restaurants is a monastery called **Myabyin** which has a reclining Buddha in a state of disrepair and just two monks and three novices in what is a rather sizeable compound. There are also two stupas, one made from glass mosaic, the other painted white. In the room where the monks eat is an image of the Buddha preaching to his five disciples.

About 2½ miles from the hotel is the **Lonedha jetty** where the British landed during colonial times. On the jetty you can watch the local children skilfully catching fish for their supper.

**Sandoway** itself is rather a drab town with the inevitable market (which has a decidedly smelly fish section) but an interesting cheroot factory called Naryi Taseik Seileik Khone. However, the area has a deep religious significance to Burmese Buddhists, for it is here that the Lord Buddha lived three of his previous 547 lives: a king cobra (hamadryad), a partridge-king and a *samari*, which in Burmese means either a species of bird or a yak. Most guide book compilers have taken *samari* to signify a yak, but if they had actually bothered to visit the relevant pagoda (the Shwesandaw), they would have seen a statue of a pheasant-type bird and not a yak. In fact, the Lord Buddha visited the region himself and pronounced that he had lived three of his past lives here and each of the three pagodas (Andaw, Nandaw and Shwesandaw) is said to contain one of *his* relics and not, as most books relate, relics of the animals concerned (though, of course, no one can say for certain).

So it is in this hilly area on three mountains (Andaw, Nandaw and Sandaw) that the celebrated trio of pagodas are located. It is a stiff climb up to the **Andaw Pagoda** which is under renovation and guarded by two cement *chinthes*. Built by King Minzetchok, king of Sandoway, in 761 AD, it has subsequently been renovated by the kings of Arakan, and was last repaired by the inhabitants of Sandoway in 1848 AD (there is an inscription in Burmese which records that the pagoda was repaired, gilt and crowned by a new *hti* in 1210 BE or 1848 AD). The Andaw is reputed to contain a molar tooth of the Buddha. In the pagoda precincts is a statue of a king cobra, an incarnation of the Buddha in one of his previous existences.

It is also a steep climb up to the **Nandaw Pagoda**, which is perched on a hilltop and best reached by car. Guarded by Nandawtaung Bodaw Nat, the Nandaw, like all three pagodas, is under renovation. It was originally built by King Minbya in 763 AD to enshrine a rib of the Lord Buddha (not of the partridge-king) and has four pavilions.

A newly-constructed path now makes the **Shwesandaw Pagoda** accessible by car, though if you decide to walk up, you will be greeted by two cement *chinthes*. The pagoda was constructed by Minnyokin, king of Sandoway, in 784 AD and has been repaired by successive kings of Arakan, and, prior to the current renovation, by the inhabitants of Sandoway in 1876. In BE 236 Minister Damathruya enshrined real hair relics of the Lord Buddha in the pagoda. A statue of a bird resembling a pheasant (and not a yak) stands in the pagoda precincts.

# Akyab

'... never mind that it's a backwater, never mind that this hotel is so very shabby, that there are cobwebs on the ceiling and cockroaches in the bathrooms. There is beauty here ... We could be happy here. And we were.'

Cristina Pantoja-Hidalgo, *Five Years in a Forgotten Land: A Burmese Notebook.*

Capital of Arakan State and first opened to foreign visitors in the 1980s, Akyab (known these days as Sittwe) is one of the four districts forming the Arakan Division of Lower Burma and covers an area of 5,136 square miles. The town is situated on the sea coast at the mouth of the Kaladan River and is located on well-wooded, low-lying ground between the sea face and the Kaladan.

The origin of the name Akyab is unknown, whereas the Arakanese name Sittwe literally means 'Where the war began.' Some people allege that the name came from the pagoda Akyab which is supposed to be the shrine of the jawbone of the Buddha and was built by one of the Arakanese kings. Akyab used to have the nickname 'The white man's grave' owing to regular cholera epidemics and malaria, but, don't worry, it's safe enough these days! In fact, it is an extraordinary place: a mix of Burmese Buddhists and Muslims, Indians, Bengalis, Chinese, a myriad of curious, smiling faces, wonderfully hospitable people and a fascinating culture. The town itself is rather spread out; a rambling city (somewhat reminiscent of Mandalay in that respect) where transportation is essentially by trishaw. Peaceful and relaxed as it is, as a foreigner, you must expect to be besieged by fascinated locals (particularly children). One Indian gentleman remarked to me with great astonishment: 'My God, sir, you are the first Englishman I have seen since the end of the War! Did you come by BOAC?'. With no decent accommodation, Akyab is very much a destination for the intrepid traveller, one generally en route to the ancient city of Myohaung (see below).

Akyab district has an abundance of flora, fauna and trees, a large assortment of weird and wonderful creatures: pigs, hogs, sambur, barking deer, leopards, tigers, wild cats, jackals, elephants, rhinoceros, all types of birds, pigeons, snipe, pintails and fantails, pheasants, teal and duck, hawks, kites and fish-eagles, owls, snakes, oysters and naturally fish, the main food of Akyab. In fact altogether there are no less than 139 different genera of fresh, salt-water and sea fish. Rice is the staple crop grown in the region, whilst petroleum (oil beds) are situated in the Eastern Boronga Island. Akyab also produces coal, laterite, sandstone and opium. And with its unique Arakan culture, it is truly an unmatched region of Burma. In fact Burmese joke that to be born a true Arakanese, *Ya-khaing* to the Burmese, *Ra-khaing* to the locals, is to be born within sight of the rusty, steel-framed clock-tower (**Nye-yee-sin**) which stands in the centre of Akyab. The old Burman adage that if you happen to see an Arakanese and a snake at the same time, you should kill the Arakanese first, is, so they say, a thing of the past (or so my Burmese friends assure me ...).

Akyab can only be reached by Myanma Airways: UB 403 departs from Rangoon every Wednesday, Friday and Sunday at 0630, stopping off en route at Sandoway (arrival 0740) and Kyaukpyu (arrival 0825) before touching down at Akyab at 0905. UB 409 (a non-stop flight) departs Rangoon daily at 1030, arriving at 1130 (except on Thursdays, when it leaves at 1530 and arrives at 1630). The fare from Rangoon is US$78 by twin-prop, US$88 by jet, and US$46 from Sandoway.

A word of warning: Myanma Airways *never* stick to these schedules. They simply do not have enough aircraft, probably between four and five for domestic routes (F27 propeller planes) and two jets (F28s for international flights). The poor F27s never rest, flying non-stop — until they 'drop out of the sky' — to any destination the pilot chooses. Reconfirming your return ticket is also a veritable nightmare. I had to wait seven hours outside Myanma Airways' office in Akyab before I could be guaranteed a return seat to Rangoon (again, it was 'lucky dip' time)!

Foreigners can only be accommodated at the inappropriately-named Mya Hotel (Tel 21888) which means Emerald Hotel. It is certainly no gem, in fact it is more like a prison with no 'en-suite facilities' of any description. The communal ant- and mosquito-infested showers and toilets stink and there are no fans and certainly no air-conditioning. Still, the manager, a qualified Bengali astrologer, is charming and speaks fluent English. The hotel — more accurately referred to by the Burmese as a 'rest-house' — has a good atmosphere, is located in pleasant surroundings and has an excellent coffee-shop. It only charges K50 a night for a single room, K100 for a double. More importantly, the manager and his associates can organise trips to Myohaung (despite what employees at MTT's office in Rangoon might say), the main reason for any visit to Akyab.

Akyab's most famous pagoda is the **Atulamarzein Pyilonechantha Payagyi**, which was built by U Agga Sayadaw in BE 1255. Inside is a large bronze Buddha image with neon lights whose head contains nine different types of precious stone. It has a large, bustling pavilion with glass mosaic pillars. Next to the pagoda is the **Kyaryoke Monastery** ('Picture of tiger') which has two stupas, one cylindrical with a Buddha image inside with a square relics box on top in Sinhalese style, the other in typical Burmese style. Close-by is the **Thanbutde Stupa**, with three terraces and encircled by small stupas. The **Thetkyamuni Pagoda** is an ancient pagoda with a vast Buddha image.

Perhaps of greatest interest in Akyab is the **Mahazeya Monastery** and the adjacent **Adeiktan Sima** (ordination hall). The monastery has Buddha images which are copies from Myohaung and a large pink Buddha image guarded by Thet Taw Shay Bodaw on the left and by a Brahmin fortune-teller on the right. The abbot is a delightful man called U Kula Rekhita Sayadaw.

The Adeiktan Sima, renovated in 1987, is filled with a myriad of different size Buddha images in various postures. It is guarded by two ogres: Ahalawaka on the left, Pannaka on the right.

The Agyeik Pagoda, built about 130 years ago, is said to contain a tooth relic of the Buddha, while located on a ridge called Akyatkundaw are three separate pagodas: Dattaw, Letyathalon and Letwethalon, which allegedly enshrine the hip and right and left shins of the Buddha.

The **Buddermokan Mosque** was said to have been founded over a century ago by two merchants of Chittagong in memory of a certain Budder Auliah, whom the Mussulmans regarded as an eminent saint. A fascinating account of this mosque is given by Colonel Nelson Davis, Deputy Commissioner of Akyab, in 1876 in a record preserved in the office of the Commissioner of Arakan:

'On the southern side of the island of Akyab, near the eastern shore of the Bay, there is a group of masonry buildings, one of which, in its style of construction, resembles an Indian mosque; the other is a cave, constructed of stone on the bare rock which superstructure once served as a hermit's cell. The spot where these buildings are situated is called Buddermokan, *Budder* being the name of a saint of Islam, and *mokan*, a place of abode. It is said that 140 years ago or thereabouts two brothers named Manick and Chan, traders from Chittagong, while returning from Cape Negrais in a vessel loaded with turmeric called at Akyab for water, and anchored off the Buddermokan rocks. On the following night, after Chan and Manick had procured water near these rocks, Manick had a dream that the saint Budder Auliah desired him to construct a cave or a place of abode at a locality near where they procured the water. Manick replied that he had no means wherewith he could comply with the request. Budder then said that all his (Manick's) turmeric would turn into gold, and that he should therefore endeavour to erect the building from the proceeds thereof. When morning came Manick, observing that all the turmeric had been transformed into gold, consulted his brother Chan on the subject of the dream, and they conjointly constructed a cave and also dug a well at the locality now known as Buddermokan.

There are orders in Persian in the Deputy Commissioner's Court of Akyab, dated 1834 from William Dampier, Esq., Commissioner of Chittagong, and also from T. Dickenson, Esq., Commissioner of Arakan to the effect that one Hussain Ally (then the *thugyi* or village headman of Bhudamaw Circle) was to have charge of the Buddermokan in token of his good services rendered to the British force in 1825, and to enjoy any sums that he might collect on account of alms and offerings.

In 1849 Mr R. C. Raikes, the officiating Magistrate at Akyab, ordered that Hussain Ally was to have charge of the Buddermokan buildings, and granted permission to one Mah Ming Oung, a female fakir, to erect a building; accordingly in 1849 the present masonry buildings were constructed by her; she also re-dug the tank.

The expenditure for the whole work came to about Rs. 2000. After Hussain Ally's death his son Abdoolah had charge, and after the death of the latter, his sister Me Moorazamal, the present wife of Abdool Morein, Pleader, took charge. Abdool Morein is now in charge on behalf of his wife.'

In the compound of the Deputy Commisioner is a stone inscription, belonging to the Palace hill of Myohaung which dates back over four centuries.

On West Boronga Island stands the **Sandawshin Pagoda** which is said to have been erected in the lifetime of the Buddha over eight of his hairs. The tradition about Taphussa and Phallika bringing these relics is identical to that attached to the Shwedagon in Rangoon. The current structure is relatively modern.

About 16 miles by boat on the way to Myohaung and situated on a low, steep and rocky hill opposite the village of Ponnagyun is the **Urittaung Pagoda**. The original builder is not known, but it is said that on the hill where this pagoda stands, the Buddha once lived in a former existence as a Brahman of high birth and that a pagoda was erected over his skull on his death, which was found on the same hill. The pagoda was repaired by King Gajapati, of the Myauk-U dynasty, in 1521 AD when it had fallen into ruin and has subsequently been repaired by King Thadomintara in 1641 AD, by King Varadhammaraja in 1688 AD and in the middle of this century was repaired and gilt by a private individual.

# Myohaung

Situated on the Shwenatpyin 'chaung', a branch of the Kaladan River, about 40 miles from Akyab and the Bay of Bengal is Myohaung, pronounced 'Myo-how'. The township covers 567 square miles: in 1891 it was transferred to the newly constituted Kyauktaw subdivision.

Myohaung (Mrohaung to the Arakanese, who replace the 'y' with an 'r') was a former ancient capital, founded in 1433 by King Minzawmun. In fact it was known as Mrauk-U ('Mrow-Oo' is the approximate Arakanese pronounciation; the Burmese referred to it as Myauk-U, 'Myow-Oo') until the first Anglo-Burmese War (1824-26), when it was renamed Myohaung (meaning 'old city') as the British moved their administrative headquarters to Akyab. Now it appears the SLORC refer to it as Mrauk-U, though to the Burmese it is still Myohaung.

There are three ways to reach Myohaung (which is only accessible in the dry season): by government or private motorboat service or by a special chartered boat. The government service costs K10 one way, K20 return, the private motorboat K40 per person, whilst a group of 20 tourists would pay in the region of K6,000 for their own boat, 30-40 tourists around K10,000-12,000. The government and private services run approximately as follows:

## AKYAB TO MYOHAUNG

Monday: government boat (with a night stop service at Myohaung), dep. 0730 arr. 1230.

Tuesday: private motorboat, dep. 0700 or 0730 arr. 1200.

Wednesday: private motorboat, dep. 0700 arr. 1200.

Thursday: government boat, dep. 0700 or 0730 arr. 1130. The boat then returns the same day: dep. Myohaung 1300 arr. Akyab 1800.

Friday: private motorboat.

Saturday: government boat (Kyauktaw via Myohaung).

Sunday: private motorboat.

## MYOHAUNG TO AKYAB

Monday: private motorboat.

Tuesday: government boat.

Wednesday: private motorboat.

Thursday: government boat.

Friday: private motorboat.

Saturday: private motorboat.

Sunday: government boat coming back from Kyauktaw.

If you wish to stay overnight in Myohaung, there are two rest-houses: the Myanantheingi Rest House and the Kyawsoe Rest House. Both charge K30 a night.

   Situated within eight miles of the Kaladan River, 48 miles north of Myohaung, is the **Mahamuni Temple**. Tradition ascribes this temple to Chandasuriya, king of Arakan, who built it to enshrine the image of the Buddha cast during the lifetime of the Sage himself in the 6th Century BC. The image was removed to Amarapura in 1784 as a spoil of war after the conquest of Arakan by the Einshemin, son of

Bodawpaya. It has now been placed in the Mahamuni or Arakan Pagoda in Mandalay. This temple has passed through many vicissitudes and has been repaired many times, the last occasion being in 1867 AD.

In Mrunchaungwa village, three miles west of the Mahamuni on the top of a hill, stands the Mrunchaungwa Pagoda. Tradition ascribes the foundation of this small shrine to the pious Buddhist kings of old Dhannavati (Arakan) (4th Century AD).

On either bank of the upper Kaladan River lies Kyauktaw, of which the most celebrated pagoda, the **Kyauktaw Zedi**, stands on a hill opposite Kyauktaw. It was erected by a fugitive queen of the Launggyet Dynasty (1237-1401 AD) and repaired by the villagers in the middle of this century. Kyauktaw also has a number of stone images and a footprint of the Buddha cut in stone dating from the 14th Century AD.

Myohaung's most famous temple is the **Shitthaung Pagoda**, which is built on a promontory half way up to the west side of the hill. Shitthaung means 'The shrine of 80,000 images' and it was constructed by King Minbin, the 12th of the Myauk-U dynasty, who reigned over Arakan from 1531-1553 AD. The Shitthaung served as a place of refuge for the royal family and is more like a fortress than a pagoda. As Dr Forchhammer explains:

'The Shrine is the work of Hindu architects and Hindu workmen; the skill and art displayed in its construction and ornamention are far beyond what the Arakanese themselves have ever attained to: the entire structure is alien in its main features to the native architectural style.'

Situated 86 feet to the northeast of the Shitthaung is the **Andaw Pagoda** which was built by King Minbin (1531-1553) to enshrine a tooth relic of the Buddha said to have been obtained from Ceylon. Like the Shitthaung, the Andaw is a temple fortress and place of refuge.

Located 40 feet to the north of the outer wall of the Andaw is the Ratanabon Pagoda, which was erected by King Minpalaung who ruled Arakan from 1571-1593 AD.

Opposite, and about 300 feet to the northwest of the entrance to the Shitthaung on a low elevation rise the Dukkanthein and Lemyethna Pagodas, built by King Minbin. These too are temple fortresses and places of refuge in war, chiefly for Buddhist priests. B... are constructed of massive stone blocks and layers of bricks over the roof. The Lemyethna ('The four-sided pagoda') is 150 feet northwest of the Dukkanthein.

Located a half-mile to the north of the Dukkanthein is the Pitakattaik or Library which was built by King Narapatigyi (1638-1645 AD) to store the Buddhist scriptures which were brought over from Ceylon. It was originally ornamented with exquisite carvings in stone. Over 50 feet to the north of the Pitakattaik lies the enclosure of the Linpanhmaung or Laungpwanbrauk Pagoda which was constructed in the 16th Century AD and also has some beautiful stone-carvings. 50 steps to the north are the ruins of the **Dipayon Pagoda**, made from stone also in the 16th Century.

A stone's throw to the east of the Dipayon is the partly-ruined Anoma Pagoda with an enclosing wall which was built in the 15th Century AD. The shrine stands on the battlefield on which the Arakanese were defeated by the Burmans in 1784. A half-mile to the west of the Dipayon is the Mingalamaraung Pagoda, an octagonal solid stone spire overgrown with dense jungle, which was constructed by King Narapatigyi. There are inscriptions in Burmese which were set up by King Chandavijaya (1710-1731 AD).

The Jinamanaung Pagoda stands on a low steep hill and was built by King Chandasudhamma between 1652-1684 AD. The facade of the porch exhibits some good stone-carvings. Each of the eight corners of the pagoda is guarded by a lion or griffin, each with a double body and a head with whiskers and a beard.

Located to the southeast of Alezeywa on the steep Shwedaung Hill is the **Shwedaung Pagoda** which was built by King Minbin. Though small, this pagoda is historically important. To oppose the advance of the British soldiers, the Burmans set up camp — which is still traceable — in 1825 on the top of the Shwedaung Hill. A half-mile north of the Shwedaung Pagoda (Shwedaungpaya) on another small hill called Wuntitaung is the Wunticeti, the origin of which is unknown. It is first mentioned in Arakanese history in the 14th Century AD. It is a Hindu shrine with Hindu deities represented in the sculptures and is clearly very ancient. The stone inscription is of a later date, probably 14th Century.

The Sandhikan Mosque was built of sandstone by the followers of King Minzawmun after he had returned from 24 years of exile in India in 1430 AD.

The Sakyamanaung and Ratanamanaung Pagodas are both ascribed to King Chandasudhamma, the 23rd of the Myauk-U dynasty, who reigned in Arakan from 1652-1684 AD. The latter is a solid stone structure, octagonal from the base to the top.

Located west of Waze village on a steep and narrow rocky ridge is the Letyodat Pagoda (where there are two pagodas of the same name). Tradition asserts that the bone of the fourth finger of the Buddha is enshrined in one of these pagodas erected in the 15th Century AD.

Situated on the Peinnugun, another small hill to the northwest of Waze, is the Shwegyathein Temple which was built by King Chandasudhamma. This king was also responsible for the construction of the Lokamu Pagoda which is located between Byinze and Kyaukyit villages. In the spacious temple-court, shaded by mango and tamarind trees, the pilgrims who intended to visit the distant Mahamuni Pagoda (48 miles to the north) used to assemble. The Lokamu was repaired by Chit San of Waze and the public.

Another pagoda usually visited by pilgrims on their way to the Mahamuni is the **Parabho Pagoda**, which is reached by crossing the Parabochaung. Standing on the banks of a tidal creek, the Parabho was built by King Minrajagyi, the 17th king of the Myauk-U dynasty, in the year 1603 AD and was repaired by the first Burmese governor of Myohaung in 1786 AD.

An ancient pagoda, now sadly completely demolished, is the Moktaw Pagoda (also called the Shwemawdaw Pagoda). It was built at the first foundation of Myohaung, but only the basement of the original pagoda remains. A smaller pagoda, which was built on it, has also fallen into ruin.

Standing on the central hill which rises behind the village of the same name is the **Mahati Pagoda** which was built in the 12th Century AD by the Arakanese King Koliya. The pagoda contains an image of the Buddha which was also finished in the 12th Century AD, as well as stone inscriptions and sculptures. Mahati village was once the site of a considerable town.

The celebrated **Kyauknyo** or 'Dusky stone' image stands on top of the southernmost hill of Mahati village. It was reputed to have been set up by King Koliya in 1133 AD. The **Migyaun Rock inscription**, five centuries old, in Burmese character and language, covers 21 feet of rock and is situated on the west side of the hill on which the Kyauknyo image stands. A mile to the north of Mahati village are the remains of the Paungdawdat Pagoda. The original pagoda was built by Chulataingchandra in 954 AD to enshrine the thigh-bone of Ananda, the well-known disciple of the Buddha. It was repaired in 1591 AD by Minpalaung, the 16th of the Myauk-U dynasty. There is an inscription in Burmese which records this fact.

One mile north of Kamaungdat village and ten miles due south of Launggyet is the **Kadothein** which was built by King Chandavijaya

(1710-1731 AD) in 1723 AD. This is the gem of the art of stone-sculpture in Arakan and lay buried in the jungle until around 1890. It is constructed entirely of stone and is square with the corners indented. There are fine carvings in stone and also two inscriptions recording the grants of land to the inmates of the monasteries in the neighbourhood of the pagoda. Glazed tiles have been found nearby.

*Akyab, Arakan State: an Arakanese child selling lottery tickets.*

# APPENDIX

## SUGGESTED READING

Abbott, Gerry:
*Back to Mandalay*, Impact Books, 1990.

Article 19:
*State of Fear: Censorship in Burma (Myanmar)*, Article 19 (see page 210), London, 1991.

Aung Aung Taik:
*Visions of Shwedagon*, White Lotus Co Ltd, Bangkok, 1989.

Aung San Suu Kyi:
*Aung San Of Burma*, Kiscadale Publications, 1991.
*Freedom From Fear*, Penguin Books, 1991.

Aung-Thwin, Michael:
*Irrigation in the Heartland of Burma: Foundations of the Pre-Colonial Burmese State*, Northern Illinois University, Center for Southeast Asian Studies, 1990.

Aye Saung:
*Burman in the Back Row: Autobiography of a Burmese Rebel*, White Lotus, Bangkok, 1989.

Boucaud, André and Louis:
*Burma's Golden Triangle: On the Trail of the Opium Warlords*, Asia Books, Bangkok, 1992.

Boyes, Jon and Piraban, S:
*Opium Fields*, Silkworm Books, Bangkok, 1991.

Burma Action Group:
*Burma and the United Nations: A Proposal for Constructive Involvement*, Burma Action Group, London, 1992.

Carrington, Charles:
*Rudyard Kipling: His Life and Work*, Penguin, 1986.

Clements, Alan:
*Burma: The Next Killing Fields?*, Odonian Press, Berkeley, California, 1992.

Damrong Rajanubhab, H.R.H. Prince of Thailand:
*Journey Through Burma in 1936*, River Books, Bangkok, 1991.

Dawood, Dr Richard:
*Travellers' Health: How To Stay Healthy Abroad*, Oxford University Press, 1990.

Donnison, F.S.V.:
*Burma*, Ernest Benn Limited, 1970.

Eliot, T.S.:
*A Choice of Kipling's Verse*, Faber and Faber, 1990.

Fergusson, Bernard:
*Return To Burma*, Collins, 1962.

Greenwood, Nicholas:
*Bound Tightly With Banana Leaves: A South East Asian Journal*, Right Now Books, 1992.

Hatt, John
*The Tropical Traveller*, Penguin, 1993.

Hunt, Gordon:
*The Forgotten Land*, Geoffrey Bles Ltd, London, 1967.

John, R.F.St.A.St.:
*Burmese Self-Taught*, Asian Educational Services, New Delhi, 1991.

Kanbawza Win:
*Daw Aung San Suu Kyi: The Nobel Laureate*, CPDSK Publications, Bangkok, 1992.

Khin Maung Nyunt:
*Market Research of Principal Exports and Imports of Burma with Special Reference to Thailand (1970/71 to 1985/86)*, Institute of Asian Studies (IAS), Chulalongkorn University, Bangkok, 1988.

Khin Myo Chit:
*A Wonderland of Burmese Legends*, The Tamarind Press, Bangkok, 1984.

Khin Nyunt:
*The Conspiracy of Treasonous Minions Within the Myanmar Naing-Ngan and Traitorous Cohorts Abroad*, Guardian Press, Rangoon, 1989.

King, Winston L.:
*A Thousand Lives Away: Buddhism in Contemporary Burma*, Asian Humanities Press, Berkeley, California, 1990.

Kipling, Rudyard:
*Something of Myself*, Penguin, 1992.

Leach, E.R.:
*Highland Burma: A Study of Kachin Social Structure*, The Athlone Press, London & New Jersey, 1990.

Lewis, Norman:
*Golden Earth*, Eland, London, 1991.

Lintner, Bertil:
*Outrage*, White Lotus, Bangkok, 1990.
*Aung San Suu Kyi And Burma's Unfinished Renaissance*, White Lotus, Bangkok, 1991.

Ludu U Hla:
*The Caged Ones*, The Tamarind Press, Bangkok, 1986.

Manich Jumsai, M.L.:
*History of Burma*, Chalermnit, Bangkok, 1979.

Mannin, Ethel:
*Land of the Crested Lion*, The Travel Book Club, 1954.

Maugham, W. Somerset:
*The Gentleman in the Parlour: A Record of a Journey from Rangoon to Haiphong*, Paragon House, New York, 1989.

Maung Htin Aung:
*Folk Elements in Burmese Buddhism*, Rangoon, 1959.

Mi Mi Khaing:
*The World of Burmese Women*, Zed Books Ltd, London, 1984.

Mirante, Edith T:
*Burmese Looking Glass: A Human Rights Adventure and a jungle Revolution*, Grove Press, New York, 1993.

Mya Than:
*Myanmar's External Trade: An Overview in the Southeast Asian Context*, Institute of Southeast Asian Studies (ISEAS), Singapore, 1992.

Ni Ni Myint:
*Burma's Struggle Against British Imperialism (1885-1895)*, The Universities Press, Rangoon, 1983.

Nyanatiloka:
*Manual of Buddhist Terms and Doctrines*, Singapore Buddhist Meditation Centre, 1991.

O'Brien, Harriet:
*Forgotten Land*, Michael Joseph, 1991.

O'Connor, V.C. Scott:
*Mandalay and Other Cities of the Past in Burma*, White Lotus, Bangkok, 1987.

Okell, John:
*First Steps in Burmese*, The School of Oriental and African Studies (University of London), 1989. (Includes five cassettes).

Orwell, George:
*Burmese Days*, Penguin, 1989.

Pantoja-Hidalgo, Cristina:
*Five Years in a Forgotten Land: A Burmese Notebook*, University of the Philippines Press, Diliman, Quezon City, 1991.

Rodrigues, Yves:
*Nat-Pwe: Burma's Supernatural Subculture*, Kiscadale Publications, 1992.

Rodriguez, Helen:
*Helen of Burma*, Collins, 1983.

San Tha Aung:
*The Buddhist Art of Ancient Arakan*, Rangoon, 1979.

Singer, Noel F.:
*Burmese Puppets*, Oxford University Press Pte Ltd, Singapore, 1992.

Smart, R. B.:
*Burma Gazetteer: Akyab District, Volume A*, Rangoon, 1957.

Soe Saing:
*United Nations Technical Aid in Burma: A Short Survey*, Institute of Southeast Asian Studies (ISEAS), Singapore, 1990.

Steinberg, David I.:
*Crisis in Burma: Stasis and Change in a Political Economy in Turmoil*, Institute of Security and International Studies (ISIS), Chulalongkorn University, Bangkok, 1989.

U Toke Gale:
*Burmese Timber Elephant*, Trade Corporation (9), Rangoon.

Venerable Mahasi Sayadaw of Burma:
*A Discourse on the Refinement of Character* (translated by U Aye Maung), Buddhaharma Meditation Center, Hinsdale, Illinois 60521, USA.

Wijeyewardene, Gehan:
*Ethnic Groups across National Boundaries in Mainland Southeast Asia*, Institute of Southeast Asian Studies (ISEAS), Singapore, 1990.

# POSTSCRIPT

'Democracy is an ideology that allows everyone to stand up according to his beliefs. They should not be threatened or endangered. Each one should go forward towards his own goal. Do not because of your greater strength be vengeful towards those who are of weaker strength ...

May the entire people be united and disciplined. May our people always do what is in complete accord with rightful principles. May the people be free from all harm.'

Daw Aung San Suu Kyi, Shwedagon Pagoda, August 26 1988.

Below is a list of organisations and publications relating to Burmese issues:

*All Burma Students' Democratic Front* or *ABSDF*: Aung Naing, 27 Witherington Road, Highbury, London N5 1PN, Tel 071 700 6435. They publish an occasional newsletter in Thailand: P.O. Box 1352, Bangkok, 10500.

*All Burma Students Relief Fund* or *ABSRF*: A group of individuals who have experienced life on the Thai-Burma border, where they encountered students suffering, amongst other things, from malnutrition, loss of limbs and hearing, malaria, black-water fever, and some who were dying from lack of medical attention. The group's aim is to raise funds for the relief of the plight and suffering of the students by providing medical supplies, food, clothing, educational materials and basic necessities for day to day survival. 105 Harrowes Meade, Edgware, Middx, HA8 8RS, Tel/Fax 081 958 2111.

*Amnesty International*: 99-119 Rosebery Avenue, London EC1R 4RE, Tel 071 814 6200, Fax 071 833 1510.

*Article 19*: A registered charity which takes its name and purpose from the nineteenth article of the United Nations' Universal Declaration of Human Rights which states: 'Everyone has the right to freedom of opinion and expression; this right includes freedom to hold opinions without interference and to seek, receive and impart information and ideas through any media and regardless of frontiers.' ARTICLE 19's mandate is to promote and defend freedom of expression and to combat censorship in order to protect individuals and publications and to encourage action and awareness of censorship at local, national and international levels. ARTICLE 19,

90 Borough High Street, London SE1 1LL, Tel 071 403 4822, Fax 071 403 1943.

*The Britain-Burma Society*: Established in 1957 under the patronage of, amongst others, Earl Mountbatten of Burma, the Society boasts a membership of around 270. The Society's Constitution states 'The Society shall be non-political and have as its object the fostering of friendship and understanding between British people interested in Burma and Burmese people, especially by the encouragement of cultural and social relations between the two countries.' Mrs Anna Allott, Hon. Secretary, Sorbrook Mill, Bodicote, Banbury, Oxford OX15 4AU, Tel 0295 720142.

*B.U.R.M.A.*: 'Burma Underground Movement for Action', publishes a newsletter on relevant Burmese issues. Box 1076, Silom Post Office, Bangkok 10505, Thailand.

*Burma Action Group UK* or *BAG UK*: A group, with a membership of almost 400, working for the immediate release of all political prisoners in Burma, the transfer of power to the elected representatives of the people, a political solution to the civil war and the promotion of humanitarian aid to the people of Burma. Also publishes a bi-monthly newsletter. 84 Long Lane, London SE1 4AU, Tel 071 403 6303, Fax 071 403 3997.

*Burma Affairs Monitor*: A group of Burmese expatriates in the UK monitoring Burma's issues and working towards the formation of a free, stable and democratic Burma. The group publishes a two-monthly newsletter entitled *Burma Affairs Bulletin*. 3A Chatto Road, London SW11 6LJ, Tel 071 924 3147.

*Burma Alert*: A Canadian-based Burmese newsletter. RR4, Shawville, JOX 2Y0, Quebec, Canada.

*The Burma Project USA*: A non-profit, tax exempt organisation dedicated to promoting human rights in Burma. It describes itself as 'A human rights organization dedicated to increasing international awareness about the crisis in Burma ... conducts investigative trips inside Burma to monitor human rights abuses, submitting documentation to the United Nations as well as to media sources.' 45 Oak Road, Larkspur CA 94939, USA, Tel 415 924 6447, Fax 415 924 6101.

*Burma Review*: An American-based Burmese newsletter. Box 7726, Rego Park NY 11374, USA.

*Burmese Relief Centre*: A Thai-based organisation which supports Burmese refugees in Thailand. P O Box 48, Chiang Mai University, Chiang Mai 50002, Thailand, Tel/Fax 53 216 894.

*DVB: The Democratic Voice of Burma*: A democratic opposition radio based in Oslo. It broadcasts one hour daily on 15180 KHz at 14.30 GMT. DVB, P.O. Box 6720, St Olavs Plass, 0130 Oslo, Norway. Tel/Fax: 47-22-114980/522487.

*Kiscadale Publications*: A Scottish-based independent publishing concern offering a large selection of books on 'Burma And Beyond'. Kiscadale Publications, Gartmore, Stirlingshire FK8 3RJ, Tel 08772 776, Fax 08772 778.

*Liverpool Burma Support Group*: Formed in March 1992 to raise awareness of the plight of the Burmese people, provide humanitarian aid for the oppressed Burmese people and to seek a peaceful transition towards democracy in Burma. 15 Menlove Gardens West, Liverpool L18 2DL. Tel/Fax 051 722 1121.

*Prospect Burma*: A charitable trust established to assist in educating and training Burmese students who have been forced to flee their country. 143 Rivermead Court, Ranelagh Gardens, London SW6 3SE. Tel 071-371 0887, Fax 071-371 0547.

# AND FINALLY ...

## An elderly Burmese lady's perspective on Burma today

'I am no longer proud to be Burmese. In the past none of us worried about anything, we all had enough to get by, we survived. But in the last few years things have got steadily worse, prices have shot up and our families have become hungry. Not so long ago, you could buy a chicken for 20 kyat, now it costs 200. How can we afford that on a salary of just 40 kyat? Children round here can't even recognise bars of chocolate when they see them, because they've no idea what chocolate looks like.

No one can speak English anymore and the universities are either closed or under constant surveillance by the MI. Today we're too frightened even to be seen with a foreigner; the SLORC is everywhere. *SLORC*, what a name. You know what it is in Burmese? *nyein wut pi pya — nyein* means *quiet*, *wut* means *bowed down*, *pi* means *pressed upon* and *pya* means *flattened*. Isn't that appropriate for our people?

What I say may shock you, but many of us are even disenchanted with Buddhism. The Buddha didn't tell us to spend all this money gilding the pagodas. The money should go to the people. You know, we have a joke in Rangoon about the television: 'You only see yellow and green' — the yellow of the newly-gilded pagodas and the green of the *Tatmadaw*, the military.

I'm old now, I don't care about politics, I just care about the starving people in this once rich country of ours. I am just too frightened to think about the future.'

## 'Pitch-dark World'

'In the pitch-dark world
Peace is going to disappear
I am afraid in boiling blood and
With fiery greed for victory
Human beings wage a war against each other.

God and gospel in the world
If everyone lives by it
The world will be beautiful
Make the world beautiful singing hymns
Do unto others as you want to be done unto.

Dove of peace with its wings spread
While gliding in the sky and composing a song
Has vanished into thin air.

*Battle For Peace*, Revolutionary Students (Burma), May 1992.

*Tiger standing guard outside the Kyaryoke Monastery, Akyab.*

# INDEX

*Guardian of the Shwethalyaung, the giant reclining Buddha at Pegu.*

**NOTES**

**NOTES**

**NOTES**